Opening- True Gospel of Jesus, called Christ, a new prophet sent by God to the world: according to the description of Barnabas his apostle.

Barnabas, apostle of Jesus the Nazarene, called Christ, to all them that dwell upon the earth desireth peace and consolation.

Dearly beloved the great and wonderful God hath during these past days visited us by his prophet Jesus Christ in great mercy of teaching and miracles, by reason whereof many, being deceived of Satan, under presence of piety, are preaching most impious doctrine, calling Jesus son of God, repudiating the circumcision ordained of God for ever, and permitting every unclean meat: among whom also Paul hath been deceived, whereof I speak not without grief; for which cause I am writing that truth which I have seen and heard, in the intercourse that I have had with Jesus, in order that ye may be saved, and not be deceived of Satan and perish in the judgment of God. Therefore beware of every one that preacheth unto you new doctrine contrary to that which I write, that ye may be saved eternally. The great God be with you and guard you from Satan and from every evil. Amen.

Chapter 1 The angel Gabriel visits Virgin Mary concerning the birth of Jesus.

In these last years a virgin called Mary, of the lineage of David, of the tribe of Judah, was visited by the angel Gabriel from God. This virgin, living in all holiness without any offense, being blameless, and abiding in prayer with fastings, being one day alone, there entered into her chamber the angel Gabriel, and he saluted her, saying: 'God be with thee, O Mary'.

The virgin was affrighted at the appearance of the angel; but the angel comforted her, saying: 'Fear not, Mary, for thou hast found favour with God, who hath chosen thee to be mother of a prophet, whom he will send to the people of Israel in order that they may walk in his laws with truth of heart.'

The virgin answered: 'Now how shall I bring forth sons, seeing I know not a man?' The angel answered: 'O Mary, God who made man without a man is able to generate in thee man with- out a man, because with him nothing is impossible.'

Mary answered: 'I know that God is almighty, therefore his will be done.' The angel answered: 'Now be conceived in thee the prophet, whom thou shalt name Jesus: and thou shalt keep him from wine and from strong drink and from every unclean meat, because the child is an holy one of God.' Mary bowed herself with humility, saying:

'Behold the handmaid of God, be it done according to thy word.'

The angel departed, and the virgin glorified God, saying: 'Know, O my soul, the greatness of God, and exult, my spirit, in God my Saviour; for he hath regarded the lowliness of his handmaiden, insomuch that I shall be called blessed by all the nations, for he that is mighty hath made me great, and blessed be his holy name. For his mercy extendeth from generation to generation of them that fear him. Mighty hath he made his hand, and he hath scattered the proud in the imagination of his heart. He hath put down the mighty from their seat, and hath exalted the humble. Him who hath been hungry hath he filled with good things, and the rich he hath sent empty away. For he keepeth in memory the promises made to Abraham and to his son for ever'.

Chapter 2   The warning of the angel Gabriel given to Joseph concerning the conception of the Virgin Mary.

Mary having known the will of God, fearing the people, lest they should take offense at her being great with child, and should stone her as guilty of fornication, chose a companion of her own lineage, a man by name called Joseph, of blameless life: for he as a righteous man feared God and served him with fastings and prayers, living by the works of his hands, for he was a carpenter. Such a man the virgin knowing, chose him for her companion and revealed to him the divine counsel.

Joseph being a righteous man, when he perceived that Mary was great with child, was minded to put her away because he feared God. Behold, whilst he slept, he was rebuked by the angel of God, saying 'O Joseph, why art thou minded to put away Mary thy wife? Know that whatsoever hath been wrought in her hath all been done by the will of God. The virgin shall bring forth a son, whom thou shalt call by the name Jesus; whom thou shalt keep from wine and strong drink and from every unclean meat, because he is an holy one of God from his mother's womb. He is a prophet of God sent unto the people of Israel, in order that he may convert Judah to his heart, and that Israel may walk in the law of the Lord, as it is written in the law of Moses. He shall come with great power, which God shall give him, and shall work great miracles, whereby many shall be saved'. Joseph, arising from sleep, gave thanks to God, and abode with Mary all his life, serving God with all sincerity.

Chapter 3 Wonderful birth of Jesus, and appearance of angels praising God.

There reigned at that time in Judaea Herod, by decree of Caesar Augustus, and Pilate was governor in the priesthood of Annas and Caiaphas. Wherefore, by decree of Augustus, all the world was enrolled; wherefore each one went to his own country, and they presented themselves by their own tribes to be enrolled. Joseph accordingly departed from Nazareth, a city of Galilee, with Mary his wife, great with child, to go to Bethlehem (for that it was his city, he being of the lineage of David), in order that he might be enrolled according to the decree of Caesar. Joseph having arrived at Bethlehem, for that the city was small, and great the multitude of them that were strangers there, he found no place, wherefore he took lodging outside the city in a lodging made for a shepherds' shelter. While Joseph abode there the days were fulfilled for Mary to bring forth.

The virgin was surrounded by a light exceeding bright, and brought forth her son without pain, whom she took in her arms, and wrapping him in swaddling-clothes, laid him in the manger, because there was no room in the inn. There came with gladness a great multitude of angels to the inn, blessing God and announcing peace to them that fear God. Mary and Joseph praised

the Lord for the birth of Jesus, and with greatest joy nurtured him.

Chapter 4 Angels announced to the shepherds the birth of Jesus, and they, after having found him, announce him.

At that time the shepherds were watching over their flock, as is their custom. And, behold, they were surrounded by an exceeding bright light, out of which appeared to them an angel, who blessed God. The shepherds were filled with fear by reason of the sudden light and the appearance of the angel; whereupon the angel of the Lord comforted them, saying:

'Behold, I announce to you a great joy, for there is born in the city of David a child who is a prophet of the Lord; who bringeth great salvation to the house of Israel. The

child ye shall find in the manger, with his mother, who blesseth God.'

And when he had said this there came a great multitude of angels blessing God, announcing peace to them that have good will. When the angels were departed, the shepherds spake among themselves, saying: 'Let us go even unto Bethlehem, and see the word which God by his angel hath announced to us.' There came many shepherds to Bethlehem seeking the new-born babe. and they found outside the city the child that was born. according to the word of the angel. lying in the manger.

They therefore made obeisance to him, and gave to the mother that which they had, announcing to her what they had heard and seen. Mary therefore kept all these things in her heart, and Joseph [likewise], giving thanks to God. The shepherds returned to their flock, announcing to everyone how great a thing they had seen. And so the whole hill-country of Judaea was filled with fear, and every man laid up this word in his heart, saying: 'What, think we, shall this child be?'

Chapter 5   Circumcision of Jesus

When the eight days were fulfilled according to the law of the Lord, as it is written in the book of Moses, they took the child and carried him to the temple to circumcise him. And so they circumcised the child, and gave him the name Jesus, as the angel of the Lord had said before he was conceived in the womb. Mary and Joseph perceived that the child must needs be for the salvation and ruin of many. Wherefore they feared God, and kept the child with fear of God.

Chapter 6   Three Magi are led by a star in the east to Judaea, and, finding Jesus, make obeisance to him and gifts.

In the reign of Herod, king of Judaea, when Jesus was born, three magi in the parts of the east were observing the stars of heaven. Whereupon appeared to them a star of great brightness, wherefore having concluded among themselves, they came to Judaea, guided by the star, which went before them, and having arrived at Jerusalem they asked where was born the King of the Jews. And when Herod heard this he was affrighted, and all the city was troubled. Herod therefore called together the priests and the scribes, saying: 'Where should Christ be born?' They answered that he should be born in Bethlehem; for thus it is written by the prophet:

'And thou, Bethlehem, art not little among the princes of Judah: for out of thee shall come forth a leader, who shall lead my people Israel.'

Herod accordingly called together the magi and asked them concerning their coming: who answered that they had seen a star in the east, which had guided them thither, wherefore they wished with gifts to worship this new King manifested by his star.

Then said Herod: 'Go to Bethlehem and search out with all diligence concerning the child; and when ye have found him, come and tell it to me, because I also would fain

come and worship him.' And this he spake deceitfully.

Chapter 7 The visitation of Jesus by magi, and their return to their own country, with the warning of Jesus given to them in a dream.

The magi therefore departed out of Jerusalem, and lo, the star which appeared to them in the east went before them. Seeing the star the magi were filled with gladness. And so having come to Bethlehem, outside the city, they saw the star standing still above the inn where Jesus was born. The magi therefore went thither, and entering the dwelling found the child with his mother, and bending down they did obeisance to him. And the magi presented unto him spices, with silver and gold, recounting to the virgin all that they had seen. Whereupon, while sleeping, they were warned by the child not to go to Herod: so departing by another way they returned to their own home, announcing all that they had seen in Judaea.

Chapter 8 Jesus is carried in flight to Egypt, and herod massacres the innocent children.

Herod seeing that the magi did not return, believed himself mocked of them; whereupon he determined to put to death the child that was born. But behold while Joseph was sleeping there appeared to him the angel of the Lord, saying: 'Arise up quickly, and take the child with his mother and go into Egypt for Herod willeth to slay him'. Joseph arose with great fear, and took Mary with the child, and they went into Egypt, and there they abode until the death of Herod: who, believing himself derided of the magi, sent his soldiers to slay all the new-born children in Bethlehem. The soldiers therefore came and slew all the children that were there, as Herod had commanded them. Whereby were fulfilled the words of the prophet, saying: 'Lamentation and great weeping are there in Ramah; Rachel lamenteth for her sons, but consolation is not given her because they are not.'

Chapter 9 Jesus, heving returned to Judaea, holds a wondrous disputation with doctors, having come to the age of twelve years.

When Herod was dead, behold the angel of the Lord appeared in a dream to Joseph, saying: 'Return into Judaea, for they are dead that willed the death of the child.' Joseph therefore took the child with Mary (he having come to the age of seven years), and came to Judaea; whence, hearing that Archelaus, son of Herod, was reigning in Judaea, he went into Galilee, fearing to remain in Judaea; and they went to dwell at Nazareth. The child grew in grace and

wisdom before God and before men.

Jesus, having come to the age of twelve years, went up with Mary and Joseph to Jerusalem, to worship there according to the law of the Lord written in the book of Moses. When their prayers were ended they departed, having lost Jesus, because they thought that he was returned home with their kinsfolk. Mary therefore returned with Joseph to Jerusalem, seeking Jesus among kinsfolk and neighbours. The third day they found the child in the temple, in the midst of the doctors, disputing with them concerning the law. And every one was amazed at his questions and answers, saying: "How can there be such doctrine in him, seeing he is so small and hath not learned to read?'

Mary reproved him, saying: 'Son, what hast thou done to us? Behold I and thy father have sought thee for three days sorrowing.' Jesus answered: 'Know ye not that the service of God ought to come before father and mother?' Jesus then went down with his mother and Joseph to Nazareth, and was subject to them with humility and reverence.

Chapter 10

Jesus having come to the age of thirty years, as he himself said unto me, went up to

Mount Olives with his mother to gather olives. Then at midday as he was praying, when he came to these words: 'Lord, with mercy . . . ,' he was surrounded by an exceeding bright light and by an infinite multitude of angels, who were saying: 'Blessed be God.' The angel Gabriel presented to him as it were a shining mirror, a book, which descended into the heart of Jesus, in which he had knowledge of what God hath done and what hath said and what God willeth insomuch that everything was laid bare and open to him; as he said unto me: 'Believe, Barnabas, that I know every prophet with every prophecy, insomuch that whatever I say the whole bath come forth from that book.'

Jesus, having received this vision, and knowing that he was a prophet sent to the house of Israel, revealed all to Mary his mother, telling her that he needs must suffer great persecution for the honour of God, and that he could not any longer abide with her to serve her. Whereupon, having heard this, Mary answered: 'Son. ere thou west born all was announced to me; wherefore blessed be the holy name of God. Jesus departed therefore that day from his mother to attend to his prophetic office.

Chapter 11   Jesus Miraculously healeth a leper, and goeth into Jerusalem.

Jesus descending from the mountain to come into Jerusalem, met a leper, who by divine inspiration knew Jesus to be a prophet. Therefore with tears he prayed him, saying: 'Jesus, thou son of David, have mercy on me.' Jesus answered: 'What wilt thou, brother, that I should do unto thee?'

The leper answered: 'Lord, give me health.'

Jesus reproved him, saying: 'Thou art foolish; pray to God who created thee, and he will give thee health; for I am a man, as thou art.'

The leper answered: 'I know that thou, Lord, art a man, but an holy one of the Lord. Wherefore pray thou to God, and he will give me health.'

Then Jesus, sighing, said: 'Lord God Almighty, for the love of thy holy prophets give health to this sick man.' Then, having said this, he said, touching the sick man with his hands in the name of God: 'O brother, receive thy health!' And when he had said this the leprosy was cleansed, insomuch that the flesh of the leper was left unto him like that of a child. Seeing which namely, that he was healed, the leper with a loud voice cried out: 'Come hither, Israel, to receive the prophet whom God sendeth unto thee'. Jesus prayed him, saying: 'Brother, hold thy peace and say nothing,' but the more he prayed him the more he cried out, saying: 'Behold the prophet! behold the holy one of God!' At which words many that were going out of Jerusalem ran back, and entered with Jesus into Jerusalem, recounting that which God through Jesus had done unto the leper.

Chapter 12 First sermon of Jesus delivered to the people: wonderful in doctrine concerning the name of God.

The whole city of Jerusalem was moved by these words, wherefore they all ran together to the temple to see Jesus, who had entered therein to pray, so that they could scarce be contained there. Therefore the priests besought Jesus, saying: 'This people desireth to see thee and hear thee; therefore ascend to the pinnacle, and if God give thee a word speak it in the name of the Lord.'

Then ascended Jesus to the place whence the scribes were wont to speak. And having beckoned with the hand for silence, he opened his mouth, saying: 'Blessed be the holy name of God, who of his goodness and mercy willed to create his creatures that they might glorify him. Blessed be the holy name of God, who created the splendour of all the saints and prophets before all things to send him for the salvation of the world, as he spoke by his servant David, saying: "Before Lucifer in the brightness of the saints I created thee." Blessed be the holy name of God, who created the angels that they might serve him. And blessed be God, who punished and reprobated Satan and his followers, who would not reverence him whom God willeth to be reverenced. Blessed be the holy name of God, who created man out of the clay of the earth, and set him over his works. Blessed be the holy name of God, who drove man out of paradise for having transgressed his holy precept. Blessed be the holy name of God, who with mercy looked upon the tears of Adam and Eve, first parents of the human race. Blessed be the holy name of God who just punished Cain the fratricide, sent the deluge upon the earth. burned up three wicked cities, scourged Egypt, overwhelmed Pharaoh in the Red Sea, scattered the enemies of his people, chastised the unbelievers and punished the impenitent. Blessed be the holy name of God, who with mercy looked upon his creatures, and therefore sent them his holy prophets, that they might walk in truth and righteousness before him; who delivered his servants from every evil, and gave them this land, as he promised to our father Abraham and to his son for ever. Then by his servant Moses he gave us his holy law, that Satan should not deceive us: and he exalted us above all other peoples.

'But, brethren, what do we to-day, that we be not punished for our sins?'

And then Jesus with greatest vehemence rebuked the people for that they had forgotten the word of God, and gave themselves only to vanity; he rebuked the priests for their negligence in God's service and for their worldly greed; he rebuked the scribes because they preached vain doctrine, and forsook the law of God; he rebuked the doctors because they made the law of God of none effect through their traditions. And in such wise did Jesus speak to the people, that all wept, from the least to the greatest, crying mercy, and beseeching Jesus that he would pray of them; save only their priests and leaders, who on that day conceived hatred against Jesus for having thus spoken against the priests, scribes, and doctors. And they meditated upon his death, but for fear of the people, who had received him as a prophet of God, they spoke no word.

Jesus raised his hands to the Lord God and prayed, and the people weeping said: 'So be it, O Lord, so be it.' The prayer being ended, Jesus descended from the temple; and that day he departed from Jerusalem, with many that followed him. And the priests spoke evil of Jesus among themselves.

Chapter 13   The remarkable fear of Jesus and his prayer, and the wonderful comfort of the angel Gabriel.

Some days having passed, Jesus having in spirit perceived the desire of the priests, ascended the Mount of Olives to pray. And having passed the whole night in prayer, in the morning Jesus praying said: 'OLord, I know that the scribes hate me, and the priests are minded to kill me, thy servant; therefore, Lord God almighty and merciful, in mercy hear the prayers of the servant, and save me from their snares, for thou art my salvation. Thou knowest, Lord, that I thy servant seek thee alone, O Lord, and speak thy word; for thy word is truth, which endureth for ever.'

When Jesus had spoken these words, behold there came to him the angel Gabriel, saying: 'Fear not, O Jesus, for a thousand thousand who dwell above the heaven guard thy garments, and thou shalt not die till everything be fulfilled, and the world shall be near its end.'

Jesus fell with his face to the ground, saying: 'O great Lord God, how great is thy mercy upon me, and what shall I give thee, Lord, for all that thou hast granted me?' The angel Gabriel answered: 'Arise, Jesus, and remember

Abraham, who being willing to make sacrifice to God of his only-begotten son Ishmael, to fulfil the word of God, and the knife not being able to cut his son, at my word offered in sacrifice a sheep. Even so therefore shalt thou do, O Jesus, servant of God.

Jesus answered: 'Willingly, but where shall I find the lamb, seeing I have no money, and it is not lawful to steal it?' Thereupon the angel Gabriel showed unto him a sheep, which Jesus offered in sacrifice, praising and blessing God, who is glorious for ever.

Chapter 14 After the fast of forty days, Jesus chooseth twelve apostles.

Jesus descended from the mount, and passed alone by night to the farther side of Jordan, and fasted forty days and forty nights, not eating anything day nor night, making continual supplication to the Lord for the salvation of his people to whom God had sent him. And when the forty days were passed he was an hungered. Then appeared Satan unto him, and tempted him in many words, but Jesus drove him away by the power of words of God. Satan having departed, the angels came and ministered unto Jesus that whereof he had need.

Jesus, having returned to the region of Jerusalem, was found again of the people with exceeding great joy, and they prayed him that he would abide with them; for his words were not as those of the scribes, but were with power, for they touched the heart.

Jesus, seeing that great was the multitude of them that returned to their heart for to walk in the law of God, went up into the mountain, and abode all night in prayer, and when day was come he descended from the mountain, and chose twelve, whom he called apostles, among whom is Judas, who was slain upon the cross. Their names are: Andrew and Peter his brother, fishermen; Barnabas, who wrote this, with Matthew the publican, who sat at the receipt of custom; John and James, sons of Zebedee; Thaddaeus and Judas; Bartholomew and Philip; James, and Judas Iscariot the traitor. To these he always revealed the divine secrets; but the Iscariot Judas he made his dispenser of that which was given in alms, but he stole the tenth part of everything.

Chapter 15 Miracle wrought by Jesus at the marriage, turning the water into wine.

When the feast of tabernacles was nigh, a certain rich man invited Jesus with his disciples and his mother to a marriage. Jesus therefore went, and as they were feasting the wine ran short. His mother accosted Jesus, saying: 'They have

no wine.' Jesus answered: 'What is that to me, mother mine?' His mother
commanded the servants that whatever Jesus should command them they should obey.
There were there six vessels for water according to the custom of Israel to
purify themselves for prayer. Jesus said: 'Fill these vessels with water.' The
servants did so. Jesus said unto them: 'In the name of God, give to drink unto
them that are feasting.' The servants thereupon bare unto the master of the
ceremonies, who rebuked the attendants saying: 'O worthless servants why have ye
kept the better wine till now?' For he knew nothing of all that

Jesus had done.

The servants answered: 'O sir, there is here a holy man of God, for he hath made
of water, wine.' The master of the ceremonies thought that the servants were
drunken; but they that were sitting near to Jesus, having seen the whole matter,
rose from the table and paid him reverence, saying: 'Verily thou art an holy one
of God, a true prophet sent to us from God!'

Then his disciples believed on him, and many returned to their heart, saying:
'Praised be God, who hath mercy upon Israel, and visiteth the house of Judah
with love, and blessed be his holy name.'

Chapter 16   Wonderful teaching giving by Jesus to his apostles concerning
conversion from the evil life.

One day Jesus called together his disciples and went up on to the mountain, and
when he had sat down there his disciples came near unto him; and he opened his
mouth and taught them, saying: 'Great are the benefits which God bath bestowed
on us wherefore it is necessary that we should serve him with truth of heart.
And forasmuch as new wine is put into new vessels, even so ought ye to become
new men, if ye will contain the new doctrine that shall come out of my mouth.
Verily I say unto you, that even as a man cannot see with his eyes the heaven
and the earth at one and the same time, so it is impossible to love God and the
world.

'No man can in any wise serve two masters that are at enmity one with the other:
for if the one shall love you, the other will hate you. Even so I tell you in
truth that ye cannot serve God and the world for the world lieth in falsehood,
covetousness, and malignity. Ye cannot therefore find rest in the world, but
rather persecution and loss. Wherefore serve God and despise the world, for from
me ye shall find rest for your souls, Hear my words for I speak unto you in
truth.

'Verily, blessed are they that mourn this earthly life, for they shall be
comforted.

'Blessed are the poor who truly hate the delights of the world, for they shall
abound in the delights of the kingdom of God.

'Verily, blessed are they that eat at the table of God, for the angels shall
minister unto them.

'Ye are journeying as pilgrims. Doth the pilgrim encumber himself with palaces
and fields and other earthly matters upon the way? Assuredly not: but he beareth
things light and prized for their usefulness and convenience upon the road. This
now should be an example unto you; and if ye desire another example I will give
it you, in order that ye may do all that I tell you.

'Weigh not down your hearts with earthly desires, saying: "Who shall clothe us?"
or "Who shall give us to eat?" But behold the flowers and the trees, with the
birds, which God our Lord clotheth and nourisheth with greater glory than all
the glory of Solomon. And he is able to nourish you, even God who created you
and called you to his service; who for forty years caused the manna to fall from
heaven for his people Israel in the wilderness, and did not suffer their
clothing to wax old or perish, they being six hundred and forty thousand men,
besides women and children. Verily I say unto you, that heaven and earth shall
fail, yet shall not fail his mercy unto them that fear him. But the rich of the
world in their prosperity are hungry and perish. There was a rich man whose
incomings increased, and he said, "What shall I do, O my soul? I will pull down
my barns because they are small, and I will build new and greater ones:
therefore thou shalt triumph my soul!" Oh, wretched ban! for that night he died.
He ought to have been mindful of the poor, and to have made himself friends with
the alms of unrighteous riches of this world; for they bring treasures in the
kingdom of heaven.

'Tell me, I pray you, if ye should give your money into the bank to a publican,
and he should give unto you tenfold and twentyfold, would ye not give to such a
man everything that ye had? But I say unto you, verily, that whatsoever ye shall
give and shall forsake for love of God, ye receive it back an hundred-fold, and
life everlasting. See then how much ye ought to be content to serve God.

Chapter 17   In this chapter is clearly perceived the unbelief of Christians,
and the true faith of Mumin.

When Jesus had said this, Philip answered: 'We are content to serve God, but we
desire, however, to know God, for Isaiah the prophet said: "Verily thou art a
hidden God," and God said to Moses his servant: "I am that which I am."

Jesus answered: 'Philip, God is a good without which there is naught good; God
is a being without which there is naught that is; God is a life without which
there is naught that liveth; so great that he filleth all and is everywhere. He
alone hath no equal. He hath had no beginning, nor will he ever have an end, but
to everything hath he given a beginning, and to everything shall he give an end.
He hath no father nor mother; he hath no sons. nor brethren. nor companions. And
because God hath no body, therefore he eateth not, sleepeth not, dieth not,
walketh not, moveth not, but abideth eternally without human similitude, for
that he is incorporeal, uncompounded, immaterial, of the most simple substance.
He is so good that he loveth goodness only; he is so just that when he punisheth
or pardoneth it cannot be gainsaid. In short, I say unto thee, Philip, that here
on earth thou canst not see him nor know him perfectly; but in his kingdom thou
shalt see him for ever: wherein consisteth all our happiness and glory.'

Philip answered: 'Master, what sayest thou? It is surely written in Isaiah that
God is our father; how, then, hath he no sons?'

Jesus answered: 'There are written in the prophets many parables, wherefore thou
oughtest not to attend to the letter, but to the sense. For all the prophets,
that are one hundred and forty-four thousand, whom God hath sent into the world,
have spoken darkly. But after me shall come the Splendour of all the prophets
and holy ones, and shall shed light upon the darkness of all that the prophets
have said, because he is the messenger of God' And having said this, Jesus
sighed and said: 'Have mercy on Israel, O Lord God; and look with pity upon
Abraham and upon his seed, in order that they may serve thee with truth of
heart.

His disciples answered: 'So be it, O Lord our God!'

Jesus said: 'Verily I say unto you, the scribes and doctors have made void the law of God with their false prophecies, contrary to the prophecies of the true prophets of God: wherefore God is wrath with the house of Israel and with this faithless generation.' His disciples wept at these words, and said: 'Have mercy, O God, have mercy upon the temple and upon the holy city, and give it not into contempt of the nations that they despise not thy holy covenant.' Jesus answered: 'So be it, Lord God of our fathers.'

Chapter 18 Here is shown forth the persecution of the servants of God by the world, and God's protection saving them.

Having said this, Jesus said: 'Ye have not chosen me, but I have chosen you, that ye may be my disciples. If then the world shall hate you, ye shall be truly my disciples; for the world hath been ever an enemy of servants of God. Remember [the] holy prophets that have been slain by the world, even as in the time of Elijah ten thousand prophets were slain by Jezebel, insomuch that scarcely did poor Elijah escape, and seven thousand sons of prophets who were hidden by the captain of Ahab's host. Oh, unrighteous world, that knowest not God! Fear not therefore ye, for the hairs of your head are numbered so that they shall not perish. Behold the sparrows and other

birds, whereof falleth not one feather without the will of God. Shall God, then, have more care of the birds than of man, for whose sake he hath created everything. Is there any man, perchance, who careth more for his shoes than for his own son? Assuredly not. Now how much less ought ye to think that God would abandon you, while taking care of the birds! And why speak I of the birds? A leaf of a tree falleth not without the will of God.

'Believe me, because I tell you the truth, that the world will greatly fear you if ye shall observe my words. For if it feared not to have its wickedness revealed it would not hate you, but it feareth to be revealed, therefore it will hate you and persecute you. If ye shall see your words scorned by the world lay it not to heart, but consider how that God is greater than you; who is in such wise scorned by the world that his wisdom is counted madness If God endureth the world with patience, wherefore will ye lay it to heart, O dust and clay of the earth? In your patience ye shall possess your soul. Therefore if one shall give you a blow on one side of the face, offer him the other that he may smite it. Render not evil for evil, for so do all the worst animals; but render good for evil, and pray God for them that hate you. Fire is not extinguished with fire, but rather with water; even so I say unto you that ye shall not overcome evil with evil, but rather with good. Behold God, who causeth the sun to come upon the good and evil, and likewise the rain. Soought ye to do good to all; for it is written in the law: "Be ye holy, for I your God am holy; be ye pure, for I am pure; and be ye perfect, for I am perfect." Verily I say unto you that the servant studieth to please his master, and so he putteth not on any garment that is displeasing to his master. Your garments are your will and your love. Beware, then, not to will or to love a thing that is displeasing to God, our Lord. Be ye sure that God hateth the pomps and lusts of the world, and therefore hate ye the world.'

Chapter 19 Jesus foretelleth his betrayal, and, descending from the mountain, healeth ten lepers.

When Jesus had said this, Peter answered: 'O teacher, behold we have felt all to follow thee, what shall become of us?' Jesus answered: 'Verily ye in the day of judgment shall sit beside me, giving testimony against the twelve tribes of Israel.' And having said this Jesus sighed, saying: 'O Lord, what thing is this? for I have chosen twelve, and one of them is a devil.'

The disciples were sore grieved at this word; whereupon he who writeth secretly questioned Jesus with tears, saying: 'O master, will Satan deceive me, and shall I then become reprobate?'

Jesus answered: "Be not sore grieved, Barnabas; for those whom God hath chosen before the creation of the world shall not perish. Rejoice, for thy name is written in the book of life.' Jesus comforted his disciples, saying: 'Fear not, for he who shall hate me is not grieved at my saying, because in him is not the divine feeling.' At his words the chosen were comforted. Jesus made his prayers, and his disciples said: 'Amen, so be it, Lord God almighty and merciful.' Having finished his devotions, Jesus came down from the mountain with his disciples, and met ten lepers, who from afar off cried out: 'Jesus, son of David, have mercy on us!'

Jesus called them near to him, and said unto them: 'What will ye of me, O brethren?' They all cried out: 'Give us health!' Jesus answered: 'Ah, wretched that ye are, have ye so lost your reason for that ye say: "Give us health?" See ye not me to be a man like yourselves. Call unto our God that hath created you: and he that is almighty and merciful will heal you. With tears the lepers answered: 'We know that thou art man like us, but yet an holy one of God and a prophet of the Lord; wherefore pray thou to God, and he will heal us.

Thereupon the disciples prayed Jesus, saying: 'Lord, have mercy upon them.' Then groaned Jesus and prayed to God, saying: 'Lord God almighty and merciful, have mercy and hearken to the words of thy servant: and for love of Abraham our father and for thy holy covenant have mercy on the request of these men, and grant them health.' Whereupon Jesus, having said this, turned himself to the lepers and said: 'Go and show yourselves to the priests according to the law of God.'

The lepers departed and on the way were cleansed. Whereupon one of them. seeing that he was healed, returned to find Jesus, and he was an Ishmaelite. And having found Jesus he bowed himself, doing reverence unto him, and saying: 'Verily thou art an holy one of God' and with thanks he prayed him that he would receive him for servant. Jesus answered: 'Ten have been cleansed; where are the nine?' And he said to him that was cleansed: 'I am not come to be served, but to serve: wherefore go to shine home, and recount how much God hath done in thee, in order that they may know that the promises made to Abraham and his son, with the kingdom of God, are drawing nigh.' The cleansed leper departed, and having arrived in his own neighbourhood recounted how much God through Jesus had wrought in him.

Chapter 20   Miracle on the sea wrought by Jesus, and Jesus declares where the prophet is received.

Jesus went to the sea of Galilee, and having embarked in a ship sailed to his city of Nazareth; whereupon there was a great tempest in the sea, insomuch that the ship was nigh unto sinking. And Jesus was sleeping upon the prow of the ship. Then drew near to him his disciples, and awoke him, saying: 'O master, save thyself, for we perish!' They were encompassed with very great fear, by reason of the great wind that was contrary and the roaring of the sea. Jesus arose, and raising his eyes to heaven, said: 'O Elohim Sabaoth, have mercy upon thy servants.' Then, when Jesus had said this, suddenly the wind ceased, and the sea became calm. Wherefore the

seamen feared, saying: 'And who is this, that the sea and the wind obey him?"

Having arrived at the city of Nazareth the seamen spread through the city all that Jesus had wrought, whereupon the house where Jesus was, was surrounded by as many as dwelt in the city. And the scribes and doctors having presented themselves unto him said: 'We have heard how much thou hast wrought in the sea and in Judaea: give us therefore some sign here in thine own country.'

Jesus answered: 'This faithless generation seek a sign, but it shall not be given them, because no prophet is received in his own country. In the time of Elijah there were many widows in Judaea, but he was not sent to be nourished save unto a widow of Sidon. Many were the lepers in the time of Elisha in Judaea; nevertheless only Naaman the Syrian was cleansed.'

Then were the citizens enraged and seized him and carried him on to the top of a precipice to cast him down. But Jesus walking through the midst of them, departed from them.

Chapter 21   Jesus healeth a demoniac, and the swine are cast into the sea. Afterwards he healeth the daughter of the Canaanites.

Jesus went up to Capernaum, and as he drew near to the city behold there came out of the tombs one that was possessed of a devil, and in such wise that no chain could hold him, and he did great harm to the man.

The demons cried out through his mouth, saying: 'O holy one of God, why art thou come before the time to trouble us?' And they prayed him that he would not cast them forth.

Jesus asked them how many they were. They answered: 'Six thousand six hundred and sixty-six.' When the disciples heard this they were affrighted, and prayed Jesus that he would depart. Then said Jesus: 'Where is your faith? It is necessary that the demon should depart, and not I.' The demons therefore cried: 'We will come out, but permit us to enter into those swine.' There were feeding there, near to the sea, about ten thousand swine belonging to the Canaanites. Thereupon Jesus said: 'Depart, and enter into the swine.' With a roar the demons entered into the swine, and cast them headlong into the sea. Then fled into the city they that fed the swine, and recounted all that had been brought to pass by Jesus.

Accordingly the men of the city came forth and found Jesus and the man that was healed. The men were filled with fear and prayed Jesus that he would depart out of their borders. Jesus accordingly departed from them and went up into the parts of Tyre and Sidon.

And lo! a woman of Canaan with her two sons, who had come forth out of her own country to find Jesus. Having therefore seen him come with his disciples, she cried out: 'Jesus, son of David, have mercy on my daughter, who is tormented of the devil! Jesus did not answer even a single word, because they were of the uncircumcised people. The disciples were moved to pity, and said: 'O master, have pity on them! Behold how much they cry out and weep!'

Jesus answered: 'I am not sent but unto the people of Israel.' Then the woman, with her sons, went before Jesus, weeping and saying: 'O son of David, have mercy on me!' Jesus answered: 'It is not good to take the bread from the children's hands and give it to the dogs.' And this said Jesus by reason of their uncleanness, because they were of the un- circumcised people.

The woman answered: 'O Lord, the dogs eat the crumbs that fall from their masters' table.' Then was Jesus seized with admiration at the words of the woman, and said: 'O woman, great is thy faith.' And having raised his hands to heaven he prayed to God, and then he said: 'O woman, thy daughter is freed, go thy way in peace.' The woman departed, and returning to her home found her daughter, who was blessing God.' Wherefore the woman said: 'Verily there is none other God than the God of Israel.' Whereupon all her kinsfolk joined themselves unto the law of [God], according to the law written in the book of Moses.

Chapter 22 Miserable condition of the uncircumcised in that a dog is better than they.

The disciples questioned Jesus on that day, saying: 'O master, why didst thou make such answer to the woman, saying that they were dogs?'

Jesus answered: 'Verily I say unto you that a dog is better than an uncircumcised man.' Then were the disciples sorrowful, saying: 'Hard are these words, and who shall be able to receive them?'

Jesus answered: "If ye consider, O foolish ones, what the dog doth, that hath no reason, for the service of his master, ye will find my saying to be true. Tell me, doth the dog guard the house of his master, and expose his life against the robber? Yea, assuredly. But what receiveth he? Many blows and injuries with little bread, and he always showeth to his master a joyful countenance. Is this true?'

'True it is, O master,' answered the disciples.

Then said Jesus: 'Consider now how much God hath given to man, and ye shall see how unrighteous he is in not observing the covenant of God made with Abraham his servant. Remember that which David said to Saul king of Israel, against Goliath the Philistine: "My lord," said David, "while thy servant was keeping thy servant's flock there came the wolf, the bear, and the lion and seized thy servant's sheep: whereupon thy servant went and slew them, rescuing the sheep. And what is this uncircumcised one but like unto them ? Therefore will thy servant go in the name of the Lord God of Israel, and will slay this unclean one that blasphemeth the holy people of God."

Then said the disciples: 'Tell us O master for what reason man must needs be circumcised?"

Jesus answered: 'Let it suffice you that God hath commanded it to Abraham. saying: "Abraham, circumcise thy foreskin and that of all thy house, for this is a covenant between me and thee for ever.''

Chapter 23 Orgin of Circumcision, and covenant of God with Abraham, and damnation of the uncircumcised.

And having said this, Jesus sat nigh unto the mountain which they looked upon. And his disciples came to his side to listen to his words. Then said Jesus: 'Adam the first man having eaten, by fraud of Satan, the food forbidden of God in paradise, his flesh rebelled against the spirit; whereupon he swore, saying: "By God, I will cut thee!"

And having broken a piece of rock, he seized his flesh to cut it with the sharp edge of the stone: whereupon he was rebuked by the angel Gabriel. And he answered: "I

have sworn by God to cut it; I will never be a liar!"

'Then the angel showed him the superfluity of his flesh, and that he cut off. And hence, just as every man taketh flesh from the flesh of Adam, so is he bound to observe all that Adam promised with an oath. This did Adam observe in his sons, and from generation to generation came down the obligation of circumcision. But in the time of Abraham there were but few circumcised upon the earth, because that idolatry was multiplied up the earth. Whereupon God told to Abraham the fact concerning circumcision, and made this covenant, saying: "The soul that shall not have his flesh circumcised, I will scatter him from among my people for ever." '

The disciples trembled with fear at these words of Jesus, for with vehemence of spirit he spoke. Then said Jesus: Leave fear to him that hath not circumcised his foreskin, for he is deprived of paradise. And having said this, Jesus spoke again, saying: 'The spirit in many is ready in the service of God, but the flesh is weak. The man therefore that feareth God ought to consider what the flesh is, and where it had its origin, and whereto it shall be reduced. Of the clay of the earth created God flesh, and into it he breathed the breath of life, with an inbreathing therein. And therefore when the flesh shall hinder the service of God it ought to be spurned like clay and

trampled on, forasmuch as he that hateth his soul in this world shall keep it in life eternal.

'What the flesh is at this present its desires make manifest -that it is a harsh enemy of all good: for it alone desireth sin.

'Ought then man for the sake of satisfying one of his enemies to leave off pleasing God, his creator? Consider ye this. All the saints and prophets have been enemies of their flesh for service of God: wherefore readily and with gladness they went to their death, so as not to offend against the law of God given by Moses his servant, and go and serve the false and lying gods.

'Remember Elijah, who fled through desert places of the mountains, eating only grass, clad in goats' skin. Ah, how many days he supped not! Ah, how much cold he endured! Ah, how many showers drenched him, and [that] for the space of seven years, wherein endured that fierce persecution of the unclean Jezebel!

Remember Elisha, who ate barley-bread, and wore the Coarsest raiment. Verily I say unto you that they, not fearing to spurn the flesh, were feared with great terror by the king and princes. This should suffice for the spurning of the flesh, O men. But if ye will gaze at the sepulchres, ye shall know what the flesh is.'

Chapter 24   Natable example how one ought to flee from banqueting and feasting.

Having said this, Jesus wept, saying: 'Woe to those who are servants to their flesh, for they are sure not to have any good in the other life, but only torments for their sins. I tell you that there was a rich glutton who paid no heed to aught but gluttony, and so every day held a splendid feast. There stood at his gate a poor man by name Lazarus, who was full of wounds, and was fain to

have those crumbs that fell from the glutton's table. But no one gave them to
him; nay, all mocked him. Only the dogs had pity on him, for they licked his
wounds. It came to pass that the poor man died, and the angels carried him to
the arms of Abraham our father. The rich man also died, and the devils carried
him to the arms of Satan; whereupon, undergoing the greatest torment, he lifted
up his eyes and from afar saw Lazarus in the arms of Abraham. Then cried the
rich man: "O father Abraham, have mercy on me, and send Lazarus, who upon his
fingers may bring me a drop of water to cool my tongue, which is tormented in
this flame."

'Abraham answered: "Son, remember that thou receivedst thy good in the other
life and Lazarus his evil; wherefore now thou shalt be in torment, and Lazarus
in consolation."

'The rich man cried out again, saying: "O father Abraham, in my house there are
three brethren of mine. Therefore send Lazarus to announce to them how much I am
suffering, in order that they may repent and not come hither."

'Abraham answered: "They have Moses and the prophets, let them hear them."

'The rich man answered: "Nay, father Abraham; but if one dead shall arise they
will believe."

'Abraham answered: "Whoso believeth not Moses and the prophets will not believe
even the dead if they should arise.

'See then whether the poor are blessed,' said Jesus, 'who have patience, and
only desire that which is necessary, hating the flesh. O wretched they, who bear
others to the burial, to give their flesh for food of worms, and do not learn
the truth. So far from it that they live here like immortals, for they build
great houses and purchase great revenues and live in pride.'

Chapter 25 How one ought to despise the flesh, and how one ought to live in the
world.

Then said he who writeth: 'O master, true are thy words and therefore have we
forsaken all to follow thee. Tell us, then how we ought to hate our flesh: for
to kill oneself is not lawful, and living we needs must give it its livelihood.'

Jesus answered: 'Keep thy flesh like a horse, and thou shalt live securely. For
unto a horse food is given by measure, and labour without measure, and the
bridle is put on him that he may walk at thy will, he is tied up that he may not
annoy any one, he is kept in a poor place, and beaten when he is not obedient:
so do thou, then, O Barnabas, and thou shalt live always with God.

'And be not offended at my words, for David the prophet did the same thing, as
he confesseth , saying: "I am as an horse before thee: and am always by thee."

'Now tell me, whether is poorer he who is content with little, or he who
desireth much? Verily I say unto you, that if the world had but a sound mind
no one would amass anything for himself, but all would be in common. But in
this is known its madness, that the more it amasseth the more it desireth, And
much as it amasseth, for the fleshly repose of others doth it amass the same.
Therefore let one single robe suffice for you, cast away your purse, carry no
wallet, no sandals on your feet; and do not think, saying: "What shall happen to
us ?" but have thought to do the will of God, and he will provide for your need,
insomuch that nothing shall be lacking unto you.

'Verily I say unto you. that the amassing much in this life giveth sure witness
of not having anything to receive in the other. For he that hath Jerusalem for
his native country buildeth not houses in Samaria, for that there is enmity
between there cities. Understand ye?'

'Yea, answered the disciples.

Chapter 26   How one ought to love God. And in this chapter is contained the
wonderful contention of Abraham with his father.

Then Jesus said: "There was a man on a journey who, as he was walking,
discovered a treasure in a field that was to be sold for five pieces of money.
Straightway the man, when he knew this, sold his cloak to buy that field. Is
that credible?" The disciples answered: "He who would not believe this is mad."

Thereupon Jesus said: "You will be mad if you do not give your senses to God to
buy your soul in which resides the treasure of love; for love is an incomparable
treasure. For he that loves God has God for his own; and whoever has God has
everything." Peter answered: "O master, how can one love God with true love?
Tell us."

Jesus replied: "Truly I say to you that he who shall not hate his father and his
mother, and his own life, and children and wife for love of God, such is not
worthy to be loved of God." Peter answered: "O master, it is written in the Law
of God in the Book of Moses: Honour your father, that you may live long upon the
earth. And further he says: Cursed be the son that obeys not his father and his
mother" God commanded that such a disobedient son should be stoned by the wrath
of the people before the gate of the city. [Why] do you bid us to hate father
and mother?"

Jesus replied: "Every word of mine is true, because it is not mine, but God's,
who has sent me to the House of Israel. Therefore I say to you that all that
which you possess God has bestowed it upon you: and so, what is more precious,
the gift or the giver? When your father and your mother with every other thing
is a stumbling block to you in the service of God, abandon them as enemies. Did
not God say to Abraham: Go forth from the house of your father and of your
kindred, and come to dwell in the land which I will give to you and to your
seed? Why did God say this, except that the father of Abraham was an image-
maker, who made and worshipped false gods? [For this reason] there was enmity
between them, such that the father wished to burn his son." Peter answered:
"Your words are true. I pray you tell us how Abraham mocked his father."

Jesus replied: "Abraham was seven years old when he began to seek God. So one
day he said to his father: 'Father, what made man?' The foolish father answered:
'Man [made man]; for I made you, and my father made me.' Abraham answered:
'Father, it is not so; for I have heard an old man weeping and saying: 'O my
God, why have you not given me children?'' His father replied: 'It is true, my
son, that God helps man to make man, but he does not put his hands to [the
task]; it is only necessary that man come to pray to his God and to give him
lambs and sheep, and his God will help him.' Abraham answered: 'How many gods
are there, father?' The old man replied: 'They are infinite in number, my son.'

Then Abraham said: 'O father, what shall I do if I serve one god and another
[god] wishes me evil because I do not serve him? In any case discord will come
between them, and so war will arise among the gods. And if, perhaps, the god
that wills me evil shall slay my own god, what shall I do? It is certain that he

will slay me also. The old man, laughing, answered: "O son, have no fear, for no god makes war upon another god; no, in the great temple there are a thousand gods with the great god Baal; and I am now near seventy years old, and yet never have I seen that one god has smitten another god. And assuredly all men do not serve one god, but one man one, and another."

Abraham answered: "So, then, they have peace among themselves?" His father said: "They have." Then said Abraham: "O father, what be the gods like?" The old man answered: "Fool, every day I make a god, which I sell to others to buy bread, and you know not what the gods are like!" And then at that moment he was making an idol. "This," said he, "is of palm wood, that one is of olive, that little one is of ivory: see how fine it is! Does it not seem as though it were alive? Assuredly, it lacks but breath!"

Abraham answered: "And so, father, the gods are without breath? Then how do they give breath? And being without life, how give they life? It is certain, father, that these are not God." The old man was wroth at these words, saying: "If you were of age to understand, I would break your head with this axe: But hold your peace, because you have not understanding!" Abraham answered: "Father, if the gods help to make man, how can it be that man should make the gods? And if the gods are made of wood, it is a great sin to burn wood. But tell me, father, how is it that, when you have made so many gods, the gods have not helped you to make so many other children that you should become the most powerful man in the world?"

The father was beside himself, hearing his son speak so; the son went on: "Father, was the world for some time without men?" Yes," answered the old man, "and why?" "Because," said Abraham, "I should like to know who made the first God." "Now go out of my house!" said the old man, "and leave me to make this god quickly, and speak no words to me; for, when you are hungry you desire bread and not words." Abraham said: "A fine god, truly, that you cut him as you will, and he defends not himself!" Then the old man was angry, and said: "All the world says that it is a god, and you, mad fellow, say that it is not. By my gods, if you were a man I could kill you!" And having said this, he gave blows and kicks to Abraham, and chased him from the house."

Chapter 27   In this chapter is clearly seen how improper is laughter in men: also the prudence of Abraham.

The disciples laughed over the madness of the old man, and stood amazed at the prudence of Abraham. But Jesus reproved them, saying: "You have forgotten the words of the prophet, who says: Present laughter is a herald of weeping to come, and further, You shall not go where is laughter, but sit where they weep, because this life passes in miseries." Then Jesus said, "In the time of Moses, know you not that for laughing and mocking at others God turned into hideous beasts many men of Egypt? Beware that in anywise you laugh not at any one, for you shall surely weep [for it]."

The disciples answered: "We laughed over the madness of the old man." Then Jesus said: "Truly I say to you, every like loves his like, and therein finds pleasure. Therefore, if you were not mad you would not laugh at madness. They answered: "My God have mercy on us. Jesus said: "So be it."

Then said Philip: "O master, how came it to pass that Abraham's father wished to burn his son?" Jesus answered: "One day, Abraham having come to the age of twelve years, his father said to him: "Tomorrow is the festival of all the gods; therefore we shall go to the great temple and bear a present to my god, great

Baal. And you shall choose for yourself a god, for you are of age to have a
god."

Abraham answered with guile: "Willingly, O my father." And so betimes in the
morning they went before every one else to the temple. But Abraham bare beneath
his tunic an axe hidden. Whereupon, having entered into the temple, as the crowd
increased Abraham hid himself behind an idol in a dark part of the temple. His
father, when he departed, believed that Abraham had gone home before him,
wherefore he did not stay to seek him.

Chapter 28

When every one had departed from the temple, the priests closed the temple and
went away. Then Abraham took the axe and cut off the feet of all the idols,
except the great god Baal. At its feet he placed the axe, amid the ruins which
the statues made, for they, through being old and composed of pieces, fell in
pieces. Thereupon, Abraham, going forth from the temple, seen by certain men,
who suspected him of having gone to thieve something from the temple. So they
laid hold on him, and having arrived at the temple, when they saw their gods so
broken in pieces, they cried out with lamentation: "Come quickly, O men, and let
us slay him who has slain our gods!" There ran together there about ten thousand
men, with the priests, and questioned Abraham of the reason why he had destroyed
their gods.

Abraham answered: "You are foolish! Shall then a man slay God? It is the great
God that has slain them. See you not that axe which he has near his feet?
Certain it is that he desires no fellows." Then arrived there the father of
Abraham, who, mindful of the many discourses of Abraham against their gods, and
recognizing the axe wherewith Abraham had broken in pieces the idols, cried out:
"It has been this traitor of a son of mine, who has slain our gods! for this axe
is mine." And he recounted to them all that had passed between him and his son.
Accordingly the men collected a great quantity of wood, and having bound
Abraham's hands and feet put him upon the wood, and put fire underneath.

'Lo! God, through his angel, commanded the fire that it should not burn Abraham
his servant. The fire blazed up with great fury, and burned about two thousand
men of those who had condemned Abraham to death. Abraham truly found himself
free, being carried by the angel of God near to the house of his father, without
seeing who carried him; and thus Abraham escaped death."

Chapter 29

Then Philip said: "Great is the mercy of God upon whoever loves him. Tell us, O
master, how Abraham came to [have] the knowledge of God." Jesus answered:
"Having arrived near to the house of his father, Abraham feared to go into the
house; so he removed [himself] some distance from the house and sat under a palm
tree, where, being by himself, he said:"There must be a God who has life and
power more than man, since he makes man, and man without God could not make
man."

Thereupon, looking round upon the stars, the moon, and the sun, he thought that
they had been God. But after considering their variableness with their
movements, hesaid: "It must be [necessarily] that God does not move and that
clouds do not hide him [as they hide the planets]; otherwise men would be
reduced to nothing." Remaining thus in suspense, he heard himself called by
name, "Abraham!" And so, turning round and not seeing any one on any side, he

said: "I am sure I heard myself called by name, 'Abraham. " Then, two other times in a similar manner, he heard himself called by name, "Abraham!"

He answered: "What calls me?" Then he heard [the voice] say: "I am the angel of God, Gabriel." Abraham was filled with fear; but the angel comforted him, saying: "Do not fear, Abraham, for you are friend of God When you broke in pieces the gods of men, you were chosen [by] the God of the angels and prophets such that you are written in the Book of Life." Then said Abraham: "What should I do [so as] to serve the God of the angels and holy prophets?" The angel answered: "Go to that fount and wash yourself, for God wishes to speak with you."

Abraham answered: "How should I wash myself?" Then the angel appeared to him as a beautiful youth, and washed himself in the fount, saying: "Do the same as this, O Abraham." When Abraham had washed himself, the angel said: "Go up that mountain, for God wilshes to speak to you there." Abraham ascended the mountain as the angel [had instructed him], and having sat down upon his knees he said to himself: "When will the God of the angels speak to me?" He heard himself called with a gentle voice: "Abraham!" Abraham answered him: "Who calls me?" The voice answered: "I am your God, O Abraham."

Abraham, filled with fear, bent his face to earth, saying: "How shall your servant who is dust and ashes hearken to you!" Then said God: "Fear not, but rise up, for I have chosen you as my servant, and I will bless you and make you increase into a great people. Therefore go forth from the house of your father and of your kindred, and come to dwell in the land which I will give to you and to your seed."

Abraham answered: "I will do everything, Lord; but guard me [so] that no other god may harm me." Then God spoke, saying: "I am God alone, and there is none other god but me. I strike down, and make whole; I slay, and give life; I lead down to hell, and I bring out thereof, and no-one is able to deliver himself out of my hands." Then God gave him the covenant of circumcision; and so our father Abraham knew God." And having said this, Jesus lifted up his hands, saying: "To you be honour and glory, O God. So be it!"

Chapter 30

Jesus went to Jerusalem, near to the Senofegia, a feast of our nation . The scribes and Pharisees having perceived this, took counsel to catch him in his talk. Whereupon, there came to him a doctor, saying: "Master, what must I do to have eternal life?" Jesus answered: "How is it written in the Law?" The tempter answered, saying: "Love the Lord your God, and your neighbour. You shall love your God above all things, with all your heart and your mind, and your neighbour as yourself." Jesus answered: "You have answered well: therefore go and do you so, I say, and you shall have eternal life." He said to him: "And who is my neighbour?"

Jesus answered, lifting up his eyes: "A man was going down from Jerusalem to go to Jericho, a city rebuilt under a curse. This man on the road was seized by robbers, wounded and stripped; whereupon they departed, leaving him half dead. It chanced that a priest passed by that place, and he, seeing the wounded man, passed on without greeting him. In like manner passed a Levite, without saying a word. It chanced that there passed [also] a Samaritan, who, seeing the wounded man, was moved to compassion, and alighted from his horse, and took the wounded man and washed his wounds with wine, and anointed them with ointment, and binding up his wounds for him and comforting him, he set him upon his own horse.

Whereupon, having arrived in the evening at the inn, he gave him into the charge
of the host. And when he had risen on the morrow, he said: "Take care of this
man, and I will pay you all." And having presented four gold pieces to the sick
man for the host, he said: "Be of good cheer, for I will speedily return and
conduct you to my own home." "Tell me," said Jesus, "which of these was the
neighbour?" The doctor answered: "He who showed mercy." Then Jesus said: "You
have answered rightly; therefore go and do you likewise." The doctor departed in
confusion.

Chapter 31

Then drew near to Jesus the priests, and said: "Master, is it lawful to give
tribute to Caesar?" Jesus turned round to Judas, and said: "Have you any money?"
And taking a penny in his hand, Jesus turned himself to the priests, and said to
them: "This penny has an image: tell me, whose image is it?" They answered:
"Caesar"s". "Give therefore," said Jesus, "that which is Caesar's to Caesar, and
that which is God's give it to God." Then they departed in confusion.

And behold there drew near a centurion, saying: "Lord, my son is sick; have
mercy on my old age!" Jesus answered: "The Lord God of Israel have mercy on
you!" The man was departing; and Jesus said: "Wait for me, for I will come to
your house, to make prayer over your son." The centurion answered: "Lord, I am
not worthy that you, a prophet of God, should come to my house, sufficient to me
is the word that you have spoken for the healing of my son; for your God has
made you lord over every sickness, even as his angel said to me in my sleep."

Then Jesus marvelled greatly, and turning to the crowd, he said: "Behold this
stranger, for he has more faith than all that I have found in Israel." And
turning to the centurion, he said: "Go in peace, because God, for the great
faith that he has given you, has granted health to your son." The centurion went
his way, and on the road he met his servants, who announced to him how his son
was healed. The man answered: "At what hour did the fever leave him?" They said:
"Yesterday, at the sixth hour, the heat departed from him."

The man knew that when Jesus said: "The Lord God of Israel have mercy on you,"
his son received his health. *Whereupon the man believed in our God, and having
entered into his house, he brake in pieces all his own gods, saying: "There is
only the God of Israel, the true and living God." Therefore said he: "None shall
eat of my bread that does not worship the God of Israel."

Chapter 32

One skilled in the Law invited Jesus to supper, in order to tempt him. Jesus
came thither with his disciples, and many scribes, to tempt him, waited for him
in the house. Whereupon, the disciples sat down to table without washing their
hands. The scribes called Jesus, saying: "Wherefore do not your disciples
observe the traditions of our elders, in not washing their hands before they eat
bread?" Jesus answered: "And I ask you, for what cause have you annulled the
precept of God to observe your traditions? You say to the sons of poor fathers:
"Offer and make vows to the Temple."

And they make vows of that little wherewith they ought to support their fathers.
And when their fathers wish to take money, the sons cry out: "This money is
consecrated to God"; whereby the fathers suffer. O false scribes, hypocrites,
does God use this money? Assuredly not, for God eats not, as he says by his
servant David the prophet: Shall I then eat the flesh of bulls and drink the

blood of sheep? Render to me the sacrifice of praise, and offer to me your vows; for if I should be hungry I will not ask aught of you, seeing that all things are in my hands, and the abundance of paradise is with me. Hypocrites! you do this to fill your purse, and therefore you tithe rue and mint.

Oh miserable ones! for to others you show the most clear way, by which you will not go. 'You scribes and doctors lay upon the shoulders of others weights of unbearable weight, but you yourselves the while are not willing to move them with one of your fingers. Truly I say to you, that every evil has entered into the world under the pretext of the elders. Tell me, who made idolatry to enter into the world, if not the usage of the elders? For there was a king who exceedingly loved his father, whose name was Baal.

Whereupon, when the father was dead, his son for his own consolation, caused to be made an image like to his father, and set it up in the market-place of the city. And he made a decree that every one who approached that statue within a space of fifteen cubits should be safe, and no one any account should do him hurt. Hence the malefactors, by reason of the benefit they received therefrom, began to offer to the statue roses and flowers, and in a short time the offerings were changed into money and food, insomuch that they called it god, to honour it. Which thing from custom was transformed into a law, insomuch that the idol of Baal spread through all the world;

and how much does God lament this by the prophet Isaiah, saying: "Truly this people worships me in vain, for they have annulled my Law given to them by my servant Moses, and follow the traditions of their elders.

Truly I say to you, that to eat bread with unclean hands defiles not a man, because that which enters into the man defiles not the man, but that which comes out of the man defiles the man." Thereupon, said one of the scribes: "If I shall eat pork, or other unclean meats, will they not defile my conscience?" Jesus answered: "Disobedience will not enter into the man, but will come out of the man, from his heart; and therefore will he be defiled when he shall eat forbidden food."

Then said one of the doctors: "Master, you have spoken much against idolatry as though the people of Israel had idols, and so you have done us wrong." Jesus answered: "I know well that in Israel today there are not statues of wood; but there are statues of flesh." Then answered all the scribes in wrath: "And so we are idolaters?" Jesus answered: "Truly I say to you, the precept says not "You shall worship", but "You shall love the Lord your God with all your soul, and with all your heart, and with all your mind." Is this true?" said Jesus. "It is true" answered every one.

Chapter 33

Then Jesus said: "Truly all that which a man loves, for which he leaves everything else but that, is his god. And so the fornicator has for his image the harlot, the glutton and drunkard has for image his own flesh, and the covetous has for his image silver and gold, and so likewise every other sinner." Then said he who had invited him: "Master, which is the greatest sin?"

Jesus answered: "Which is the greatest ruin of a house?" Every one was silent, when Jesus with his finger pointed to the foundation, and said: "If the foundation give way, immediately the house falls in ruin, in such wise that it is necessary to build it up anew: but if every other part give way it can be repaired. Even so then say I to you, that idolatry is the greatest sin, because it deprives a man entirely of faith, and consequently of God; so that he can have no spiritual affection. But every other sin leaves to man the hope of obtaining mercy: and therefore I say that idolatry is the greatest sin." All stood amazed at the speaking of Jesus, for they perceived that it could not in any wise be assailed.

Then Jesus continued: "Remember that which God spoke and which Moses and Joshua wrote in the Law, and you shall see how grave is this sin. God said, speaking to Israel: "You shall not make to yourself any image of those things which are in heaven nor of those things which are under the heaven, nor shall you make it of those things which are above the earth, nor of those which are under the earth; nor of those things which are above the water, nor of those which are under the water. For I am your God, strong and jealous, who will take vengeance for this sin upon the fathers and upon their children even to the fourth generation."

Remember how, when our people had made the calf, and when they had worshipped it, by commandment of God Joshua and the tribe of Levi took the sword and slew of them one hundred and twenty thousand of those that did not crave mercy of God. Oh, terrible judgment of God upon the idolaters!"

Chapter 34

There stood before the door one who had his right hand shrunken in such fashion that he could not use it. Whereupon Jesus, having lift up his heart to God, prayed, and then said: "In order that you may know that my words are true, I say, "In the name of God, man, stretch out your infirm hand! " He stretched it out whole, as if it had never had anything wrong with it.

Then with fear of God they began to eat. And having eaten somewhat, Jesus said again: "Truly I say to you, that it were better to burn a city than to leave an evil custom. For on account of such is God wroth with the princes and kings of the earth, to whom God has given the sword to destroy iniquities."

Afterwards said Jesus: "When you are invited, remember not to set yourself in the highest place, in order that if a greater friend of the host come the host say not to you: "Arise and sit lower down!' which were a shame to you. But go and sit in the meanest place, in order that he who invited you may come and say: "Arise, friend, and come and sit here, above!" For then shall you have great honour: for every one that exalts himself shall be humbled, and he that humbles himself shall be exalted.

'Truly I say to you, that Satan became not reprobate for any other sin than for his pride. Even as says the prophet Isaiah;, reproaching him with these words: "How are you fallen from heaven, O Lucifer, that were the beauty of the angels, and did shine like the dawn: truly to earth is fallen your pride!"

'Truly I say to you, that if a man knew his miseries, he would always weep here on earth and account himself most mean, beyond every other thing. For no other cause did the first man with his wife weep for a hundred years without ceasing, craving mercy of God. For they knew truly where they had fallen through their pride."

And having said this, Jesus gave thanks; and that day it was published through Jerusalem how great things Jesus had said, with the miracle he had wrought, insomuch that the people gave thanks to God blessing his holy name.

But the scribes and priests, having understood that he spoke against the traditions of the elders, were kindled with greater hatred. And like Pharaoh they hardened their heart: wherefore they sought occasion to slay him, but found it not.

Chapter 35

Jesus departed from Jerusalem, and went to the desert beyond Jordan: and his disciples that were seated round him said to Jesus: "O master, tell us how Satan fell through pride, for we have understood that he fell through disobedience, and because he always tempts man to do evil."

Jesus answered: "God having created a mass of earth, and having left it for twenty-five thousand years without doing aught else; Satan, who was as it were priest and head of the angels, by the great understanding that he possessed, knew that God of that mass of earth was to take one hundred and forty and four thousand signed with the mark of prophecy, and the Messenger of God, the soul of which messenger he had created sixty thousand years before aught else;. Therefore, being indignant, he instigated the angels, saying: "Look you, one day God shall will that this earth be revered by us. Wherefore consider that we are spirit, and therefore it is not fitting so to do." Many therefore forsook God. Whereupon said God, one day when all the angels were assembled: "Let each one that holds me for his lord straightway do reverence to this earth."

They that loved God bowed themselves, but Satan, with them that were of his mind, said: "O Lord, we are spirit, and therefore it is not just that we should do reverence to this clay;." Having said this, Satan became horrid and of fearsome look, and his followers became hideous; because for their rebellion God took away from them the beauty wherewith he had endued them in creating them. Whereat the holy angels, when, lifting their heads, they saw how terrible a monster Satan ;had become, and his followers, cast down their face to earth in fear. Then said Satan: "O Lord, you have unjustly made me hideous, but I am content thereat, because I desire to annul all that

you shall do. And the other devils said: "Calf him not Lord, O Lucifer;, for you are Lord."

Then said God to the followers of Satan: "Repent you, and recognize me as God, your creator." They answered: "We repent of having done you any reverence, for that

you are not just; but Satan is just. Then said God: "Depart from me, O you cursed, for I have no mercy on you." And in his departing Satan spat up that mass of earth,

and that spittle the angel Gabriel lifted up with some earth, so that therefore now man has the navel in his belly."

Chapter 36

The disciples stood in great amazement at the rebellion of the angels. Then Jesus said: "Truly I say to you, that he who makes not prayer is more wicked than Satan, and shall suffer greater torments. Because Satan had, before his fall, no example of fearing, nor did God so much as send him any prophet to invite him to repentance: but man now that all the prophets are come except the Messenger of God who shall come after me, because so God wills, and that I may prepare his way and man, I say, albeit he have infinite examples of the justice of God, lives carelessly without any fear, as though there were no God. Even as of such spoke the prophet David;: "The fool has said in his heart, there is no God. Therefore are they corrupt and become abominable, without one of them doing good."

Make prayer unceasingly, O my disciples' 'in order that you may receive. For he who seeks finds, and he who knocks to him it is opened, and he who asks receives. And in your prayer do not look to much speaking, for God looks on the heart; as he said through Solomon;: "O my servant, give me your heart." Truly I say to you, as God lives, the hypocrites make much prayer in every part of the city in order to be seen and held for saints by the multitude: but their heart is full of wickedness, and therefore they do not mean that which they ask. It is needful that you mean your prayer if you will that God receive it. Now tell me: who would go to speak to the Roman governor

to Herod, except he first have made up his mind to whom he is going, and what he is going to do? Assuredly none. And if man does so in order to speak with man, what ought man to do in order to speak with God, and ask of him mercy for his sins, while thanking him for all that he has given him?

Truly I say to you, that very few make true prayer, and therefore Satan has power over them, because God wills not those who honour him with their lips: who in the Temple ask [with] their lips for mercy, and their heart cries out for justice. Even as he says to Isaiah the prophet, saying: "Take away this people that is irksome to me, because with their lips they honour me, but their heart is far from me." Truly I say to you, that he that goes to make prayer without consideration mocks God.

Now who would go to speak to Herod with his back towards him, and before him speak well of Pilate the governor, whom he hates to the death? Assuredly none. Yet no less does the man who goes to make prayer and prepares not himself. He turns his back to God and his face to Satan, and speaks well of him. For in his heart is the love of iniquity, whereof he has not repented. If one, having injured you, should with his lips say to you, "Forgive me,' and with his hands should strike you a blow, how would you forgive him? Even so shall God have mercy on those who with their lips say: "Lord, have mercy on us," and with their heart love iniquity and think on fresh sins."

Chapter 37

The disciples wept at the 'words of Jesus and besought him, saying: "Lord, teach us to make prayer." Jesus answered: "Consider what you would do if the Roman governor seized you to put you to death, and that same do you when you go to make prayer. And let your words be these:

"O Lord our God, hallowed be your holy name, your kingdom come in us, your will be done always, and as it is done in heaven so be it done in earth; give us the bread for every day, and forgive us our sins, as we forgive them that sin against us, and suffer us not to fall into temptations, but deliver us from evil, for you are alone our God, to whom pertains glory and honour for ever."

Chapter 38

Then answered John: "Master let us wash ourselves as God commanded by Moses." * Jesus said: "Do you think that I have come to destroy the Law and the prophets? Truly I say to you, as God lives, I have not come to destroy it, but rather to observe it. For every prophet has observed the Law of God and all that God by the other prophets has spoken. As God lives, in whose presence my soul stands, no one that breaks one least precept can be pleasing to God, but shall be least in the kingdom of God, for he shall have no part there. Moreover I say to you, that one syllable of the Law of God cannot be broken without the. gravest sin. But I do you to wit that it is necessary to observe that which God says by Isaiah the prophet, with these words: "Wash you and be clean, take away your thoughts from my eyes. 'Truly I say to you, that all the water of the sea will not wash him who with his heart loves iniquities.

And furthermore I say to you, that no one will make prayer pleasing to God if he be not washed, but will burden his soul with sin like to idolatry. 'Believe me, in sooth, that if man should make prayer to God as is fitting, he would obtain all that he should ask. Remember Moses the servant of God, who with his prayer scourged Egypt, opened the Red Sea, and there drowned Pharaoh and his host. Remember Joshua, who made the sun stand still, Samuel, who smote with fear the innumerable host of the Philistines; , Elijah, who made the fire to rain from heaven, Elisha raised a dead man, and so many other holy prophets, who by prayer obtained all that they asked. But those men truly did not seek their own in their matters, but sought only God and his honour."

Chapter 39

Then said John: "Well have you spoken, O master, but we lack to know how man sinned through pride." Jesus answered: "When God has expelled Satan, and the angel Gabriel had purified that mass of earth whereon Satan spat, God created everything that lives, both of the animals that fly and of them that walk and swim, and he adorned the world with all that it has. One day Satan approached to the gates of paradise, and, seeing the horses eating grass, he announced to them that if that mass of earth should receive a soul there would be for them grievous labour; and that therefore it would be to their advantage to trample that piece of earth in such wise that it should be no more good for anything.

The horses aroused themselves and impetuously set themselves to run over that piece of earth which lay among lilies and roses;. Whereupon God gave spirit to that unclean portion of earth upon which lay the spittle of Satan, which Gabriel had taken up from the mass; and raised up the dog, who, barking, filled the horses with fear, and they fled. Then God gave his soul to man, while all the holy angels sang: "Blessed be your holy name, O God our Lord." "Adam, having sprung upon his feet, saw in the air a writing that shone like the sun;, which said: "There is only one God, and Muhammad is the Messenger of God."

Whereupon Adam opened his mouth and said: "I thank you, O Lord my God, that you have deigned to create me; but tell me. I pray you, what means the message of these words: "Muhammad is Messenger of God. Have there been other men before me?" 'Then said God: "Be you welcome, O my servant Adam. . I tell you that you are the first man whom I have created. And he whom you have seen [mentioned] is your son, who shall come into the world many years hence, and shall be my Messenger, for whom I have created all things; who shall give light to the world when he shall come; whose soul was set in a celestial splendour ;sixty thousand years before I made any. thing."

Adam besought God, saying: "Lord, grant me this writing upon the nails of the fingers of my hands." Then God gave to the first man upon his thumbs that writing; upon the thumb-nail of the right hand it said: "There is only one God;," and upon the thumb-nail of the left it said: "Muhammad is Messenger ;of

God." Then with fatherly affection the first man kissed those words, and rubbed his eyes, and said: "Blessed be that day when you shall come to the world."

Seeing the man alone, God said: "It is not well that he should remain alone." Wherefore he made him to sleep, and took a rib from near his heart, filling the place with flesh. * Of that rib made he Eve, and gave her to Adam for his wife. He set the twain of them as lords of Paradise, to whom he said: "Behold I give to you every fruit to eat, except the apples and the corn" whereof he said: "Beware that in no wise you eat of these fruits, for you shall become unclean, insomuch that I shall not suffer. You to remain here, but shall drive you forth, and you shall suffer great miseries."

Chapter 40

When Satan had knowledge of this he became mad with indignation, and so he drew near to the gate of paradise where a horrid serpent with legs like a camel, and nails on his feet [that] cut like a razor on every side, stood on guard. The enemy said to him: 'Let me to enter into paradise.'

The serpent answered: 'How shall I let you enter [since] God has commanded me to cast you out?' Satan answered: 'You see how much God loves you; he has set you outside of paradise to keep guard over a lump of clay, which is man! If you bring me into paradise I will make you so terrible that every one shall flee you, and so you shall go and stay at your pleasure.' Then the serpent said: 'And how shall I set you within [paradise]?'

Satan said, 'You are great: therefore, open your mouth, and I will enter into your belly, and so [when] you enter into paradise [you] shall place me near to those two lumps of clay that are newly walking upon the earth.' Then the serpent did so, and placed Satan near Eve, for Adam, her husband, was sleeping. Satan presented himself before the woman like a beauteous angel, and said to her: 'Why do you not eat of those apples and corn?' Eve answered: 'Our God has said to us that [if we] eat [them] we shall be unclean, and he will drive us from paradise.'

Satan answered: 'He does not speak the truth! You must know that God is wicked and envious, and suffers no equals, but keeps every one as a slave. [This is] why he has said this [to you]; in order that you may not become equal to him. But if you and your companion do according to my counsel, you shall eat of those fruits as [you eat] of the other [fruits], and you shall not remain subject to others but like God you shall know good and evil, and you shall do whatever you please, because you shall be equal to God.'

Then Eve took and ate of those [fruits], and when her husband awoke she told [him everything] that Satan had said; and he took and ate the fruit [when] his wife offered them to him. But, as the food was going down, he remembered the words of God, and, wishing to stop the food, he put his hand into his throat, where every man has the mark.

Chapter 41

Then both of them knew that they were naked, and, being ashamed, they took fig leaves and made a clothing for their secret parts. When midday was passed, God appeared to them, and called Adam, saying: 'Adam, where are you?' He answered: 'Lord, I hid myself from your presence because my wife and I are naked, and so we are ashamed to present ourselves before you.' Then God said: 'And who has robbed you of your innocence, unless you have eaten the fruit [that makes you] unclean, and will not be able to abide [any] longer in paradise?'

Adam answered: 'O Lord, the wife whom you have given me [urged] me to eat [it] and so I have eaten it.' Then God said to the woman: 'Why did you give [this] food to your husband?' Eve answered: 'Satan deceived me, and so I ate [the fruit].' 'And how did that reprobate enter into [the garden]?' said God. Eve answered: 'A serpent that stands at the northern gate brought him near to me.'

Then God said to Adam: 'Because you have [listened to] your wife and have eaten the fruit, cursed be the earth in your works; it shall bring forth brambles and thorns for you, and you shall eat bread by the sweat of your face. Remember that you are earth, and to earth you return.' And he spoke to Eve, saying: 'And you who did [listen] to Satan, and gave the food to your husband, shall abide under the dominion of man, who shall keep you as a slave, and you shall bear children with travail.'

And having called the serpent, God called the angel Michael, who holds the sword of God, [and] said: 'First drive this wicked serpent forth from paradise, and when outside cut off his legs: for if he wants to walk, he must trail his body upon the earth.' Afterwards God called Satan, who came laughing, and he said to him: 'Because you, reprobate, have deceived [Adam and Eve] and have made them unclean, I will that every uncleanness [from] them and [from] all their children - [of which] they shall be truly penitent and shall serve me - in going forth from their body shall enter through your mouth, and so shall you be satiated with uncleanness.'

Satan then gave a horrible roar, and said: 'Since you will to make me [continually] worse, I will make me that which I shall be able!' Then said God: 'Depart, cursed one, from my presence!' Then Satan departed, and God said to Adam [and] Eve, who were both weeping: 'Go forth from paradise, and do penance, and do not let your hope fail, for I will send your son so that your seed shall lift the dominion of Satan from off the human race: for I will give all things to he who shall come, my Messenger.'

God hid himself [from Adam and Eve], and the angel Michael drove them forth from paradise. Then, Adam, turning around, saw written above the gate, There is only one God, and Muhammad is Messenger of God. Weeping, he said: 'May it be pleasing to God, O my son, that you come quickly and draw us out of misery.' And thus," said Jesus, "Satan and Adam sinned through pride, the one by despising man, the other by wishing to make himself equal with God."

Chapter 42

Then the disciples wept after this discourse, and Jesus was weeping, when they saw many who came to find him, for the chiefs of the priests took counsel among themselves to catch him in his talk. Wherefore they sent the Levites and some of the scribes to question him, saying: "Who are you?"

Jesus confessed, and said the truth: "I am not the Messiah." They said: "Are you Elijah or Jeremiah, or any of the ancient prophets?" Jesus answered: "No." Then said they: "Who are you? Say, in order that we may give testimony to those who sent us." Then Jesus said: "I am a voice that cries through all Judea, and cries: "Prepare you the way for the messenger of the Lord," even as it is written in Esaias;."

They said: "If you be not the Messiah nor Elijah, or any prophet, wherefore do you preach new doctrine, and make yourself of more account than the Messiah?" Jesus answered: "The miracles which God works by my hands show that I speak that which God wills; nor indeed do I make myself to be accounted as him of whom you speak. For I am not worthy to unloose the ties of the hosen or the ratchets of the shoes of the Messenger of God whom you call "Messiah," who was made before me, and shall come after me, and shall bring the words of truth, so that his faith shall have no end."

The Levites and scribes departed in confusion, and recounted all to the chiefs of the priests, who said: "He has the devil on his back who recounts all to him." Then Jesus said to his disciples: "Truly I say to you, that the chiefs and the elders of our people seek occasion against me." Then said Peter: "Therefore go not you any more into Jerusalem." Therefore said Jesus to him: "You are foolish, and know not what you say, for it is necessary that I should suffer many persecutions, because so have suffered all the prophets and holy one of God. But fear not, for there be that are with us and there be that are against us."

And having said this, Jesus departed and went to the mount Tabor, and there ascended with him Peter ;and James ;and John ;his brother, with him who writes this. Whereupon there shone a great light above him, and his garments became white like snow and his face glistened as the sun;, and lo! there came Moses and Elijah; speaking with Jesus concerning all that needs must come upon our race and upon the holy city.

Peter spoke, saying: "Lord, it is good to be here. Therefore, if you will, we will make here three tabernacles, one for you and one for Moses and the other for Elijah." And while he spoke they were covered with a white cloud, and they heard a voice saying: "Behold my servant, in whom I am well pleased; hear you him."

The disciples were filled with fear, and fell with their face upon the earth as dead. Jesus went down and raised up his disciples, saying: "Fear not, for God loves you, and has done this in order that you may believe on my words."

Chapter 43

Jesus went down to the eight disciples who were awaiting him below. And the four narrated to the eight all that they had seen: and so there departed that day from their heart all doubt of Jesus, save [from] Judas Iscariot, who believed nothing. Jesus seated himself at the foot of the mountain, and they ate ofthe wild fruits, because they had not bread. Then said Andrew: "You have told us many things of the Messiah, therefore of your kindness tell us clearly all." And in like

manner the other disciples besought him.

Accordingly Jesus said: "Everyone that works works for an end in which he finds satisfaction. Wherefore I say to you that God, truly because he is perfect, has not need of satisfaction, seeing that he has satisfaction himself. And so, willing to work, he created before all things the soul of his Messenger, for whom he determined to create the whole, in order that the creatures should find joy and blessedness in God, whence his Messenger should take delight in all his creatures, which he has appointed to be his slaves. And wherefore is this, so save because thus he has willed?

Truly I say to you, that every prophet when he is come has borne to one nation only the mark of the mercy of God. And so their words were not extended save to that people to which they were sent. But the Messenger of God, when he shall come, God shall give to him as it were the seal of his hand, insomuch that he shall carry salvation and mercy to all the nations of the world that shall receive his doctrine. He shall come with power upon the ungodly, and shall destroy idolatry, insomuch that he shall make Satan confounded; for so promised God to Abraham, saying: "Behold, in your seed I will bless all the tribes of the earth; and as you have broken in pieces the

idols, O Abraham;, even so shall your seed do.""

James answered: "O master, tell us in whom this promise was made; for the Jews say "in Isaac," and the Ishmaelites say "in Ishmael;." Jesus answered: David, whose son was he, and of what lineage?" James answered: "Of Isaac; for Isaac was father of Jacob, and Jacob was father of Judah, of whose lineage is David."

Then Jesus said: "And the Messenger of God when he shall come, of what lineage will he be?" The disciples answered: "Of David." Whereupon Jesus said: "You deceive yourselves; for David in spirit calls him lord, saying thus: God said to my lord, sit you on my right hand until I make your enemies your footstool. God shall send forth your rod which shall have lordship in the midst of your enemies. If the Messenger of God whom you call Messiah were son of David, how should David call him lord? Believe me, for truly I say to you, that the promise was made in Ishmael, not in Isaac."

Chapter 44

The disciples said: "O master, it is written in the Book of Moses, that the promise was made in Isaac." Jesus answered with a groan: "It is so written, but Moses did not write it, nor Joshua, but rather our rabbins, who do not fear God! Truly I say to you, that if you consider the words of the angel Gabriel, you shall discover the malice of our scribes and doctors. For the angel said: "Abraham, all the world shall know how God loves you; but how shall the world know the love

that you bear to God? Assuredly it is necessary that you do something for love of God." Abraham answered: 'Behold the servant of God, ready to do all that which God shall will.'

Then spoke God, saying to Abraham: "Take your son, your firstborn Ishmael;, and come up the mountain to sacrifice him." How is Isaac firstborn, if when Isaac was born Ishmael was seven years old? Then said the disciples: "Clear is the deception of our doctors: therefore tell us you the truth, because we know that you are sent from God." Then answered Jesus: "Truly I say to you, that Satan ever seeks to annul the laws of God; and therefore he with his followers, hypocrites and evil-doers, the former with false doctrine, the latter with lewd living, to day have contaminated almost all things, so that scarcely is the truth found. Woe to the hypocrites! for the praises of this world shall turn for them into insults and torments in hell.

"I therefore say to you that the Messenger of God is a splendour that shall give gladness to nearly all that God has made, for he is adorned with the spirit of understanding and of counsel, the spirit of wisdom and might, the spirit of fear and love, the spirit of prudence and temperance, he is adorned with the spirit of charity and mercy, the spirit of justice and Piety, the spirit of gentleness and patience, which he has received from God three times more than he has given to all his creatures.

O blessed time, when he shall come to the world! Believe me that I have seen him and have done. him reverence, even as every prophet has seen him: seeing that of his spirit God gives to them prophecy. And when I saw him my soul was filled with consolation, saying: "O Muhammad;, God be with you, and may he make me worthy to untie, your shoelatchet;, for obtaining this I shall be a great prophet and holy one of God." And having said this, Jesus rendered his thanks to God.

Chapter 45

Then came the angel Gabriel to Jesus, and spoke to him in such wise that we also heard his voice, which said: "Arise, and go to Jerusalem!" Accordingly Jesus departed and went up to Jerusalem. And on the sabbath day he entered into the Temple;, and began to teach the people. Whereupon the people ran together to the Temple with the high priest and priests, who drew near to Jesus, saying: "O master, it has been said to us that you say evil of us; therefore beware lest

some evil befall you." Jesus answered: "Truly I say to you, that I speak evil of the hypocrites; therefore if you be hypocrites I speak against you." They answered: "Who is a hypocrite? Tell us plainly."

Jesus said: "Truly I say to you, that he who does a good thing in order that men may see him, even he is a hypocrite, forasmuch as his work penetrates not the heart which men cannot see, and so leaves therein every unclean thought and every filthy lust. Know you who is hypocrite? He who with his tongue serves God, but with his heart serves men. O wretched man! for dying he loses all his reward. For on this matter says the prophet David: "Put not your confidence in princes, [nor] in the children of men, in whom is no salvation; for at death their thoughts perish": no, before death they find themselves deprived of reward, for "man is," as said Job the prophet of

God, "unstable, so that he never continues in one stay." So that if today he praises you, tomorrow he will abuse you, and if today he wills to reward you, tomorrow he will be fain to despoil you. Woe, then, to the hypocrites, because their reward is vain. As God lives, in whose presence I stand, the hypocrite is a robber and commits sacrilege, inasmuch as he makes use of the Law to appear good, and thieves the honour of God, to whom alone pertains praise and honour for ever.

Furthermore I say to you, that the hypocrite has not faith, forasmuch as if he believed that God sees all and with terrible judgment would punish wickedness, he would purify his heart, which, because he has not faith, he keeps full of iniquity. Truly I say to you, that the hypocrite is as a sepulchre, that [on the outside] is white, but within is full of corruption and worms. So then if you, O priests, do the service of God because God has created you and asks it of you, I speak not against you, for you are servants of God; but if you do all for gain, and so buy and sell in the Temple as in a market-place, not regarding that the Temple of God is a house of prayer and not of merchandise, which you convert into a cave of robbers: if you do all to please men, and have put God out of your mind; then cry I against you that you are sons of the devil, and not sons of Abraham, who left his father's house for love of God, and was willing to slay his own son. Woe to you, priests and doctors, if you be such, for God will take away from you the priesthood!"

Chapter 46

Again spoke Jesus, saying: "I set before you an example. There was a householder
who planted a vineyard, and made a hedge for it in order that it should not be
trampled down of beasts. And in the midst of it he built a press for the wine,
and thereupon let it out to husbandman. Whereupon, when the time was come to
collect the wine he sent his servants; whom when the husbandman saw, they stoned
some and burned some, and others they ripped open with a knife. And this they
did many times. Tell me, what will the lord of the vineyard do to the
husbandmen"

Every one answered: "In evil wise will he make them to perish, and his vineyard
will he give to other husbandman." Therefore said Jesus: "Know you not that the
vineyard is the House of Israel, and the husbandman are the people of Judah and
Jerusalem? Woe to you; for God is wroth with you, having ripped open so many
prophets of God; so that at the time of Ahab ;there was not found one to bury
the holy ones of God!" And when he had said this the chief priests wished to
seize him, but they feared the common people, which magnified him.

Then Jesus, seeing a woman who from her birth had remained with her head bent
toward the ground, said: "Raise your head, O woman, in the name of our God, in
order that these may know that I speak truth, and that he wills that I announce
it." Then the woman raised herself up whole, magnifying God. The chief of the
priests cried out, saying: "This man is not sent of God, seeing he keeps not the
sabbath; for today he has healed an infirm person."

Jesus answered: "Now tell me, is it not lawful to speak on the sabbath day, and
to make prayer for the salvation of others? And who is there among you who, if
on the sabbath his ass or his ox fell into the ditch, would not pull him out on
the sabbath? Assuredly none. And shall I then have broken the sabbath day by
having given health to a daughter of Israel? Surely, here is known your
hypocrisy! Oh, how many are there today that fear the smiting of a straw in
another's eye, while a beam is ready to cut off their own head! Oh, how many
there are that fear an ant, but reck not of an elephant!" And having said this,
he went forth from the Temple;. But the priests chafed with rage among
themselves, because they were not able to seize him and to work their will upon
him, even as their fathers have done against the holy ones of God.

Chapter 47

Jesus went down, in the second year of his prophetic ministry, from Jerusalem,
and went to Nain. Whereupon, as he drew near to the gate of the city, the
citizens were bearing to the sepulchre the only son of his mother, a widow, over
whom every one was weeping. Whereupon, when Jesus had arrived, the men
understood how that Jesus, a prophet of Galilee;, was come: and so they set
themselves to beseech him for the dead man, that he being a prophet should raise
him up; which also his disciples did. Then Jesus feared greatly, and turning
himself to God, said: "Take me from the world, O Lord, for the world is mad, and
they well near call me God!". And having said this, he wept.

Then came the angel Gabriel, and said: "O Jesus, fear not, for God has given you
power over every infirmity, insomuch that all that you shall grant in the name
of God shall be entirely accomplished." Hereupon Jesus gave a sigh, saying: "Thy
will be done, Lord God almighty and merciful. And having said this, he drew near
to the mother of the dead, and with pity said to her: "Woman, weep not." And
having taken the hand of the dead , he said: "I say to you, young man, in the
name of God arise up healed!" Then the boy revived, whereupon all were filled

with fear, saying: "God has raised up a great prophet amongst us, and he has visited his people."

Chapter 48

At that time the army of the Romans was in Judea, our country being subject to them for the sins of our forefathers. Now it was the custom of the Romans to call god and to worship him that did any new thing of benefit to the common people. And so [some] of these soldiers finding themselves in Nain, they rebuked now one, now another, saying: "One of your gods has visited you, and you make no account of it. Assuredly if our gods should visit us we would give them all

that we have. And you see how much we fear our gods, since to their images we give the best of all we have."

Satan did so instigate this manner of speaking that he aroused no small sedition among the people of Nain. But Jesus did not tarry in Nain, but turned to go into Capernaum. The discord of Nain was such that some said: "He is our God who has visited us"; others said: "God is invisible, so that none has seen him, not even Moses, his servant; therefore it is not God, but rather his son." Others said: "He is not God, nor son of God, for God has not a body to beget anything; but he is a great prophet of God." And so did Satan instigate that, in the third year of the prophetic ministry of Jesus, great ruin to our people was like to arise therefrom.

Jesus went into Capernaum: whereupon the citizens, when they knew him, assembled together all the sick folk they had, and placed them in front of the porch of the house where Jesus was lodging with his disciples. And having called Jesus forth, they besought him for the health of them. Then Jesus laid his hands upon each of them, saying: "God of Israel, by your holy name, give health to this sick person." Whereupon each one was healed. On the sabbath Jesus entered into the synagogue, and all the people ran there together to hear him speak.

Chapter 49

The scribe that day read the psalm of David, where says David: When I shall find a time, I will judge uprightly. Then, after the reading of the prophets, arose Jesus, and made sign of silence with his hands, and opening his mouth he spoke thus: "Brethren, you have heard the words spoken by David the prophet, our father, that when he should have found a time he would judge uprightly. I tell you in truth that many judge, in which judgment they fall for no other reason than

because they judge that which is not meet for them, and that which is meet for them they judge before the time. Wherefore the God of our fathers cries to us by his prophet David, saying: Justly judge, O sons of men.

Miserable therefore are those who set themselves at street corners, and do nothing but judge all those who pass by, saying: "That one is fair, this one is ugly, that one is good, this one is bad." Woe to them, because they lift the sceptre of his judgment from the hand of God, who says: "I am witness and judge, and my honour I will give to none.'" Truly I tell you that these testify of that which they have not seen nor really heard, and judge without having been constituted judges. Therefore are they abominable on the earth before the eyes of God, who will pass tremendous judgment upon them in the last day.

Woe to you, woe to you who speak good of the evil, and call the evil good, for you condemn as a malefactor God, who is the author of good, and justify as good Satan, who is the origin of all evil. Consider what punishment you shall have, and that it is horrible to fall into the judgment of God, which shall be then upon those who justify the wicked for money, and judge not the cause of the orphans and widows. Truly I say to you, that the devils shall tremble at the judgment of such, so terrible shall it be. You man who are set as a judge, regard no other thing; neither kinsfolk nor friends, neither honour nor gain, but look solely with fear of God to the truth, which you shall seek with greatest diligence, because it will secure you in the judgment of God. But I warn you that without mercy shall he be judged who judges without mercy".

Chapter 50

Tell me, O man, you that judge another man, do you not know that all men had their

origin in the same clay? Do you not know that none is good save God alone? wherefore every man is a liar and a sinner. Believe me man, that if you judge others of a fault your own heart has whereof to be judged. Oh, how dangerous it is to judge! oh, how many have perished by their false judgment! Satan judged man to be more vile than himself; therefore he rebelled against God, his creator: whereof he is impenitent, as I have knowledge by speaking with him. Our first parents judged the speech of Satan to be good, therefore they were cast out of paradise, and condemned all their progeny. Truly I say to you, as God lives in whose presence I stand, false judgment is the father of all sins. Forasmuch as none sins without will, and none wills that which he does not know. Woe, therefore, to the sinner who with the judgment judges sin worthy and goodness unworthy, who on that account rejects goodness and chooses sin. Assuredly he shall bear an intolerable punishment when God shall come to judge the world.

Oh, how many have perished through false judgment, and how many ha+ve been near to perishing! Pharaoh judged Moses and the people of Israel to be impious, Saul judged David to be worthy of death, Ahab judged Elijah, Nebuchadnezzar the three children who would not worship their lying gods. The two elders judged Susanna, and all the idolatrous princes judged the prophets. Oh, tremendous judgment of God! the judge perishes, the judged is saved. And wherefore this, O man, if not because [in] rashness they falsely judge the innocent?

How nearly then the good approached to ruin by judging falsely, is shown by the brethren of Joseph, who sold him to the Egyptians, by Aaron and Miriam, sister of Moses, who judged their brother. Three friends of Job ;judged the innocent friend of God, Job. David judged Mephibosheth and Uriah. Cyrus judged Daniel to be meat for the lions; and many others, the which were near to their ruin for this. Therefore I say to you, Judge not and you shall not be judged."

And then, Jesus having finished his speech, many forthwith were converted to repentance, bewailing their sins; and they would fain have forsaken all to go with him. But Jesus said: "Remain in your homes, and forsake sin and serve God with fear, and thus shall you be saved; because I am not come to receive service, but rather to serve." And having said thus, he went out of the synagogue and the city, and retired into the desert to pray, because he loved solitude greatly.

Chapter 51

When he had prayed to the Lord, his disciples came to him and said: "O master, two things we would know; one is, how you talked with Satan, who nevertheless you say is impenitent; the other is, how God shall come to judge in the day of judgment.' Jesus replied: "Truly I say to you I had compassion on Satan, knowing his fall; and I had compassion on mankind whom he tempts to sin. Therefore I prayed and fasted to our God, who spoke to me by his angel Gabriel: "What seek you, O Jesus, and what is your request?" I answered: "Lord, you know of what evil Satan is the cause, and that through his temptations many perish; he is your creature, Lord, whom you did create; therefore, Lord, have mercy upon him." God answered: "Jesus, behold I will pardon him. Only cause him to say, "Lord, my God, I have sinned, have mercy upon me," and I will pardon him and restore him to his first state." 'I rejoiced greatly," said Jesus, when I heard this, believing that I had made this peace. Therefore I called Satan, who came, saying: "What must I do for you, O Jesus?"I answered: "You shall do it for yourself, O Satan, for I love not your services, but for your good have I called you."

Satan replied: "If you desire not my services neither desire I yours; for I am nobler than you, therefore you are not worthy to serve me you who are clay, while I am spirit." "Let us leave this," I said, "and tell me if it were not well you should return to your first beauty and your first state. You must know that the angel Michael must needs on the day of judgment strike you with the sword of God one hundred thousand times, and each blow will give you the pain of ten hells." Satan replied: "We shall see in that day who can do most; certainly I shall have on my side many angels and most potent idolaters who will trouble God, and he shall know how great a mistake he made to banish me for the sake of a vile [piece of] clay." Then I said: "O Satan, you are infirm in mind, and know not what you say."

Then Satan, in a derisive manner wagged his head, saying: "Come now, let us make up this peace between me and God; and what must be done say you, O Jesus, since you are sound in mind." I answered: "Two words only need be spoken." Satan replied: "What words?" I answered: "These: I have sinned; have mercy on me." Then Satan said: "Now willingly will I make this peace if God will say these words to me." "Now depart from me," I said, "O cursed one, for you are the wicked author of all injustice and sin, but God is just and without any sin." Satan departed shrieking, and said: "It is not so, O Jesus, but you tell a lie to please God." Now consider," said Jesus to his disciples, "how he will find mercy. They answered: "Never, Lord, because he is impenitent. Speak to us now of the judgment of God."

Chapter 52

The judgment day of God will be so dreadful that, truly I say to you, the reprobates would sooner choose ten hells than go to hear God speak in wrath against them against whom all things created will witness. Truly I say to you, that not alone shall the reprobates fear, but the saints and the elect of God, so that Abraham shall not trust in his righteousness, and Job shall have no confidence in his innocence. And what say I? Even the Messenger of God shall fear, for that God, to make known his majesty, shall deprive his Messenger of memory, so that he shall have no remembrance how that God has given him all things. Truly I say to you that, speaking from the heart, I tremble because by the world I shall be called God, and for this I shall have to render an account.

As God lives, in whose presence my soul stands, I am a mortal man as other men are, for although God has placed me as prophet over the House of Israel for the health of the feeble and the correction of sinners, I am the servant of God, and of this you are witness, how I speak against those wicked men who after my departure from the world shall annul the truth of my gospel by the operation of Satan. But I shall return towards the end, and with me shall come Enoch and Elijah, and we will testify against the wicked, whose end shall be accursed."

And having thus spoken, Jesus shed tears, whereat his disciples wept aloud, and lifted their voices, saying: "Pardon O Lord God, and have mercy on your innocent servant." Jesus answered: "Amen, Amen."

Chapter 53

"Before that day shall come," said Jesus, "great destruction shall come upon the world, for there shall be war so cruel and pitiless that the father shall slay the son, and the son shall slay the father by reason of the factions of peoples. Wherefore the cities shall be annihilated, and the country shall become desert. Such pestilences shall come that none shall be found to bear the dead to burial, so that they shall be left as food for beasts. To those who remain upon the earth

God shall send such scarcity that bread shall be valued above gold, and they shall eat all manner of unclean things. O miserable age, in which scarce any one shall be heard to say: "I have sinned, have mercy on me, O God"; but with horrible voices they shall blaspheme him who is glorious and blessed for ever.

After this, as that day draws near, for fifteen days, shall come every day a horrible sign over the inhabitants of the earth.

The first day the sun shall run its course in heaven without light, but black as the dye of cloth; and it shall give groans, as a father who groans for a son near to death. The second day the moon shall be turned into blood, and blood shall come upon the earth like dew. The third day the stars shall be seen to fight among themselves like an army of enemies. The fourth day the stones and rocks shall dash against each other as cruel enemies. The fifth day every plant and herb shall weep blood. The sixth day the sea shall rise without leaving its place to the height of one hundred and fifty cubits, and shall stand all day like a wall. The seventh day it shall on the contrary sink so

low as scarcely to be seen. The eighth day the birds and the animals of the earth and of the water shall gather themselves close together, and shall give forth roars and cries. The ninth day there shall be a hailstorm so horrible that it shall kill [such] that scarcely the tenth part of the living shall escape. The tenth day shall come such horrible lightning and thunder [such] that the third part of the mountains shall be split and scorched. The eleventh day every river shall run backwards, and shall run blood and not water. The twelfth day every created thing shall groan and cry. The thirteenth day the heaven shall be rolled up like a book, and it shall rain fire, so that every living thing shall die. The fourteenth day there shall be an earthquake so horrible that the tops of the mountains shall fly through the air like birds, and all the earth shall become a plain. The fifteenth day the holy angels shall die, and God alone shall remain alive; to whom be honour and glory."

And having said this, Jesus smote his face with both his hands, and then smote the ground with his head. And having raised his head, he said: "Cursed be every one who shall insert into my sayings that I am the son of God." At these words the disciples fell down as dead, whereupon Jesus lifted them up, saying: 'Let us fear God now, if we would not be affrighted in that day.'

Chapter 54

When these signs be passed, there shall be darkness over the world forty years,
God alone being alive, to whom be honour and glory forever. When the forty years
have passed, God shall give life to his Messenger, who shall rise again like the
sun, but resplendent as a thousand suns. He shall sit, and shall not speak, for
he shall be as it were beside himself. God shall raise again the four angels
favoured of God, who shall seek the Messenger of God, and, having found him,
shall

station themselves on the four sides of the place to keep watch upon him. Next
shall God give life to all the angels, who shall come like bees circling round
the Messenger of God. Next shall God give life to all his prophets, who,
following Adam, shall go every one to kiss the hand of the Messenger of God,
committing themselves to his protection. Next shall God give life to all the
elect, who shall cry out: "O Muhammad be mindful of us!" At whose cries pity
shall awake in the

Messenger of God, and he shall consider what he ought to do, fearing for their
salvation.

Next shall God give life to every created thing and they shall return to their
former existence, but every one shall besides possess the power of speech. Next
shall God give life to all the reprobates, at whose resurrection, by reason of
their hideousness, all the creatures of God shall be afraid, and shall cry: "Let
not your mercy forsake us, O Lord our God." After this shall God cause Satan ;to
be raised up, at whose aspect every creature shall be as dead, for fear of the
horrid form of his appearance. May it please God," said Jesus, "that I behold
not that monster on that day. The Messenger of God alone shall not be affrighted
by such shapes, because he shall fear God only.

"Then the angel, at the sound of whose trumpet all shall be raised, shall sound
his trumpet again, saying: "Come to the judgment, O creatures, for your Creator
wills to judge you." Then shall appear in the midst of heaven over the valley of
Jehoshaphat; a glittering throne over which shall come a white cloud, whereupon
the angels shall cry out: "Blessed be you our God, who has created us and saved
us from the fall of Satan." Then the Messenger ;of God shall fear, for that he
shall perceive that none has loved God as he should. For he who would get in
change a piece of gold must have sixty mites; wherefore, if he have but one mite
he cannot change it. But if the Messenger of God shall fear, what shall the
ungodly do who are full of wickedness?"

Chapter 55

The Messenger of God shall go to collect all the prophets, to whom he shall
speak praying them to go with him to pray God for the faithful. And every one
shall excuse himself for fear; nor, as God lives, would I go there, knowing what
I know. Then God, seeing this, shall remind his Messenger how he created all
things for love of him, and so his fear shall leave him, and he shall go near to
the throne with love and reverence, while the angels sing: "Blessed be your holy
name O God, our God."

And when he has drawn near to the throne, God shall open [his mind] to his
Messenger, even as a friend to a friend when for a long while they have not met.
The first to speak shall be the Messenger of God, who shall say: "I adore and
love you, O my God, and with all my heart and soul I give you thanks for that
you did vouchsafe to create me to be your servant, and made all for love of me,

so that I might love you for all things and in all things and above all things; therefore let all your creatures praise you, O my God." Then God shall say: "We give you thanks, O Lord, and bless your holy name." Truly I say to you, the demons and reprobates with Satan shall then weep so that more water shall flow from the eyes of one of them than is in the river of Jordan. Yet shall they not see God "And God shall speak to his Messenger, saying: "You are welcome, O my faithful servant; therefore ask what you will, for you shall obtain all." The Messenger of God shall answer. "O Lord, I remember that when you did create me, you said that you had willed to make for love of me the world and paradise, and angels and men, that they might glorify you by me your servant. Therefore, Lord God, merciful and just. I pray you that you recollect your promise made to your servant."

And God shall make answer even as a friend who jests with a friend, and shall say: 'Have you witnesses of this, my friend Muhammad?' And with reverence he shall say: "Yes, Lord." Then God shall answer: "Go, call them, O Gabriel;." The angel Gabriel shall come to the Messenger of God, and shall say: "Lord who are your 'witnesses?" The Messenger of God shall answer: "They are Adam;, Abraham, Ishmael;, Moses;, David;, and Jesus son of Mary.?" "Then shall the angel departs and he shall call the aforesaid witnesses, who with fear shall go thither. And when they are present God shall say to them: Remember you that which my Messenger affirms?" They shall reply: "What thing, O Lord?" God shall say: "That I have made all things for love of him, so that all things might praise me by him."

Then every one of them shall answer: "There are with us three witnesses better than we are, O Lord." And God shall reply: "Who are these three witnesses?" Then Moses shall say: "The book that you gave to me is the first"; and David shall say: "The book that you gave to me is the second"; and he who speaks to you shall say: "Lord the whole world, deceived by Satan, that I was your son and your fellow, but the book that you gave me said truly that I am your servant; and that book confesses that which your Messenger affirms." Then shall the Messenger of God speak, and shall say: "Thus says the book that you gave me O Lord." And when the Messenger

of God has said this, God shall speak, saying: ,All that I have now done, I have done in order that every one should know how much I love you." And when he has thus spoken, God shall give to his Messenger a book, in which are written all the names of the elect of God. Wherefore every creature shall do reverence to God, saying: "To you alone O God, be glory and honour, because you have given us to your Messenger.

Chapter 56

God shall open the book in the hand of his Messenger, and his Messenger reading therein shall call all the angels and prophets and all the elect, and on the forehead of each one shall be written the mark of the Messenger of God. And in the book shall be written the glory of paradise.

Then shall each pass to the right hand of God; next to whom shall sit the Messenger of God. and the prophets shall sit near him, and the saints shall sit near the prophets, and the blessed near the saints, and the angel shall then sound the trumpet, and shall call Satan to judgment.

Chapter 57

Then that miserable one shall come, and with greatest contumely shall be accused of every creature. Wherefore God shall call the angel Michael, who shall strike him one hundred thousand times with the sword of God. He shall strike Satan, and every stroke is heavy as ten hells, and he shall be the first to be cast into the abyss. The angel shall call his followers, and they shall in like manner be abused and accused. Wherefore the angel Michael, by commission from God, shall strike some a hundred times, some fifty, some twenty, some ten, some five. And then shall they descend into the abyss, because God shall say to them: "Hell is your dwelling-place, O cursed ones."

After that shall be called to judgment all the unbelievers and reprobates, against whom shall first arise all creatures inferior to man, testifying before God how they have served these men, and how the same have outraged God and his creatures. And the prophets every one shall arise, testifying against them; wherefore they shall be condemned by God to infernal flames. Truly I say to you, that no idle lord or thought shall pass unpunished in that tremendous day. Truly I say to you, that the hair-shirt shall shine like the sun, and every louse a man shall have borne for love of God shall be turned into pearl. O, thrice and four times blessed are the poor, who in true poverty shall have served God from the heart, for in this world are they destitute of worldly cares, and shall therefore be freed from many sins, and in that day they shall not have to render an account of how they have spent the riches of the world, but they shall be rewarded for their patience and their poverty. Truly I say to you, that if the world knew his it would choose the hair-shirt sooner than purple, lice sooner than gold, fasts sooner than feasts.

When all have been examined, God shall say to his Messenger: "Behold, O my friend, their wickedness, how great it has been, for I their creator did employ all created things in their service and in all things have they dishonoured me. It is most just, therefore, that I have no mercy on them." The Messenger of God shall answer:, "It is true, Lord, our glorious God, not one of your friends and servants could ask you to have mercy on them; no, I your servant before all ask justice against them."

And he having said these words, all the angels and prophets, with all the elect of God no, why say I the elect? truly I say to you, that spiders and flies, stones and sand shall cry out against the impious, and shall demand justice. Then shall God cause to return to earth every living soul inferior to man, and. he shall send the impious to hell. Who, in going, shall see again that earth, to which dogs and horses and other vile animals shall be reduced. Wherefore shall they say: "O Lord God, cause us also to return to that earth." But that which they ask shall not be granted to them."

Chapter 58

While Jesus was speaking the disciples wept bitterly. And Jesus wept many tears. Then after he had wept, John spoke: "O master, we desire to know two things. The one is, how it is possible that the Messenger of God, who is full of mercy and pity, should have no pity on reprobates that day, seeing that they are of the same clay as himself? The other is, how is it to be understood that the sword of Michael is [as] heavy as ten hells? Is there more than one hell?"

Jesus replied: "Have you not heard what David the prophet says, how the just shall laugh at the destruction of sinners, and shall deride him with these words, saying: I saw the man who put his hope in his strength and his riches, and forgot God. Truly, therefore, I say to you, that Abraham shall deride his father, and Adam [shall deride] all reprobate men: and this shall be because the elect shall rise again so perfect and united to God that they shall not conceive in their minds the small[est] thought against his justice. Each of them shall demand justice, and above all the Messenger of God. As God lives, in whose presence I stand, though now I weep for pity of mankind, on that day I shall demand justice without mercy against those who despise my words, and most of all against those who defile my gospel.

Chapter 59

Hell is one, O my disciples, and in it the damned shall suffer punishment eternally. Yet has it seven rooms or regions, one deeper than the other, and he who goes to the deep shall suffer greater punishment. Yet my words [are] true concerning the sword of the angel Michael, for he that commits but one sin merits hell, and he that commits two sins merits two hells. Therefore in one hell the reprobates shall feel punishment as though they were in ten, or in a hundred or in a

thousand; and the omnipotent God, through his power and by reason of his justice, shall cause Satan to suffer as though he were in ten hundred thousand hells, and the rest each one according to his wickedness."

Then Peter answered: "O master, truly the justice of God is great, and today this discourse has made you sad; therefore, we pray you, rest, and tomorrow tell us what hell is like." Jesus answered: "O Peter, you tell me to rest; O Peter, you do not know what you say, [or] else you would not have spoken thus.

Truly I say to you, that rest in this present life is the poison of piety and the fire which consumes every good work. Have you forgotten how Solomon, God's prophet, with all the prophets, has reproved sloth? It is true that he says: The idle will not work the soil for fear of the cold, therefore in summer shall he beg. [And for this reason] he said: All that your hand can do, do it without rest. And what says Job, the most innocent friend of God: As the bird is born to fly, man is born to work. Truly I say to you, I hate rest above all things."

Chapter 60

Hell is one, and is contrary to paradise, as winter is contrary to summer, and cold to heat. Therefore, he who would describe the misery of hell must have seen the paradise of God's delights. O place accursed by God's justice for the malediction of the faithless and reprobate, of which Job, the friend of God, said: There is no order there, but everlasting fear! And Isaiah the prophet, against the reprobate, says: Their flame shall not be quenched nor their worm die.

And David our father, weeping said: Then lightning and bolts and brimstone and great tempest shall rain upon them." O miserable sinners, how loathsome delicate meats, costly raiment, soft couches, and [the] concord of sweet song shall seem to them! How sick shall raging hunger, burning flames, scorching cinders, and cruel torments with bitter weeping make them!"

And then Jesus uttered a lamentable groan, saying: "Truly, it is better never to have been formed than to suffer such cruel torments, for imagine a man suffering torments in every part of his body, who has no one to show him compassion, but is mocked by everyone; tell me, would not this be great pain?" The disciples answered: "The greatest."

Then Jesus said: "This is a delight [in comparison] to hell. For I tell you in truth, that if God should place in one balance all the pain which all men have suffered in this world and shall suffer till the Day of Judgment, and in the other [balance] one single hour of the pain of hell, the reprobates would without doubt choose the worldly tribulations, for the worldly [tribulations] come from the hand of man, but the others from the hand of devils, who are utterly without compassion.

O what cruel fire they shall give to miserable sinners! O what bitter cold, which yet shall not temper their flames! What gnashing of teeth and sobbing and weeping! For the Jordan has less water than the tears which shall flow from their eyes every moment. Their tongues shall curse all created things, with their. father and mother, and their Creator, who is blessed for ever."

Chapter 61

Having said this, Jesus washed himself, with his disciples, according to the Law of God written in the Book of Moses; and then they prayed. And the disciples, seeing [Jesus] sad did not speak at all to him that day, but each stood terror-struck at his words. Then Jesus, opening his mouth after the evening [prayer], said: * "What father of a family, if he knew that a thief meant to break into his house, would sleep? None surely; for he would watch and stand prepared to slay the thief. Do you not know then that Satan is as a roaring lion that goes about seeking whom he may devour. Thus he seeks to make man sin. Truly I say to you, that if man would act as the merchant he should have no fear in that day, because he would be well prepared.

There was a man who gave money to his neighbours that they might trade with it, and the profit should be divided in a just proportion. And some traded well, so that they doubled the money. But some used the money in the service of the enemy of him who gave them the money, speaking evil of him. Tell me now, when the neighbour shall call the debtors to account how shall the matter go? Assuredly he will reward those who traded well, but against the others his anger shall vent itself in reproaches. And then he will punish them according to the Law.

As God lives, in whose presence my soul stands, the neighbour is God, who has given to man all that he has, with life itself, so that, [man] living well in this world, God may have praise, and man the glory of paradise. For those who live well double their money by their example, because sinners, seeing their example, are converted to repentance; wherefore men who live well shall be rewarded with a great reward. But wicked sinners, who by their sins halve what God has given them, by their lives spent in the service of Satan the enemy of God, blaspheming God and giving offence to others tell me what shall be their punishment?" "It shall be without measure," said the disciples.

Chapter 62

Then Jesus said: "He who would live well should take example from the merchant who locks up his shop, and selling guards it day and night with great diligence. And again the things which he buys he is fain to make a profit; for if he perceives that he will lose thereby he will not sell, no, not to his own brother. Thus then should you do; for in truth your soul is a merchant, and the body is the shop: wherefore what it receives from outside, through the senses, is bought and sold by it. And the money is love. See then that with your love you do not sell nor buy the small thought by which d work be all for you cannot profit. But let thought, speech, and love of God; for so shall you find safety in that day.

Truly I say to you, that many make ablutions and go to pray, many fast and give
alms, many study and preach to others, whose end is abominable before God;
because they cleanse the body and not the heart, they cry with the mouth not
with the heart; they abstain from meats, and fill themselves with sins; they
give to others things not good for them, in order that they may be held good;
they study that they may know to speak, not to work; they preach to others
against that which they do themselves, and thus are condemned by their own
tongue. As God lives, these do not know God with their hearts; for if they knew
him they would love him; and since whatsoever a man has he has received it from
God,, even so should he spend all for the love of God."

Chapter 63

After certain days Jesus passed near to a city of the Samaritans; and they would
not let him enter the city, nor would they sell bread to his disciples.
Wherefore said James and John: "Master, may it please you that we pray God that
he send down fire from heaven upon these people?"

Jesus answered: "You know not by what spirit you are led, that you so speak.
*Remember that God determined to destroy Nineveh because he did not find one who
feared God in that city; the which was so wicked that God, having called Jonah
;the prophet to send him to that city, he would fain for fear of the people have
fled to Tarsus;, wherefore God caused him to be cast into the sea, and received
by a fish and cast up near to Nineveh. And he preaching there, that people was
converted to repentance, so that God had mercy on them.

Woe to them that call for vengeance; for on themselves it shall come, seeing
that every man has in himself cause for the vengeance of God. Now tell me, have
you created this city with this people? O madmen that you are, assuredly no. For
all creatures united together could not create a single new fly from nothing,
and this it is to create. If the blessed God who has created this city now
sustains it, why desire you to destroy it? Why did you not say: "May it please
you, master, that we pray to the Lord our God that this people may be converted
to penitence?" Assuredly this is the proper act of a disciple of mine, to pray
to God for those who do evil. Thus did Abel when his brother Cain, accursed of
God, slew him.

Thus did Abraham ;for Pharaoh;, who took from him his wife, and whom therefore,
the angel of God did not slay, but only struck with infirmity. Thus did
Zechariah when, by decree of the impious king, he was slain in the Temple. Thus
did Jeremiah, Isaiah, Ezekiel, Daniel, and David, with all the friends of God
and holy prophets. Tell me, if a brother were stricken with frenzy, would you
slay him because he spoke evil and struck those who came near him? Assuredly you
would not do so; but rather would you endeavour to restore his health with
medicines suitable to his infirmity."

Chapter 64

"As God lives, in whose presence my soul stands, a sinner is of infirm mind when
he persecutes a man. For tell me, is there anyone who would break his head for
the sake of tearing the cloak of his enemy? Now how can he be of sane mind who
separates himself from God, the head of his soul, in order that he may injure
the body of his enemy?

"Tell me, O man, who is your enemy? Assuredly your body, and every one who
praises you. Wherefore if you were of sane mind you would kiss the hand of those

who revile you, and present gifts to those who persecute you and strike you much; because, O man because the more that for your sins you are reviled and persecuted in this life the less shall you be in the day of judgment. But tell me, O man, if the saints and prophets of God have been persecuted and defamed by the

world even though they were innocent, what shall be da one to you, O sinner? and if they endured all with patience, praying for their persecutors, what shouldst you do, O man, who are worthy of hell?

Tell me, O my disciples, do you not know that Shimei cursed the servant of God, David the prophet, and threw stones at him? Now what said David to those who would fain have killed Shimei? "What is it to you, O Joab, that you would kill Shimei? let him curse me, for this is the will of God, who will turn this curse into a blessing." And thus it was; for God saw the patience of David and delivered him from the persecution of his own son, Absalom.

Assuredly not a leaf stirs without the will of God. Wherefore, when you are in tribulation do not think of how much you have borne, nor of him who afflicts you; but consider how much for your sins you are worthy to receive at the hand of the devils of hell. You are angry with this city because it would not receive us, nor sell bread to us. Tell me, are these people your slaves? have you given them this city? have you given them their corn? or have you helped them to reap it? Assuredly no; for you are strangers in this land, and poor men. What thing is this then that you say?" The two disciples answered: "Lord, we have sinned; may God have mercy on us." And Jesus answered: "So be it."

Chapter 65

The Passover drew near, so Jesus, with his disciples, went up to Jerusalem. And he went to the pool called Probatica. And the bath was so called because every day the angel of God troubled the water, and whoever first entered the water after its movement was cured of every kind of infirmity. For this reason a great number of sick persons remained beside the pool, which had five porticoes. And Jesus saw there an impotent man, who had been there thirty-eight years sick with a grievous infirmity. So Jesus, knowing this by divine inspiration, had compassion on the sick man, and said to him: "Do you want to be made whole?"

The impotent man answered: "Sir, when the angel troubles the waters I do not have anyone to put me into it, but while I am coming [to the water] another steps down before me and enters." Then Jesus lifted up his eyes to heaven and said: "Lord our God, God of our fathers, have mercy upon this impotent man." And having said this, Jesus said: "In God's name, brother, be whole; rise and take up your bed."

Then the impotent man arose, praising God, and carried his bed upon his shoulders, and went to his house praising God. Those who saw him cried: "It is the Sabbath day; it is not lawful for you to carry your bed." He answered: "He that made [me] whole said to me, 'Pick up your bed, and go your way to your home.'" Then asked they him: "Who is he?" He answered: "I do not know his name."

So among themselves they said: "It must have been Jesus the Nazarene." Others said: "No, for [Jesus the Nazarene] is a holy one of God, whereas he who has done this thing is a wicked man, for he causes the sabbath to be broken." And Jesus went into the Temple, and a great multitude drew near to him to hear his words [for which reason] the priests were consumed with envy.

Chapter 66

One of them came to him, saying: "Good master, you teach well and truly; tell me therefore, what reward shall God give us in paradise?" Jesus answered: "You call me good, and do not know that God alone is good, even as Job, the friend of God, said: A child of a day old is not clean; yes, even the angels are not faultless in God's presence. Moreover he said: The flesh attracts sin, and sucks up iniquity even as a sponge sucks up water. The priest was silent, being confounded. And Jesus said: "Truly I say to you, nothing is more perilous than speech. For so said Solomon: Life and death are in the power of the tongue. "

And he turned to his disciples, and said: "Beware of those who bless you, because they deceive you. With the tongue Satan blessed our first parents, but the outcome of his words was miserable. So did the sages of Egypt bless Pharaoh. So did Goliath bless the Philistines. So did four hundred false prophets bless Ahab; but false were their praises, so that the praised one perished with the praisers. Wherefore not without cause did God say by Isaiah the prophet: O My people, those that bless you deceive you. Woe to you, scribes and Pharisees! Woe to you, priests and Levites! because you have corrupted the sacrifice of the Lord, so that those who come to sacrifice believe that God eats cooked flesh [in the manner of] a man.

Chapter 67

For you say to them: 'Bring your sheep and bulls and lambs to the Temple of your God, and do not eat it all, but give to your God a share of that which he has given you'; and you do not tell them of the origin of sacrifice, that it is for a witness of the life granted to the son of our father Abraham, so that the faith and obedience of our father Abraham, with the promises made to him by God and the blessing given to him, should never be forgotten. But God says by Ezekiel the prophet: Remove from me these your sacrifices, your victims are abominable to me.

For the time draws near when that shall be done of which our God spoke by Hosea the prophet, saying: I will call chosen the people not chosen. And as he says in Ezekiel the prophet: God shall make a new covenant with his people, not according to the covenant which he gave to your fathers, which they did nott and he shall take from them a heart of stone, and give them a new heart" : and all this shall be because you do not walk now in his Law. And you have the key and do not open: rather you block the road for those who would walk in it." The priest was departing to report everything to the high priest, who stood near the sanctuary, but Jesus said: "Stay, for I will answer your question."

Chapter 68

You ask me to tell you what God will give us in paradise. Truly I say to you that those who think of the wages do not love the master. A shepherd who has a flock of sheep, when he sees the wolf coming, prepares to defend them; contrariwise, the hireling when he sees the wolf leaves the sheep and flees. As God lives, in whose presence I stand, if the God of our fathers were your God you would not have thought of saying: "What will God give me?" But you would have said, as did David his prophet: What shall I give to God for all that he has given to me?

"I will speak to you by a parable that you may understand. There was a king who found by the wayside a man stripped by thieves;, who had wounded him to death. And he had compassion on him, and commanded his slaves to bear that man to the

city and tend him, and this they did with all diligence. And the king conceived
a great love for the sick man, so that he gave him his own daughter in marriage,
and made him his heir. Now assuredly this king was most merciful; but the man
beat the slaves, despised the medicines, abused his wife, spoke evil of the
king, and caused his vassals to rebel against him. And when the king required
any service, he was wont to say: "What will the king give me as reward?" Now
when the king heard this, what did he do to so impious a man?" They all replied:
"Woe to him, for the king deprived him of all, and cruelly punished him."

Then Jesus said: "O priests, and scribes, and Pharisees, and you high-priest
that hear my voice, I proclaim to you what God has said to you by his prophet
Isaiah: "I have nourished slaves and exalted them, but they have despised me."
"The king is our God, who found Israel in this world full of miseries, and gave
him therefore to his servants Joseph, Moses and Aaron, who tended him. And our
God conceived such love for him that for the sake of the people of Israel he
smote Egypt, drowned Pharaoh, and discomfited an hundred and twenty kings of the
Canaanites and Madianites; he gave him his laws, making him heir of all that
[land] wherein our people dwells.

"But how does Israel bear himself? How many prophets has he slain; how many
prophecies has he contaminated; how has he violated the Law of God: how many for
that cause have departed from God and gone to serve idols, through your offence,
O priests! And how do you dishonour God with your manner of life! And now you
ask me: "What will God give us in paradise?" You ought to have asked me: What
will be the punishment that God will give you in hell; and then what you ought
to do for true penitence in order that God may have mercy on you: for this I can
tell you, and to this end am I sent to you."

Chapter 69

As God lives, in whose presence I stand, you will not receive adulation from me,
but truth. Wherefore I say to you, repent and turn to God even as our fathers
did after sinning, and harden not your heart. The priests were consumed with
rage at this speech, but for fear of the common people they spoke not a word.

And Jesus continued, saying: "O doctors, O scribes, O Pharisees, O priests, tell
me. You desire horses like knights, but you desire not to go forth to war: you
desire fair clothing like women, but you desire not to spin and nurture
children; you desire the fruits of the field, and you desire not to cultivate
the Earth; you desire the fishes of the sea, but you desire not to go a fishing;
you desire honour as citizens, but you desire not the burden of the republic;
and you desire tithes and first fruits as priests, but you desire not to serve
God in truth. What then shall God do with you, seeing you desire here every good
without any evil? Truly I say to you that God will give you a place where you
will have every evil without any good."

And when Jesus had said this, there was brought to him a demoniac who could not
speak nor see, and was deprived of hearing. Whereupon Jesus, seeing their faith,
raised his eyes to heaven and said: "Lord God of our fathers, have mercy on this
sick man and give him health, in order that this people may know that you have
sent me."

And having said this Jesus commanded the spirit to depart, saying: "In the power
of the name of God our Lord, depart, evil one, from the man. The spirit departed
and the dumb man spoke, and saw with his eyes. Whereupon every one was filled
with fear, but the scribes said: "In the power of Beelzebub, prince of the
demons, he casts out the demons."

Then Jesus said: "Every kingdom divided against itself destroys itself, and house falls upon house. If in the power of Satan, Satan be cast out, how shall his kingdom stand? And if your sons cast out Satan with the scripture that Solomon the prophet gave them, they testify that I cast out Satan in the power of God. As God lives, blasphemy against the Holy Spirit is without remission in this and in the other world; because the wicked man of his own will reprobates himself, knowing the reprobation."

And having said this Jesus went out of the Temple. And the common people magnified him, for they brought all the sick folk whom they could gather together, and Jesus having made prayer gave to all their health: whereupon on that day in Jerusalem the Roman soldiery, by the working of Satan, began to stir up the common people, saying that Jesus was the God of Israel, who was come to visit his people.

Chapter 70

Jesus departed from Jerusalem after the Passover, and entered into the borders of Caesarea Philippi. Whereupon, the angel Gabriel having told him of the sedition which was beginning among the common people, he asked his disciples, saying: "What do men say of me?" They said: "Some say that you are Elijah, others Jeremiah, and others one of the old prophets." Jesus answered: "And you; what say you that I am?" Peter answered: "You are Christ, son of God."

Then was Jesus angry, and with anger rebuked him, saying: "Begone and depart from me, because you are the devil and seek to cause me offences And he threatened the eleven, saying: "Woe to you if you believe this, for I have won from God a great curse against those who believe this." And he was fain to cast away Peter; whereupon the eleven besought Jesus for him, who cast him not away, but again rebuked him saying: "Beware that never again you say such words, because God would reprobate you!" Peter wept and said: "Lord, I have spoken foolishly; beseech God that he pardon me."

Then Jesus said: "If our God willed not to show himself to Moses his servant, nor to Elijah whom he so loved, nor to any prophet, will you think that God should show himself to this faithless generation? But know you not that God has created all things of nothing with one single word, and all men have had their origin out of a piece of clay? Now, how shall God have likeness to man? Woe to those who suffer themselves to be deceived of Satan!" And having said this, Jesus besought God for Peter, the eleven and Peter weeping, and saying: "So be it, so be it, O blessed Lord our God." Afterwards Jesus departed and went into Galilee, in order that this vain opinion which the common folk began to hold concerning him might be extinguished.

Chapter 71

Jesus having arrived in his own country, it was spread through all the region of Galilee how that Jesus the prophet was come to Nazareth. Whereupon with diligence sought they the sick and brought them to him, beseeching him that he would touch them with his hands. And so great was the multitude that a certain rich man, sick of the palsy, not being able to get himself carried through the door, had himself carried up to the roof of the house in which Jesus was, and having caused the roof to be uncovered, had himself let down by sheets in front of Jesus. Jesus stood for a moment in hesitation, and then he said: "Fear not, brother, for your sins are forgiven you." Every one was offended hearing this, and they said: "And who is this who forgives sins?"

Then Jesus said: "As God lives, I am not able to forgive sins, nor is any man, but God alone forgives. But as servant of God I can beseech him for the sins of others: and so I have besought him for this sick man, and I am sure that God has heard my prayer. Wherefore, that you may know the truth, I say to this sick man: "In the name of the God of our fathers, the God of Abraham and his sons, rise up healed!"" And when Jesus had said this the sick man rose up healed, and glorified God.

Then the common people besought Jesus that he would beseech God for the sick who stood outside. Whereupon Jesus went out to them, and, having lifted up his hands, said: "Lord God of hosts, the living God, the true God, the holy God, that never will die; having mercy upon them!" Whereupon every one answered: "Amen.". And this having been said, Jesus laid his hands upon the sick folk, and they all received their health. Thereupon they magnified God, saying: "God has visited us by his prophet, and a great prophet has God sent to us."

Chapter 72

At night Jesus spoke in secret with his disciples, saying: "Truly I say to you that Satan desires to sift you as wheat; but I have besought God for you, and there shall not perish of you save he that lays snares for me." And this he said of Judas, because the angel Gabriel said to him how that Judas had hand with the priests, and reported to them all that Jesus spoke.

With tears drew near to Jesus he who writes this saying: "O master, tell me, who is he that should betray you?" Jesus answered, saying: "O Barnabas, this is not the hour for you to know him, but soon will be wicked one reveal himself, because I shall depart from the world." Then wept the apostles, saying: "O master, wherefore will you forsake us? It is much better that we should die than be forsaken of you!"

Jesus answered: "Let not your heart be troubled, neither be you fearful: for I have not created you, but God our creator who has created you will protect you. As for me, I am now come to the world to prepare the way for the Messenger of God, who shall bring salvation to the world. But beware that you be not deceived, for many false prophets shall come, who shall take my words and contaminate my gospel."

Then said Andrew: "Master tell us some sign, that we may know him." Jesus answered: "He will not come in your time, but will come some years after you, when my gospel shall be annulled, insomuch that there shall be scarcely thirty faithful. At that time God will have mercy on the world, and so he will send his Messenger, over whose head will rest a white cloud, whereby he shall be known of one elect of God, and shall be by him manifested to the world. He shall come with great power against the ungodly, and shall destroy idolatry upon the earth. And it rejoices me because that through him our God shall be known and glorified, and I shall be known to be true; and he will execute vengeance against those who shall say that I am more than man.

Truly I say to you that the moon shall minister sleep to him in his boyhood, and when he shall be grown up he shall take her in his hands. Let the world beware of casting him out because he shall slay the idolaters, for many more were slain by Moses, the servant of God, and Joshua, who spared not the cities which they burnt, and slew the children; for to an old wound one applies fire. "He shall come with truth more clear than that of all the prophets, and shall reprove him who use the world amiss. The towers of the city of our father shall greet one another for joy: and so when idolatry shall be seen to fall to the ground and confess me a man like other men, truly I say to you the Messenger of God shall be come."

Chapter 73

"Truly I say to you, that if Satan shall try whether you be friends of God; because no one assails his own cities if Satan should have his will over you he would suffer you to glide at your own pleasure; but because he knows that you be enemies to him he will do every violence to make you perish. But fear not you, for he will be against you as a dog that is chained, because God has heard my prayer." John answered: "O master, not only for us, but for them that shall

believe the gospel, tell us how the ancient tempter lays wait for man."

Jesus answered: "In four ways tempts that wicked one. The first is when he tempts by himself, with thoughts. The second is when he tempts with words and deeds by means of his servants; the third is when he tempts with false doctrine; the fourth is when he tempts with false visions. Now how cautious ought men to be, and all the more according as he has in his favour the flesh of man, which loves sin as he who has fever loves water. Truly I say to you, that if a man fear God he shall have victory over all, as says David his prophet: "God shall give his angels charge over you, who shall keep your ways, so that the devil shall not cause you to stumble. A thousand shall fall on your left hand, and ten thousand on your right hand, so that they shall not come near you."

"Furthermore, our God with great love promised to us by the same David to keep us, saying: "I give to you understanding, which shall teach you; and in your ways wherein you shall walk I will cause My eye to rest upon you." "But what shall I say? He has said by Isaiah: "Can a mother forget the child of her womb? But I say to you, that when she forget, I will not forget you." "Tell me, then, who shall fear Satan, having for guard the angels and for protection the living God? Nevertheless, it is necessary, as says the prophet Solomon, that "You, my son, that are come to fear the Lord, prepare your soul for temptations." Truly I say to you, that a man ought to do as the banker who examines money, examining his thoughts, that he sin not against God his creator."

Chapter 74

There have been and are in the world men who hold not thought for sin [and] who are in the greatest error. Tell me, how [did] Satan sin? It is certain that he sinned in the thought he was more worthy than man. Solomon sinned in thinking to invite all the creatures of God to a feast, [so] a fish corrected him by eating all that he had prepared. Not without cause, our father David says, that to ascend in one's heart sets one in the valley of tears. And why does God cry by his prophet Isaiah, saying: Take away your evil thoughts from my eyes? And to what purpose [does] Solomon say, With all your keeping, keep your heart?"

As God lives, in whose presence my soul stands, all [scripture speaks] against the evil thoughts with which sin is committed, for without thinking it is not possible to sin. Now tell me, when the husbandman plants the vineyard does he set the plants deep? Assuredly yes. Satan does [the same]. In planting sin [he] does not stop at the eye or the ear, but passes into the heart, which is God's dwelling, as Moses his servant, [said]: I will dwell in them, in order that they may walk in my Law.

Now tell me, if Herod the king gave you a house to keep in which he desired to dwell, would you let Pilate, his enemy, enter there or place his goods in it? Surely not. Then how much less ought you let Satan enter into your heart, or place his thoughts [in your heart]. Our God has given you your heart to keep, which is his dwelling.

Observe, therefore, [how] the banker considers [his] money. [He considers] whether the image of Caesar is right, whether the silver is good or false, and whether it is of due weight. He turns it over much in his hand. Ah, mad world! How prudent you are in your business; in the last day you will reprove and judge the servants of God of negligence and carelessness, for without doubt your servants are more prudent than the servants of God. Tell me, now, who is he who examines a thought as the banker a silver coin? No one."

Chapter 75

Then said James: "O master, how is the examination of a thought like to [that of] a coin?" Jesus answered: "The good silver in the thought is piety, because every impious thought comes of the devil. The right image is the example of the holy ones and prophets, which we ought to follow; and the weight of the thought is the love of God by which all ought to be done. Whereupon the enemy will bring there impious thoughts against your neighbour, [thoughts] conformed to the world, to corrupt the flesh; [thoughts] of earthly love to corrupt the love of God."

Bartholomew answered: "O master, what ought we to do to think little, in order that we may not !fall into temptation?" Jesus answered: "Two things are necessary for you. The first is to exercise yourselves much, and the second is to talk little: for idleness is a sink wherein is gathered every unclean thought, and too much talking is a sponge which picks up iniquities. It is, therefore, necessary not only your working should hold the body occupied, but also that the soul be occupied with prayer. For it needs never to cease from prayer.

"I tell you for an example: There was a man who paid ill, wherefore none that knew him would go to till his fields. Whereupon he, like a wicked man, said: 'I will go to the market-place to find idle ones who are doing nothing, and will therefore come to till my vines.' This man went forth from his house, and found many strangers who were standing in idleness, and had no money. To them he spoke, and led them to his vineyard. But truly none that knew him and had work for his hands went thither.

He is Satan, that one who pays ill; for he gives labour, and man receives for it the eternal fires in his service. Wherefore he has gone forth from paradise, and goes in search of labourers. Assuredly he sets to his labours those who stand in idleness whoever they be, but much more those who do not know him. It is not in any wise enough for any one to know evil in order to escape it, but it behoves to work at good in order to overcome it."

Chapter 76

I tell you for an example. There was a man who had three vineyards, which he let out to three husbandman. Because the first knew not how to cultivate the vineyard the vineyard brought forth only leaves. The second taught the third how the vines ought to be cultivated; and he most excellently hearkened to his words; and he cultivated his, as he told him, insomuch that the vineyard of the third bore much. But the second left his vineyard uncultivated, spending his time solely in talking. When the time was come for paying the rent to the lord of the vineyard, the first said: "Lord, I know not how your vineyard ought to be cultivated: therefore I have not received any fruit this year." The lord answered: "O fool, do you dwell alone in the world, that you has not asked counsel of my second vinedresser, who knows well how to cultivate the land? Certain it is that you shall pay me."

And having said this he condemned him to work in prison until he should pay his lord; who moved with pity at his simplicity liberated him, saying: "Begone, for I will not that you work longer at my vineyard; it is enough for you that I give you your debt."

The second came, to whom the lord said: "Welcome, my vinedresser! Where are the fruits that you owe me? Assuredly, since you know well how to prune the vines, the vineyard that I let out to you must needs have borne much fruit." The second answered: "O lord, your vineyard is backward because I have not pruned the wood nor worked up the soil; but the vineyard has not borne fruit, so I cannot pay you." Whereupon the lord called the third and with wonder said: "You said to me that this man, to whom I let out the second vineyard, taught you perfectly to cultivate the vineyard which I let out to you. How then can it be that the vineyard I let out to him should not have borne fruit, seeing it is all one soil."

The third answered: "Lord, the vines are not cultivated by talking only, but he needs must sweat a shirt every day who wills to make it bring forth its fruit. And how shall your vineyard of your vinedresser bear fruit, O lord, if he does nothing but waste the time in talking? Sure it is, O lord, that if he had put into practice his own words, [while] I who cannot talk so much have given you the rent for two years, he would have given you the rent of the vineyard for five years." The lord was wroth, and said with scorn to the vinedresser, "And so you have wrought a great work in not cutting away the wood and levelling the vineyard, wherefore there is owing to you a great reward!" And having called his servants he had him beaten without any mercy. And then he put him into prison under the keeping of a cruel servant who beat him every day, and never was willing to set him free for prayers of his friends."

Chapter 77

Truly I say to you, that on the day of judgment many shall say to God: "Lord, we have preached and taught by your Law." Against them even the stones shall cry out, saying: "When you preached to others, with your own tongue you condemned yourselves, O workers of iniquity." "As God lives," said Jesus, "he who knows the truth and works the contrary shall be punished with such grievous penalty that Satan shall almost have compassion on him. Tell me, now has our God given us the Law for knowing or for working? Truly I say to you, that all knowledge has for end that wisdom which works all it knows. "Tell me, if one were sitting at table and with his eyes beheld delicate meats, but with his hands should choose unclean things and eat those, would not he be mad?" "Yes, assuredly," said the disciples.

Then Jesus said: "O mad beyond all madmen are you, O man, that with your understanding know heaven, and with your hands choose earth; with your understanding know God, and with your affection desire the world; with your understanding know the delights of paradise, and with your works choose the miseries of hell. Brave soldier, that leaves the sword and carries the scabbard to fight! Now, know you not that he who walks by night desires light, not only to see the light, but rather to see the good road, in order that he may pass safely to the inn?

O miserable world, to be a thousand times despised and abhorred! since our God by his holy prophets has ever willed to grant it to know the way to go to his country and his rest: but you, wicked one, not only wiliest not to go, but, which is worse, have despised the light! True is the proverb of the camel, that it likes not clear water to drink, because it desires not to see its own ugly face. So does the ungodly who works ill; for he hates the light lest his evil works should be known. But he who receives wisdom, and not only works not well, but, which is worse, employs it for evil, is like to him who should use the gifts as instruments to slay the giver."

Chapter 78

Truly I say to you, that God had not compassion on the fall of Satan, but yet [had compassion on the fall of Adam;. And let this suffice you to know the unhappy condition of him who knows good and does evil." Then said Andrew: "O master, it is a good thing to leave learning aside, so as not to fall into such condition."

Jesus answered: "If the world is good without the sun, man without eyes, and the soul without understanding, then is it good not to know. Truly I say to you, that bread is not so good for the temporal life as is learning for the eternal life. Know you not that it is a precept of God to learn? For thus says God: Ask of your elders, and they shall teach you. And of the Law says God: See that my precept be before your eyes, and when you sit down, and when you walk, and at all times meditate thereon. Whether, then, it is good not to learn, you may now know. Oh, unhappy he who despises wisdom, for he is sure to lose eternal life."

James answered: "O master, we know that Job learned not from a master, nor Abraham; nevertheless they became holy ones and prophets." Jesus answered: "Truly I say to you, that he who is of the bridegroom's house does not need to be invited to the marriage, because he dwells in the house where the marriage is held; but they that are far from the house. Now know you not that the prophets of God are in the house of God's grace and mercy, and so have the Law of God manifest in them: as David our father says on this matter: The Law of his God is in his heart; therefore his path shall not be digged up.

Truly I say to you that our God in creating man not only created him righteous, but inserted in his heart a light that should show to him that it is fitting to serve God. Wherefore, even if this light be darkened after sin, yet is it not extinguished. For every nation has this desire to serve God, though they have lost God and serve false and lying gods. Accordingly it is necessary that a man be taught of the prophets of God, for they have clear the light to teach the way to go to paradise, our country, by serving God well: just as it is necessary that he who has his eyes diseased should be guided and helped."

Chapter 79

James answered: "And how shall the prophets teach us if they are dead; and how shall he be taught who has not knowledge of the prophets?" Jesus answered: "Their doctrine is written down, so that it ought to be studied, for [the writing] is to you for a prophet. Truly, truly, I say to you that he who despises the prophecy despises not only the prophet, but despises also God who has sent the prophet. But concerning such as know not the prophet, as are the nations, I tell you that if there shall live in those regions any man who lives as his heart shall show him, not doing to others that which he would not receive from others, and giving to his neighbour that which he would receive from others, such a man shall not be forsaken of the mercy of God.

Wherefore at death, if not sooner, God will show him and give him his Law with mercy. Perhaps you think that God has given the Law for love of the Law? Assuredly this is not true, but rather has God given his Law in order that man might work good for love of God. And so if God shall find a man who for love of him works good, shall he perhaps despise him? No, surely, but rather will he love him more than those to whom he has given the Law.

I tell you for an example: There was a man who had great possessions; and in his territory he had desert land that only bore unfruitful things. And so, as he was walking out one day through such desert land, he found among such unfruitful plants a plant that had delicate fruits. Whereupon this man said: "Now how does this plant here bear these so delicate fruits? Assuredly I will not that it be cut down and put on the fire with the rest." And having called his servants he made them dig it

up and set it in his garden. Even so, I tell you, that our God shall preserve from the flames of hell those who work righteousness;, wheresoever they be."

Chapter 80

"Tell me, where dwelt Job but in Uz among idolaters? And at the time of the flood, how writes Moses? Tell me. He says: "Noah truly found grace before God." Our father Abraham had a father without faith, for he made and worshipped false idols. Lot abode among the most wicked men on earth. Daniel as a child, with Ananias, Azarias, and Misael, were taken captive by Nebuchadnezzar in such wise that they were but two years old when they were taken; and they

were nurtured among the multitude of idolatrous servants. As God lives, even as the fire burns dry things and converts them into fire, making no difference between olive and cypress and palm; even so our God has mercy on every one that works righteously, making no difference between Jew, Scythian, Greek, or Ishmaelite.

But let not your heart stop there, O James, because where God has sent the prophet it is necessary entirely to deny your own judgment and to follow the prophet, and not to say: 'Why says he thus? Why does he thus forbid and command?' But say: 'Thus God wills. Thus God commands.' Now what said God to Moses when Israel despised Moses? They have not despised you, but they have despised me. Truly I say to you, that man ought to spend all the time of his life not in learning how to speak or to read, but in learning how to work well. Now tell me, who is that servant of Herod who would not study to please him by serving him with all diligence? Woe to the world that studies only to please a body that is clay and dung, and studies not but forgets the service of God who has made all things, who is blessed for evermore."

Chapter 81

Tell me, would it have been a great sin of the priests if when they were carrying the ark of the testimony of God they had let it fall to the ground? The disciples trembled hearing this, for they knew that God slew Uzzah for having wrongly touched the ark of God. And they said: "Most grievous would be such a sin." Then Jesus said: "As God lives, it is a greater sin to forget the word of God, wherewith he made all things, whereby he offers you eternal life." And having said this Jesus made prayer; and after the prayer he said: "Tomorrow we needs must pass into Samaria;, for so has said to me the holy angel of God."

Early on the morning of a certain day, Jesus arrived near the well which Jacob made and gave to Joseph his son. Whereupon Jesus being wearied with the journey, sent his disciples to the city to buy food. And so he sat himself down by the well, upon the stone of the well. And, lo, a woman of Samaria comes to the well to draw water. Jesus says to the woman: "Give me to drink." The woman answered: "Now, are you not ashamed that you, being an Hebrew, ask drink of me which am a Samaritan woman?" Jesus answered: "O woman, if you knew who he is that asks you for drink, perhaps you would have asked of him for drink." The woman answered: "Now how should you give me to drink, seeing you have no vessel to draw the water, nor rope, and the well is deep?"

Jesus answered: "O woman, whoever drinks of the water of this well, thirst comes to him again, but whosoever drinks of the water that I give has thirst no more; but to them that have thirst give they to drink, insomuch that they come to eternal life." Then said the woman: "O Lord, give me of this your water." Jesus answered: "Go call your husband, and to both of you I will give to drink." The woman said: "I have no husband." Jesus answered: "Well have you said the truth, for you have had five husbands, and he whom you now have is not your husband."

The woman was confounded hearing this, and said: "Lord, hereby perceive I that you are a prophet; therefore tell me, I pray: the Hebrews make prayer on mount Sion in the Temple built by Solomon in Jerusalem, and say that there and nowhere else [men] find grace and mercy of God. And our people worship on these mountains, and say that only on the mountains of Samaria ought worship to be made. Who are the true worshippers?"

Chapter 82

Then Jesus gave a sigh and wept, saying: "Woe to you, Judea, for you glory, saying: "The Temple of the Lord, the Temple of the Lord," and live as though there were no God; given over wholly to the pleasures and gains of the world; for this woman in the day of judgment shall condemn you to hell; for this woman seeks to know how to find grace and mercy before God."

And turning to the woman he said: "O woman, you Samaritans worship that which you know not, but we Hebrews worship that which we know. Truly, I say to you, that God is spirit and truth, and so in spirit and in truth must he be worshipped. For the promise of God was made in Jerusalem, in the Temple of Solomon, and not elsewhere. But believe me, a time will come that God will give his mercy in another city, and in every place it will be possible to worship him in truth. And God in

every place will have accepted true prayer with mercy.

The woman answered: "We look for the Messiah; when he comes he will teach us." Jesus answered: "Know you, woman, that the Messiah must come?" *She answered: "Yes, Lord." Then Jesus rejoiced, and said: "So far as I see, O woman, you are faithful: know therefore that in the faith of the Messiah shall be saved every one that is elect of God; therefore it is necessary that you know the coming of the Messiah;." The woman said: "O Lord, perhaps you are the Messiah." Jesus answered: "I am indeed sent to the House of Israel as a prophet of salvation; but after me shall come the Messiah, sent of God to all the world; for whom God has made the world.

And then through all the world will God be worshipped, and mercy received, insomuch that the year of jubilee, which now comes every hundred years, shall by the Messiah be reduced to every year in every place." Then the woman left her waterpot and ran to the city to announce all that she had heard from Jesus.

Chapter 83

 Whilst the woman was talking with Jesus came his disciples, and marvelled that Jesus was speaking so with a woman. Yet no one said to him: "Why speak you thus with a Samaritan woman;?" Whereupon, when the woman was departed, they said: "Master, come and eat." Jesus answered: "I must eat other food."

Then said the disciples one to another: "Perhaps some wayfarer has spoken with Jesus and has gone to find him food." And they questioned him who writes this ;-, saying: "Has there been any one here, O Barnabas, who might have brought food to the master?" Then answered he who writes: "There has not been here any other than the woman whom you saw, who brought this empty vessel to fill it with water." Then the disciples stood amazed, awaiting the issue of the words of Jesus. Whereupon Jesus said: "You know not that the true food is to do the will of God; because it is not bread that sustains man and gives him life, but rather the word of God, by his will. And so for this reason the holy angels eat not, but live nourished only by the will of God. And thus we, Moses and Elijah and yet another, have been forty days and forty nights; without any food."

And lifting up his eyes, Jesus said: "How far off is the harvest;?" The disciples answered: "Three months." Jesus said: "Look now, how the mountain is white with corn; truly I say to you, that today there is a great harvest ;to be reaped." And then he pointed to the multitude who had come to see him. For the woman having entered into the city had moved all the city, saying: "O men, come and see a new prophet sent of God to the House of Israel"; and she recounted to them all that she had heard from Jesus. When they were come thither they besought Jesus to abide with them; and he entered into the city and abode there two days, healing all the sick, and teaching concerning the kingdom of God;. *Then said the citizens to the woman: "We believe more in his words and miracles than we do in what you said; for he is indeed a holy one of God, a prophet sent for the salvation of those that shall believe on him."

After the prayer of midnight; the disciples came near to Jesus, and he said to them: "This night shall be in the time of the Messiah, Messenger of God, the jubilee every year that now comes every hundred years. Therefore I will not that we sleep, but let us make prayer, bowing our head a hundred times, doing reverence to our God, mighty and merciful, who is blessed for evermore, and therefore each time let us say: "I confess you our God alone, that has not had beginning, nor shall ever have end; for by your mercy gave you to all things their beginning, and by your justice you shall give to all an end; that has no likeness among men, because in your infinite goodness you are not subject to motion nor to any accident. Have mercy on us, for you have created us, and we are the works of your hand.""

Chapter 84

Having made the prayer, Jesus said: "Let us give thanks to God because he has given to us this night great mercy; for that he has made to come back the time that needs must pass in the night, in that we have made prayer in union with the Messenger of God. And I have heard his voice." The disciples rejoiced greatly at hearing this, and said: "Master, teach us some precepts this night." Then Jesus said: "Have you ever seen dung mixed with balsam?" They answered: "No, Lord, for no one is so mad as to do this thing."

"Now I tell you that there be in the world greater madmen, said Jesus, "because with the service of God they mingle the service of the world. So much so that many of blameless life have been deceived of Satan, and while praying have mingled with their prayer worldly business, whereupon they have become at that time abominable in the sight of God. Tell me, when you wash yourselves for prayer, do you take care that no unclean thing touch you? Yes, assuredly. But what do you when you are making prayer? You wash your soul from sins through the mercy of God. Would you be willing then, while you are making prayer, to speak of worldly things? Take care not to do so, for every worldly word becomes dung of the devil upon the soul of him that speaks."

Then the disciples trembled, because he spoke with vehemence of spirit; and they said: "O master, what shall we do if when we are making prayer a friend shall come to speak to us?" Jesus answered: "Suffer him to wait, and finish the prayer." Bartholomew said;: "But what if he shall be offended and go his way, when he see that we speak not with him?" Jesus answered: "If he shall be offended, believe me he will not be a friend of yours nor a believer, but rather an unbeliever and a companion of Satan. Tell me, if you went to speak with a stable boy of Herod;, and found him speaking into Herod's ears, would you be offended if he made you to wait?' No,

assuredly; but you would be comforted at seeing your friend in favour with the king. Is this true?" said Jesus.

The disciples answered: "It is most true." Then Jesus said: "Truly I say to you, that every one when he prays speaks with God. Is it then right that you should leave speaking with God in order to speak with man? Is it right that your friend should for this cause be offended, because you have more reverence for God than for him? Believe me that if he shall be offended when you make him wait, he is a good servant of the evil. For this desires the devil, that God should be forsaken for man. As God lives, in every good work he that fears God ought to separate himself from the works of the world, so as not to corrupt the good work."

Chapter 85

"When a man works ill or talks ill, if one go to correct him, and hinder such work, what does such an one?" said Jesus. The disciples answered: "He does well, because he serves God, who always seeks to hinder evil, even as the sun that always seeks to chase away the darkness." Jesus said: "And I tell you on the contrary that when one works well or, speaks well, whosoever seeks to hinder him, under pretext of aught that is not better, he serves the devil, no, he even becomes his companion. For the devil attends to nought else but to hinder every good thing. "But what shall I say to you now? I will say to you as said Solomon ;the prophet, holy one, and friend of God: "Of a thousand whom you know, one be your friend."

Then said Matthew: "Then shall we not be able to love any one." Jesus answered: "Truly I say to you, that it is not lawful for you to hate anything save only sin: insomuch that you cannot hate even Satan as creature of God, but rather as enemy of God. Know you wherefore? I will tell you; because he is a creature of God, and all that God has created is good and perfect. Accordingly, whoever hates the creature hates also the creator. But the friend is a singular thing, that is not easily found, but is easily lost. For the friend will not suffer contradiction against him whom he supremely loves. Beware, be you cautious, and choose not for friend one who loves not him whom you love. Know you what friend means? Friend means nothing but physician of the soul;.

And so, just as one rarely finds a good physician who knows the sicknesses and understands to apply the medicines thereto, so also are friends rare who know the faults and understand how to guide to good. But herein is an evil, that there are many who have friends that feign not to see the faults of their friend; others excuse them; others defend them under earthly pretext; and, what is worse, there are friends who invite and aid their friend to err, whose end shall be like to their villainy. Beware that you receive not such men for friends, for that in truth they are enemies and slayers of the soul.

Chapter 86

"Let your friend be such that, even as he wills to correct you, so he may receive correction; and even as he wills that you should leave all things for love of God, even so again it may content him that you forsake him for the service of God. "But tell me, if a man know not how to love God how shall he know how to love himself; and how shall he know how to love others, not knowing how to love himself? Assuredly this is impossible. Therefore when you choose you one for friend (for truly he is supremely poor who has no friend at all), see that you consider first, not his fine lineage, not his fine family, not his fine house, not his fine clothing, not his fine person, nor yet his fine words, for you shall be easily deceived.

But look how he fears God, how he despises earthly things, how he loves good works, and above all how he hates his own flesh, and so shall you easily find the true friend: if he above all things shall fear God, and shall despise the vanities of the world; if he shall be always occupied in good works, and shall hate his own body as a cruel enemy. Nor yet shall you love such a friend in such wise that your love stay in him, for [so] shall you be an idolater. But love him as a gift that God has given you, for so shall God adorn [him] with greater favour. Truly I say to you, that he who has found a true friend has found one of the delights of paradise; no, such is the key of paradise."

Thaddaeus answered: "But if perhaps a man shall have a friend who is not such as you have said, O master? What ought he to do? Ought he to forsake him?" Jesus answered: "He ought to do as the mariner does with the ship, who sails it so long as he perceives it to be profitable, but when he sees it to be a loss forsakes it. So shall you do with your friend that is worse than you: in those things wherein he is an offence to you, leave him if you would not be left of the mercy of God."

Chapter 87

"Woe to the world because of offences. It needs must be that the offence come, because all the world lies in wickedness. But yet woe to that man through whom the offence comes. It were better for the man if he should have a millstone about his neck and should be sunk in the depths of the sea than that he should offend his neighbour. If your eye be an offence to you, pluck it out. For it is better that you go with one eye only into paradise than with both of them into hell. If your hand or your foot offend you, do likewise; for it is better that you go into the kingdom of heaven with one foot or with one hand, than with two hands and two feet go into hell."

Simon, called Peter: said "Lord, how must I do this? Certain it is that in a short time I shall be dismembered." Jesus answered: "O Peter, put off fleshly prudence and straightway you shall find the truth. For he that teaches you is your eye, and he that helps you to work is your foot, and he that ministers aught to you is your hand. Wherefore when such are to you an occasion of sin leave them; for it is better for you to go into paradise ignorant, with few works, and poor, than to go into hell wise, with great works, and rich. Everything that may hinder you from serving God, cast it from you as a man casts away everything that hinders his sight."

And having said this, Jesus called Peter close to him, and said to him: * "If your brother shall sin against you, go and correct him. If he amend, rejoice, for you have gained your brother; but if he shall not amend go and call afresh two witnesses and correct him afresh; and if he shall not amend, go and tell it to the church; and if he shall not then amend, count him for an unbeliever, and therefore you shall not dwell under the same roof whereunder he dwells, you shall not eat at the same table whereat he sits, and you shall not speak with him; insomuch that if you know where he sets his foot in walking you shall not set your foot there."

Chapter 88

"But beware that you hold not yourself for better; rather shall you say thus: "Peter, Peter, if God helped you not with his grace you would be worse than he." Peter answered: "How must I correct him?" Jesus answered: "In the way that you yourself would fain be corrected And as you would fain be borne with, so bear with others. Believe me, Peter, for truly I say to you that every time you shall correct your brother with mercy you shall receive mercy of God, and your words shall bear some fruit; but if you shall do it with rigour, you shall be rigorously punished by the justice of God, and shall bear no fruit.

Tell me, Peter: Those earthen pots wherein the poor cook their food they wash them, perhaps, with stones and iron hammers? No, assuredly; but rather with hot water. Vessels are broken in pieces with iron, things of wood are burned with fire; but man is amended with mercy. Wherefore, when you shall correct your brother you shall say to yourself: "If God help me not, I shall do tomorrow worse than all that he has done today." Peter answered: "How many times must I forgive my brother, O master?" Jesus answered: "As many times as you would fain be forgiven by him."

Peter said: "Seven times a day?" Jesus answered: "Not only seven, but seventy times seven you shall forgive him every day; for he that forgives, to him shall it be forgiven, and he that condemns shall be condemned." Then said he who writes this: "Woe to princes! for they shall go to hell" Jesus reproved him, saying: "You are become foolish, O Barnabas. in that you have spoken thus. Truly I say to you, that the bath is not so necessary for the body, the bit for the horse, and the tiller for the ship, as the prince is necessary for the state. And for what cause did God give Moses, Joshua, Samuel, David, and Solomon, and so many others who passed judgment? To such has God given the sword for the extirpation of iniquity."

Then said he who writes this: "Now, how ought judgment to be given, condemning and pardoning?" Jesus answered: "Not every one is a judge: for to the judge alone it appertains to condemn others, O Barnabas. And the judge ought to condemn the guilty, even as the father commands a putrefied member to be cut off from his son, in order that the whole body may not become putrefied."

Chapter 89

Peter said: "How long must I wait for my brother to repent?" Jesus answered: "So long as you would be waited for." Peter answered: "Not every one will understand this; wherefore speak to us more plainly." Jesus answered: "Wait for your brother as long as God waits for him." "Neither will they understand this," said Peter. Jesus answered: "Wait for him so long as he has time to repent."

Then was Peter sad, and the others also, because they understood not the meaning. Whereupon Jesus answered: "If you had sound understanding, and knew that you yourselves were sinners, you would not think ever to cut off your heart from mercy to the sinner. And so I tell you plainly, that the sinner ought to be waited for that he may repent, so long as he has a soul beneath his teeth to breathe. For so does our God wait for him, the mighty and merciful. God said not: "In that hour that the sinner shall fast, do alms, make prayer, and go on pilgrimage, I will forgive him." Wherefore this have many accomplished, and are damned eternally. But he said: "In that hour that the sinner shall bewail his sins, I for my part will not remember any more his iniquities." Do you understand?" said Jesus.

The disciples answered: "Part we understand, and part not." Jesus said: "Which is the part that you understand not?" They answered: "That many who have made prayer with fastings are damned." Then Jesus said: "Truly I say to you, that the hypocrites and the Gentiles make more prayers, more alms, and more fasts than do the friends of God. But because they have not faith, they are not able to repent for love of God, and so they are damned." Then said John: "Teach us, for love of God, of the faith." Jesus answered: "It is time that we say the prayer of the dawn." Whereupon they arose, and having washed themselves made prayer to our God, who is blessed for evermore.

Chapter 90

When the prayer was done, his disciples again drew near to Jesus, and he opened his mouth and said: Draw near, John, for today will I speak to you of all that you have asked. Faith is a seal whereby God seals his elect: which seal he gave to his Messenger, at whose hands every one that is elect has received the faith. For even as God is one, so is the faith one. Wherefore God, having created before all things his Messenger, gave to him before aught else the faith which is as it were a likeness of God and of all that God has done and said. And so the faithful by faith sees all things, better than one sees with his eyes; because the eyes can err; no they do almost always err; but faith errs never, for it has for foundation God and his word. Believe me that by faith are saved all the elect of God. And it is certain that without faith it is impossible for any one to please God.

Wherefore Satan seeks not to bring to nothing fastings and prayer, alms and pilgrimages, no rather he incites unbelievers thereto, for he takes pleasure in seeing man work without receiving pay. But he takes pains with all diligence to bring faith to nought, wherefore faith ought especially to be guarded with diligence, and the safest course will be to abandon the "Wherefore," seeing that the "Wherefore" drove men out of Paradise and changed Satan from a most beautiful angel into a horrible devil."

Then said John: "Now, how shall we abandon the "Wherefore," seeing that it is the gate of knowledge?" Jesus answered: "No, rather the "Wherefore" is the gate of hell." Thereupon John kept silence, when Jesus added: "When you know that God has said a thing, who are you, O man, that you should say, "Wherefore have you

so said, O God: wherefore have you so done?" Shall the earthen vessel, perhaps,
say to its maker: "Wherefore have you made me to hold water and not to contain
balsam?" Truly I say to you, it is necessary against every temptation to
strengthen yourself with this word, saying "God has so said"; "So has God done";
"God so wills"; for so doing you shall live safely."

Chapter 91

At this time there was a great disturbance throughout Judea because of Jesus.
The Roman soldiery, through the operation of Satan, [had] stirred up the
Hebrews, saying that Jesus was God come to visit them. So great [was the]
sedition [that] arose, that near the Forty Days all Judea was in arms, such that
the son was against the father, and the brother against the brother. Some said
that Jesus was God come to the world; others said: 'No, but he is a son of God';
and others said: 'No, for God has no human similitude, and therefore does not
beget sons; but Jesus of Nazareth is a prophet of God.' This [sedition] arose
because of the great miracles which Jesus did.

To quiet the people, it was necessary that the high-priest should ride in
procession, clothed in his priestly robes, with the holy name of God, the teta
gramaton (sic), on his forehead, and the governor Pilate, and Herod rode in a
similar manner. Then, three armies assembled in Mizpeh, each one of two hundred
thousand men that bare sword. Herod spoke to them, but they were not quietened.
Then the governor and the high-priest spoke, saying: "Brothers, this war [has
been] aroused by the work of Satan, for Jesus is alive, and we ought to resort
to him, and ask him to give testimony of himself, and then believe him,
according to his word."

So at this everyone was quieted; and having laid down their arms they all
embraced one another, saying to one another: 'Forgive me, brother!' *On that
day, therefore, every one laid this in his heart, to believe [whatever] Jesus
said. The governor and the high-priest offered great rewards to whoever should
come [forward and] announce where Jesus was to be found.

Chapter 92

At this time, by the word of the holy angel, we, [had] gone to Mount Sinai with
Jesus. There Jesus [and] his disciples kept the forty days.

When this was past, Jesus drew near to the river Jordan, to go to Jerusalem. And
he was seen by one of them who believed Jesus to be God. Then, crying with great
gladness [over and over] "Our God comes!" he reached the city [and] moved the
whole city saying: Our God comes, O Jerusalem; prepare you to receive him! And
he testified that he had seen Jesus near to [the] Jordan.

Then everyone, small and great, went out from the city to see Jesus, so that the
city was left empty, for the women [carried] their children in their arms, and
forgot to take food to eat. When they [saw] this, the governor and the high-
priest rode forth and sent a messenger to Herod, who [also] rode forth to find
Jesus, in order to quiten the sedition of the people. For two days they sought
him in the wilderness near to [the] Jordan, and the third day they found him,
near the hour of midday, when he (with his disciples) was purifying himself for
prayer, according to the Book of Moses.

Jesus marvelled greatly, seeing the multitude which covered the ground with
people, and [he] said to his disciples: "Perhaps Satan has raised sedition in
Judea. May it please God to take away from Satan the dominion which he has over

sinners." And when he had said this, the crowd drew near, and when they knew him they began to cry out: "Welcome to you, O our God!" and they began to do him reverence, as to God. Jesus gave a great groan and said: "Get from before me, O madmen, for I fear [that] the earth shall open and devour me with you for your abominable words!" At this the people were filled with terror and began to weep.

Chapter 93

Then Jesus, having lifted his hand in token of silence, said: "Truly you have erred greatly, O Israelites, in calling me, a man, your God. And I fear that God may for this give heavy plague upon the holy city, handing it over in servitude to strangers;. O a thousand times accursed Satan, that has moved you to this!"

And having said this, Jesus smote his face with both his hands, whereupon arose such a noise of weeping that none could hear what Jesus was saying. Whereupon once more he lifted up his hand in token of silence;, and the people being quieted from their weeping, he spoke once more: "

I confess before heaven, and I call to witness everything that dwells upon the earth, that I am a stranger to all that you have said; seeing that I am man, born of mortal woman, subject to the judgment of God, suffering the miseries of eating and sleeping, of cold and heat, like other men. Whereupon when God shall come to judge, my words like a sword shall pierce each one [of them] that believe me to be more than man." And having said this, Jesus saw a great multitude of horsemen, whereby he perceived that there were coming the governor with Herod and the high-priest. Then Jesus said: "Perhaps they also are become mad."

When the governor arrived there, with Herod and the priest, every one dismounted, and they made a circle round about Jesus, insomuch that the soldiery could not keep back the people that were desirous to hear Jesus speaking with the priest. Jesus drew near to the priest with reverence, but he was wishful to bow himself down and worship Jesus, when Jesus cried out: "Beware of that which you do, priest of the living God! Sin not against our God!"

The priest answered: "Now is Judea so greatly moved over your signs and your teaching that they cry out that you are God; wherefore, constrained by the people, I am come here with the Roman governor and king Herod. We pray you therefore from our heart, that you will be content to remove the sedition which is arisen on your account. For some say you are God, some say you are son of God, and some say you are a prophet."

Jesus answered: "And you, O high priest of God, why have you not quieted this sedition? Are you also perhaps, gone out of your mind? Have the prophecies, with the Law of God, so passed into oblivion, O wretched Judea, deceived of Satan!"

Chapter 94

And having said this, Jesus said again: "I confess before heaven, and call to witness everything that dwells upon the earth, that I am a stranger to all that men have said of me, to wit, that I am more than man. For I am a man, born of a woman, subject to the judgment of God; that live here like as other men, subject to the common miseries. As God lives, in whose presence my soul stands, you have greatly sinned, O priest, in saying what you have said. May it please God that there come not upon the holy city great vengeance for this sin." Then said the priest: "May God pardon us, and do you pray for us. Then said the governor and

Herod: "Sir, it is impossible that man should do that which you do; wherefore we understand not that which you say.

Jesus answered: "That which you say is true, for God works good in man, even as Satan works evil. For man is like a shop, wherein whoever enters with his consent works and sells therein. But tell me, O governor, and you O king, you say this because you are strangers to our Law: for if you read the testament and covenant of our God you would see that Moses with a rod made the water turn into blood, the dust into fleas, the dew into tempest, and the light into darkness. He made the frogs and mice to come into Egypt;, which covered the ground, he slew the first-born, and opened the sea, wherein he drowned Pharaoh;. Of these things I have wrought none.

And of Moses, every one confesses that he is a dead man at this present. Joshua made the sun to stand still, and opened the Jordan, which I have not yet done. And of Joshua every one confesses that he is a dead man at this present. Elijah made fire to come visibly down from heaven, and rain, which I have not done. And of Elijah every one confesses that he is a man. And [in like manner] very many other prophets, holy men, friends of God, who in the power of God have wrought things which cannot be grasped by the minds of those who know not our God, almighty and merciful, who is blessed for evermore."

Chapter 95

Accordingly the governor and the priest and the king prayed Jesus that in order to quiet the people he should mount up into a lofty place and speak to the people. Then went up Jesus on to one of the twelve stones which Joshua made the twelve tribes take up from the midst of Jordan;, when all Israel passed over there dry shod; and he said with a loud voice: "Let our priest go up into a high place whence he may confirm my words." Thereupon the priest went up thither; to whom Jesus said distinctly, so that everyone might hear: "It is written in the testament and covenant of the living God that our God has no beginning, neither shall he ever have an end." The priest answered: "Even so is it written therein."

Jesus said: "It is written there that our God by his word alone has created all things." "Even so it is," said the priest. Jesus said: "It is written there that God is invisible and hidden from the mind of man, seeing he is incorporeal and uncomposed, without variableness." "So is it, truly" said the priest. Jesus said: "It is written there how that the heaven of heavens cannot contain him, seeing that our God is infinite." "So said Solomon the prophet," said the priest, "O Jesus." Jesus said: "It is written there that God has no need, forasmuch as he eats not, sleeps not,; and suffers not from any deficiency." "So is it," said the priest.

Jesus said: "It is written there that our God is everywhere, and that there is not any other god but he, who strikes down and makes whole, and does all that pleases him." "So is it written," replied the priest. Then Jesus, having lifted up his hands, said: "Lord our God, this is my faith wherewith I shall come to your judgment: in testimony against every one that shall believe the contrary."

And turning himself towards the people, he said: "Repent, for from all that of which the priest has said that it is written in the Book of Moses, the covenant of God for ever, you may perceive your sin; for. that I am a visible man and a morsel of clay that walks upon the earth, mortal as are other men. And I have had a beginning, and shall have an end, and [am] such that I cannot create a fly over again."

Thereupon the people raised their voices weeping, and said: "We have sinned, Lord our God, against you; have mercy upon us. And they prayed Jesus, every one, that he would pray for the safety of the holy city, that our God in his anger should not give it over to be trodden down of the nations. Thereupon Jesus, having lifted up his hands, prayed for the holy city and for the people of God, every one crying: "So be it," "Amen."

Chapter 96

When the prayer was ended, the priest said with a loud voice: "Stay, Jesus, for we need to know who you are, for the quieting of our nation." Jesus answered: "I am Jesus, son of Mary, of the seed of David, a man that is mortal and fears God, and I seek that to God be given honour and glory."

The priest answered: "In the Book of Moses it is written that our God must send us the Messiah, who shall come to announce to us that which God wills, and shall bring to the world the mercy of God. Therefore I pray you tell us the truth, are you the Messiah of God whom we expect?"

Jesus answered: "It is true that God has so promised, but indeed I am not he, for he is made before me, and shall come after me." The priest answered: "By your words and signs at any rate we believe you to be a prophet and an holy one of God, wherefore I pray you in the name of all Judea and Israel that you for love of God should tell us in what wise the Messiah will come.

Chapter 97

Jesus answered: "As God lives, in whose presence my soul stands, I am not the Messiah whom all the tribes of the earth expect, even as God promised to our father Abraham, saying: "In your seed will I bless all the tribes of the earth." But when God shall take me away from the world, Satan will raise again this accursed sedition, by making the impious believe that I am God and son of God, whence my words and my doctrine shall be contaminated, insomuch that scarcely shall there remain thirty faithful ones: whereupon God will have mercy upon the world, and will send his Messenger for whom he has made all things who shall come from the south with power, and shall destroy the idols with the idolaters who shall take away the dominion from Satan which he has over men. He shall bring with him the mercy of God for salvation of them that shall believe in him, and blessed is he who shall believe his words.

"Unworthy though I am to untie his hosen, I have received grace and mercy from God to see him." Then answered the priest, with the governor and the king, saying: "Distress not yourself, O Jesus, holy one of God, because in our time shall not this sedition be any more, seeing that we will write to the sacred Roman senate in such wise that by imperial decree none shall any more call you God or son of God." Then Jesus said: "With your words I am not consoled, because where you hope for light darkness shall come; but my consolation is in the coming of the Messenger, who shall destroy every false opinion of me, and his faith shall spread and shall take

hold of the whole world, for so has God promised to Abraham our father. And that which gives me consolation is that his faith shall have no end, but shall be kept inviolate by God."

The priest answered: "After the coming of the Messenger of God shall other prophets come?" Jesus answered: "There shall not come after him true prophets

sent by God, but there shall come a great number of false prophets, whereat I
sorrow. For Satan shall raise them up by the just judgment of God, and they
shall hide themselves under the pretext of my gospel." Herod answered: "How is
it a just judgment of God that such impious men should come?"

Jesus answered: "It is just that he who will not believe in the truth to his
salvation should believe in a lie to his damnation. Wherefore I say to you, that
the world has ever despised the true prophets and loved the false, as can be
seen in the time of Micaiah and Jeremiah. For every like loves his like."

Then said the priest: "How shall the Messiah be called, and what sign shall
reveal his coming?" Jesus answered: "The name of the Messiah is admirable, for
God himself gave him the name when he had created his soul, and placed it in a
celestial splendour. God said: "Wait Muhammad; for your sake I will to create
paradise, the world, and a great multitude of creatures, whereof I make you a
present, insomuch that whoever shall bless you shall be blessed, and whoever
shall curse you shall be accursed. When I shall send you into the world I shall
send you as my Messenger of salvation, and your word shall be true, insomuch
that heaven and earth shall fail, but your faith shall never fail." Muhammad is
his blessed name." Then the crowd lifted up their voices, saying: "O God send us
your Messenger: O Muhammad, come quickly for the salvation of the world!"

Chapter 98

And having said this, the multitude departed with the priest and the governor
with Herod, having great disputations concerning Jesus and concerning his
doctrine. Whereupon the priest prayed the governor to write to Rome to the
senate the whole matter; which thing the governor did; wherefore the senate had
compassion on Israel, and decreed that on pain of death none should call Jesus
the Nazarene, prophet of the Jews, either God or son of God. Which decree was
posted up in the Temple, engraved upon copper.

When the greater part of the crowd had departed, there remained about five
thousand men, without women and children who being wearied by the journey,
having been two days without bread, for that through longing to see Jesus they
had forgotten to bring any, whereupon they ate raw herbs therefore they were not
able to depart like the others. Then Jesus, when he perceived this, had pity on
them, and said to Philip: "Where shall we find bread for them that they perish
not of hunger?" Philip answered: "Lord, two hundred pieces of gold could not buy
so much bread that each one should taste a little." Then said Andrew: "There is
here a child which has five loaves and two fishes, but what will it be among so
many?"

Jesus answered: "Make the multitude sit down" And they sat down upon the grass
by fifties and by forties. Thereupon said Jesus: "In the name of God!" And he
took the bread, and prayed to God and then brake the bread, which he gave to the
disciples, and the disciples gave it to the multitude; and so did they with the
fishes. Every one ate and every one was satisfied. Then Jesus said: "Gather up
that which is over." So the disciples gathered those fragments, and filled
twelve baskets.

Thereupon every one put his hand to his eyes, saying: "Am I awake, or do I
dream?" And they remained, every one, for the space of an hour. as it were
beside themselves by reason of the great miracle. Afterwards Jesus, when he had
given thanks to God, dismissed them, but there were seventy-two men that willed
not to leave him; wherefore Jesus, perceiving their faith, chose them for
disciples.

Chapter 99

Jesus, having withdrawn into a hollow part of the desert in Tiro near to Jordan, called together the seventy-two with the twelve, and, when he had seated himself upon a stone, made them to sit near him. And he opened his mouth with a sigh and said: "This day have we seen a great wickedness in Judea and in Israel such that my heart trembles within my breast for fear of God. Truly I say to you, that God is jealous for his honour, and loves Israel as a lover. You know that when a youth loves a lady, and she does not love him, but another, he is moved to indignation and slays his rival. Even so, I tell you, does God: for, when Israel has loved anything such that he forgets God, God has brought such a thing to nothing.

Now what thing is more dear to God here on earth than the priesthood and the holy Temple? Nevertheless, in the time of Jeremiah the prophet, when the people had forgotten God, and boasted only of the Temple, for that there was none like it in all the world, God raised up his wrath by Nebuchadnezzar, king of Babylon, and with an army caused him to take the holy city and burn it with the sacred Temple, such that the sacred things which the prophets of God trembled to touch were trodden under foot by infidels full of wickedness.

Abraham loved his son Ishmael a little more than was right, so in order to kill that evil love out of the heart of Abraham, God commanded that he should slay his son: which he would have done had the knife cut. * David loved Absalom vehemently, and therefore God brought it to pass that the son rebelled against his father and was suspended by his hair and slain by Joab. O fearful judgment of God, that Absalom loved his hair above all things, and this was turned into a rope to hang him!

Innocent Job came near to loving his seven sons and three daughters [too much], when God gave him into the hand of Satan, who not only deprived him of his sons and his riches in one day, but also struck him with grievous sickness, such that worms came out of his flesh for the next seven years. Our father Jacob loved Joseph more than his other sons, so God caused him to be sold, and caused Jacob to be deceived by these same sons, such that he believed that the beasts had devoured his son, and so lived in mourning for ten years.

Chapter 100

As God lives, brothers, I fear that God will be angered against me. Therefore you must go through Judea and Israel, preaching the truth to the twelve tribes, that they may be undeceived." The disciples answered with fear, weeping: "We will do whatever you bid us [to do]."

Then Jesus said: "Let us make prayer and fast for three days, and from henceforth every evening when the first star shall appear, when prayer is made to God, let us make prayer three times, asking him for mercy three times: because the sin of Israel is three times more grievous than other sins." "So be it," answered the disciples.

When the third day was ended, on the morning of the fourth day, Jesus called together all the disciples and apostles and said to them: "Barnabas and John will stay with me: you others are to go through all the region of Samaria and Judea and Israel, preaching penitence: because the axe is laid near to the tree, to cut it down. And make prayer over the sick, because God has given me authority over every sickness."

Then he who writes said: "O Master, if your disciples be asked how they ought to show penitence, what shall they answer?" Jesus answered: "When a man loses a purse does he turn back only his eye, to see it? or his hand, to take it? or his tongue, to ask? No, but he turns his whole body back and employs every power of hissoul to find it. Is this true?" Then he who writes answered : "It is most true."

Chapter 101

Then Jesus said: "Penitence is a reversing of the evil life: for every sense must be turned around to the contrary of that which it wrought while sinning. Instead of delight must be mourning; for laughter, weeping; for revellings, fasts; for sleeping, vigils; for leisure, activity; for lust, chastity; let storytelling be turned into prayer and avarice into almsgiving." Then he who writes answered: "But if they are asked, how are we to mourn, how are we to weep, how are we to fast, how are we to show activity, how are we to remain chaste, how are we to make prayer and do alms; what answer shall they give? And how shall they do penance properly if they do not know how to repent."

Jesus answered: "You have asked [a good question], O Barnabas, and I wish to answer all fully if it is pleasing to God. So today I will speak to you of penitence generally, and that which I say to one I say to all. Know then that penitence more than anything [else] must be done for pure love of God; otherwise it will be vain to repent. I will speak to you by a similitude. Every building, if its foundation be removed, falls into ruin: is this true?" "It is true," answered the disciples.

Then Jesus said: "The foundation of our salvation is God, without whom there is no salvation. When man has sinned, he has lost the foundation of his salvation; so it is necessary to begin from the foundation. Tell me, if your slaves had offended you, and you knew that they did not grieve at having offended you, but grieved at having lost their reward, would·you forgive them? Certainly not. I tell you that this is what God will do to those who repent for having lost paradise. Satan, the enemy of all good, has great remorse for having lost paradise and gained hell. Yet he will he never find mercy. Do you know why? Because he does not love God; no, he hates his Creator.

Chapter 102

Truly I say to you, that every animal according to its own nature, if it loses that which it desires, mourns for the lost good. Accordingly, the sinner who will be truly penitent must have [a] great desire to punish in himself that which he has done in opposition to his Creator: [to the extent that] when he prays he dare not to crave paradise from God, or that God [will] free him from hell, but in confusion of mind, prostrate before God, he says in his prayer:

'Behold the guilty one, O Lord, who has offended You without any cause at the very time when he ought to have been serving You. Here he seeks that what he has done may be punished by Your hand, and not by the hand of Satan, Your enemy; in order that the ungodly may not rejoice over your creatures. Chastise, punish as it pleases you, O Lord, for you will never give me so much torment as this wicked one deserves.'

The sinner, holding to this manner of [penitence], will find mercy with God in proportion to [the extent that] he craves justice. Assuredly, [the] laughter of a sinner is an abominable sacrilege since this world is rightly called by our father David a vale of tears.

There was a king who adopted one of his slaves as [his] son [and] he made him lord of all that he possessed. Now it happened that by the deceit of a wicked man the wretched one fell under the displeasure of the king, so that he suffered great miseries, not only in his substance, but in being despised, and being deprived of all that he won each day by working. Do you think that such a man would laugh for any time?" "No," answered the disciples, "for if the king should have known it he would have had him slain, seeing him laugh at the king's displeasure. But it is probable that he would weep day and night."

Then Jesus wept saying: "Woe to the world, for it is sure of eternal torment. O wretched mankind, that God has chosen you as a son, granting you paradise, at which you, O wretched one, by the operation of Satan, did fall under the displeasure of God, and was cast out of paradise and condemned to the unclean world, where you receive all things with toil and every good work is taken from you by continual sinning. And the world simply laughs, and, what is worse, he that is the greatest sinner laughs more than the rest! It will be, therefore, as you have said: that God will give the sentence of eternal death upon the sinner who laughs at his sins and does not weep."

Chapter 103

The weeping of the sinner ought to be like that of a father who weeps over his son [who is] near to death. O madness of man, that weeps over the body from which the soul is departed, and [yet] does not weep over the soul from which the mercy of God has departed because of sin! Tell me, if the mariner, when his ship has been wrecked by a storm, could recover all that he had lost by weeping, what would he do? It is certain that he would weep bitterly. But I say to you truly, that in every thing [for which] a man weeps, he sins, except when he weeps for his sin. For every misery that comes to man comes to him from God for his salvation, so that he should rejoice [when it befalls him]. But sin comes from the devil for the damnation of man, and [yet] man is not sad about that. Surely here you can perceive that man seeks loss and not profit."

Bartholomew said: "Lord, what shall he do who cannot weep because his heart is a stranger to weeping? " Jesus answered: "Not all those who shed tears weep, O Bartholomew. As God lives, there are found men from whose eyes no tear has ever fallen, and they have wept more than a thousand of those who [do] shed tears. The weeping of a sinner is a consumption of earthly affection by vehemence of sorrow.

Just as the sunshine preserves from putrefaction what is placed uppermost, even so this consumption preserves the soul from sin. If God should grant as many tears to the true penitent as the sea has waters he would desire far more: and so that desire consumes that little drop that he would shed, as a blazing furnace consumes a drop of water. But they who readily burst into weeping are like the horse that goes faster the more lightly he is laden.

Chapter 104

'Truly there are men who have both the inward affection and the outward tears. But he who is thus, will be a Jeremiah. In weeping, God measures more the sorrow than the tears.' Then said John: "O master, how does man lose in weeping over things other than sin?" Jesus answered: 'If Herod; should give you a mantle to keep for him, and afterwards should take it away from you, would you have reason to weep?'

"No," said John. Then Jesus said: 'Now has man less reason to weep when he loses aught, or has not that which he would; for all comes from the hand of God. Accordingly, shall not God have power to dispose at his pleasure of his own things, O foolish man? For you have of your own, sin alone; and for that ought you to weep, and not for aught else.'

Matthew said: "O master, you have confessed before all Judea that God has no similitude like man, and now you have said that man receives from the hand of God; accordingly, since God has hands he has a similitude with man." Jesus answered: 'You are in error, O Matthew, and many have so erred, not knowing the sense of the words. For man ought to consider not the outward [form] of the words, but the sense; seeing that human speech is as it were an interpreter between us and God. Now knew you not, that when God willed to speak to our fathers on mount Sinai, our fathers cried out: "Speak you to us, O Moses, and let not God speak to us, lest we die"? And what said God by Isaiah the prophet, but that, so far as the heaven is distant from the earth, even so are the ways of God distant from the ways of men, and the thoughts of God from the thoughts of men?

Chapter 105

'God is so immeasurable that I tremble to describe him. But it is necessary that I make to you a proposition. I tell you, then, that the heavens are nine and that they are distant from one another even as the first heaven is distant from the earth, which is distant from the earth five hundred years' journey. Wherefore the earth is distant from the highest heaven four thousand and five hundred years' journey. I tell you, accordingly, that [the earth] is in proportion to the first heaven as the point of a needle and the first heaven in like manner is in proportion to the second as a point, and similarly all the heavens are inferior each one to the next. But all the size of the earth with that of all the heavens is in proportion to paradise as a point, no, as a grain of sand. Is this greatness immeasurable?'

The disciples answered: 'Yes, surely.'

Then Jesus said: 'As God lives, in whose presence my soul stands, the universe before God is small as a grain of sand, and God is as many times greater [than it] as it would take grains of sand to fill all the heavens and paradise, and more. Now consider you if God has any proportion with man, who is a little piece of clay that stands upon the earth. Beware, then, that you take the sense and not the bare words, if you wish to have eternal life.' The disciples answered: 'God alone can know himself, and truly it is as said Isaiah the prophet: "He is hidden from human senses."

Jesus answered: 'So is it true; wherefore, when we are in paradise we shall know God, as here one knows the sea from a drop of salt water. Returning to my discourse, I tell you that for sin alone one ought to weep, because by sinning man forsakes his Creator. But how shall he weep who attends at revellings and feasts? He will weep even as ice will give fire! You needs must turn revellings into fasts if you will have lordship over your senses, because even so has our God lordship. Thaddaeus said: 'So then, God has sense over which to have lordship.'

Jesus answered: 'Go you back to saying, "God has this," "God is such"? Tell me, has man sense?' 'Yes,' answered the disciples. Jesus said: 'Can a man be found who has life in him, yet in him sense works not?' 'No,' said the disciples. 'You deceive yourselves,' said Jesus, 'for he that is blind, deaf, dumb, and mutilated-where is his sense? And when a man is in a swoon?' Then were the disciples perplexed; when Jesus said: 'Three things there are that make up man: that is, the soul and the sense and the flesh, each one of itself separate. Our God created the soul and the body as you have heard, but you have not yet heard how he created the sense. Therefore to-morrow, if God please, I will tell you all.' And having said this Jesus gave thanks to God, and prayed for the salvation of our people, every one of us saying: 'Amen.'

Chapter 106

When he had finished the prayer of dawn, Jesus sat down under a palm tree, and thither his disciples drew near to him. Then Jesus said: 'As God lives, in whose presence stands my soul, many are deceived concerning our life. For so closely are the soul and the sense joined together, that the more part of men affirm the soul and the sense to be one and the same thing, dividing it by operation and not by essence, calling it the sensitive, vegetative, and intellectual soul. But truly I say to you, the soul is one, which thinks and lives. O foolish ones, where will they find the intellectual soul without life? Assuredly, never. But life without senses will readily be found, as is seen in the unconscious when the sense leaves him.' Thaddaeus answered: "O master, when the sense leaves the life, a man does not have life."

Jesus answered: "This is not true, because man is deprived of life when the soul departs; because the soul returns not any more to the body, save by miracle. But sense departs by reason of fear that it receives, or by reason of great sorrow that the soul has. For the sense has God created for pleasure, and by that alone it lives, even as the body lives by food and the soul lives by knowledge and love. This sense is now rebellious against the soul, through indignation that it has at being deprived of the pleasure of paradise through sin. Wherefore there is the greatest need to nourish it with spiritual pleasure for him who wills not that it should live of carnal pleasure. Understand you? Truly I say to you, that God having created it condemned it to hell and to intolerable snow and ice; because it said that it was God; but when he deprived it of nourishment, taking away its food from it, it confessed that it was a slave of God and the work of his hands. And now tell me, how does sense work in the ungodly? Assuredly, it is as God in them: seeing that they follow sense, forsaking reason and the Law of God. Whereupon they become abominable, and work not any good."

Chapter 107

'And so the first thing that follows sorrow for sin is fasting. For he that sees that a certain food makes him sick, for that he fears death, after sorrowing that he has eaten it, forsaken it, so as not to make himself sick. So ought the sinner to do. Perceiving that pleasure has made him to sin against God his creator by following sense in these good things of the world, let him sorrow at having done so, because it deprives him of God, his life, and gives him the eternal death of hell. But because man while living has need to take these good things of the world, fasting is needful here. So let him proceed to mortify sense and to know God for his lord. And when he sees the sense abhor fastings, let him put before it the condition of hell, where no pleasure at all but infinite sorrow is received; let him put before it the delights of paradise, that are so great that a grain of one of the delights of paradise is greater than all those of the world. For so will it easily be quieted; for that it is better to be content with little in order to receive much, than to be unbridled in little and be deprived of all and abide in torment.

'You ought to remember the rich feaster in order to fast well. For he, wishing here on earth to fare deliciously every day, was deprived eternally of a single drop of water: while Lazarus, being content with crumbs here on earth, shall live eternally in full abundance of the delights of paradise. But let the penitent be cautious; for that Satan seeks to annul every good work, and more in the penitent than in others, for that the penitent has rebelled against him, and from being his faithful slave has turned into a rebellious foe. Whereupon Satan will seek to cause that he shall not fast in any wise, under pretext of sickness, and when this shall not avail he will invite him to an extreme fast, in order that he may fall sick and afterwards live deliciously. And if he succeed not in this, he will seek to make him set his fast simply upon bodily food, in order that he may be like to himself, who never eats but always sins.

As God lives, it is abominable to deprive the body of food and fill the soul with pride, despising them that fast not, and holding oneself better than they. Tell me, will the sick man boast of the diet that is imposed on him by the physician, and call them mad who are not put on diet? Assuredly not. But he will sorrow for the sickness by reason of which he needs must be put upon diet. Even so I say to you, that the penitent ought not to boast in his fast, and despise them that fast not; but he ought to sorrow for the sin by reason whereof he fasts. Nor should the penitent that fasts procure delicate food, but he should content himself with coarse food. Now will a man give delicate food to the dog that bites and to the horse that kicks? No, surely, but rather the contrary. And let this suffice you concerning fasting.'

Chapter 108

Hearken, then, to what I shall say to you concerning watching. For just as there are two kinds of sleeping, viz. that of the body and that of the soul, even so must you be careful in watching that while the body watches the soul sleep not. For this would be a most grievous error. Tell me, in parable: there is a man who whilst walking strikes himself against a rock, and in order to avoid striking it the more with his foot, he strikes with his head what is the state of such a man?' "Miserable," answered the disciples, "for such a man is frenzied."

Then Jesus said: "Well have you answered, for truly I say to you that he who watches with the body and sleeps with the soul is frenzied. As the spiritual infirmity is more grievous than the corporeal, even so is it more difficult to cure. Wherefore, shall such a wretched one boast of not sleeping with the body, which is the foot of the life, while he perceives not his misery that he sleeps with the soul, which is the head of the life? The sleep of the soul is forgetfulness of God and of his fearful judgment. The soul, then, that watches is that which in everything and in every place perceives God, and in everything and through everything and above everything gives thanks to his majesty, knowing that always at every moment it receives grace and mercy from God.

Wherefore in fear of his majesty there always resounds in its ear that angelic utterance "Creatures, come to judgment, for your Creator wills to judge you." For it abides habitually ever in the service of God. * Tell me, whether do you desire the more: to see by the light of a star or by the light of the sun?" Andrew answered: "By the light of the sun; for by the light of the star we cannot see the neighbouring mountains, and by the light of the sun we see the tiniest grain of sand. Wherefore we walk with fear by the light of the star, but by the light of the sun we go securely."

Chapter 109

Jesus answered: "Even so I tell you that you ought to watch with the soul by the sun of justice [which is] our God, and not to boast yourselves of the watchings of the body. It is most true, therefore, that bodily sleep is to be avoided as much as is possible, but [to avoid it] altogether is impossible, the sense and the flesh being weighed down with food and the mind with business. Wherefore let him that will sleep little avoid too much business and much food. As God lives, in whose presence stands my soul, it is lawful to sleep somewhat every night, but it is never lawful to forget God and his fearful judgment: and the sleep of the soul is such oblivion."

Then answered he who writes: "O master, how can we always have God in memory? Assuredly, it seems to us impossible. Jesus said, with a sigh: "This is the greatest misery that man can suffer, O Barnabas. For man cannot here upon earth have God his creator always in memory; saving them that are holy, for they always have God in memory, because they have in them the light of the grace of God, so that they cannot forget God. But tell me, have you seen them that work quarried stones, how by their constant practice they have so learned to strike that they speak with others and all the time are striking the iron tool that works the stone without looking at the iron, and yet they do not strike their hands? Now do you likewise.

Desire to be holy if you wish to overcome entirely this misery of forgetfulness. Sure it is that water cleaves the hardest rocks with a single drop striking there for a long period. Do you know why you have not overcome this misery? Because you have not perceived that it is sin. I tell you then that it is an error, when a prince gives you a present, O man, that you shouldst shut your eyes and turn your back upon him. Even so do they err who forget God, for at all times man receives from God gifts and mercy."

Chapter 110

Now tell me, does our God at all times grant you [his bounty]? Yes, assuredly; for unceasingly he ministers to you the breath whereby you live. Truly, truly, I say to you, every time that your body receives breath your heart ought to say: "God be thanked!"' Then said John: "it is most true what you say, O master; teach us therefore the way to attain to this blessed condition."

Jesus answered: "Truly I say to you, one cannot attain to such condition by human powers, but rather by the mercy of God our Lord. It is true indeed that man ought to desire the good in order that God may give it him. Tell me, when you are at table do you take those meats which you would not so much as look at? No, assuredly. Even so I say to you that you shall not receive that which you will not desire. God is able, if you desire holiness, to make you holy in less time than the twinkling of an eye, but in order that man may be sensible of the gift and the giver our God wills that we should wait and ask.

Have you seen them that practice shooting at a mark? Assuredly they shoot many times in vain. Howbeit, they never wish to shoot in vain, but are always in hope to hit the mark. Now do you this, you who ever desire to have our God in remembrance, and when you forget, mourn; for God shall give you grace to attain to all that I have said. Fasting and spiritual watching are so united one with the other that, if one break the watch, straightway the fast is broken. For in sinning a man breaks the fast of the soul, and forgets God. So is it that

watching and fasting as regards the soul are always necessary for us and for all
men. For to none is it lawful to sin.

But the fasting of the body and its watchings, believe me, they are not possible
at all times, nor for all persons. For there are sick and aged folk, women with
child, men that are put upon diet, children, and others that are of weak
complexion. For indeed everyone, even as he clothes himself according to his
proper measure, so should choose his [manner of] fasting. For just as the
garments of a child are not suitable for a man of thirty years, even so the
watchings and fastings of one are not suitable for another."

Chapter 111

'But beware that Satan will use all his strength [to bring it to pass] that you
[shall] watch during the night, and afterward be sleeping when by commandment of
God you ought to be praying and listening to the word of God. Tell me, would it
please you if a friend of yours should eat the meat and give you the bones?"
Peter answered: "No, master, for such an one ought not to be called friend, but
a mocker."

Jesus answered with a sigh: "You have well said the truth, O Peter, for truly
every one that watches with the body more than is necessary, sleeping, or having
his head weighed down with slumber when he should be praying or listening to the
words of God, such a wretch mocks God his creator, and so is guilty of such a
sin. Moreover, he is a robber, seeing that he steals the time that he ought to
give to God, and spends it when, and as much as, pleases him.

In a vessel of the best wine a man gave his enemies to drink so long as the wine
was at its best, but when the wine came down to the dregs he gave to his lord to
drink. What, think you, will the master do to his servant when he shall know
all, and the servant be before him? Assuredly, he will beat him and slay him in
righteous indignation according to the laws of the world. And now what shall God
do to the man that spends the best of his time in business, and the worst in
prayer and study of the Law? Woe to the world, because with this and with
greater sin is its heart weighed down! Accordingly, when I said to you that
laughter should be turned into weeping, feasts into fasting, and sleep into
watching, I compassed in three words all that you have heard that here on earth
one ought always to weep, and that weeping should be from the heart, because God
our creator is offended; that you ought to fast in order to have lordship over
the sense, and to watch in order not to sin; and that bodily weeping and bodily
fasting and watching should be taken according to the constitution of each one."

Chapter 112

Having said this, Jesus said: "You needs must seek of the fruits of the field
the wherewithal to sustain our life, for it is now eight days that we have eaten
no bread. Wherefore I will pray to our God, and will await you with Barnabas."

So all the disciples and apostles departed by fours and by sixes and went their
way according to the word of Jesus. There remained with Jesus he who writes;
whereupon Jesus, weeping, said: "O Barnabas, it is necessary that I should
reveal to you great secrets, which, after that I shall be departed from the
world, you shall reveal to it." Then answered he that writes, weeping, and said:
"Suffer me to weep, O master, and other men also, for that we are sinners. And
you, that are an holy one and prophet of God, it is not fitting for you to weep
so much."

Jesus answered: "Believe me, Barnabas that I cannot weep as much as I ought. For if men had not called me God, I should have seen God here as he will be seen in paradise, and should have been safe not to fear the day of judgment. But God knows that I am innocent, because never have I harboured thought to be held more than a poor slave. No, I tell you that if I had not been called God I should have been carried into paradise when I shall depart from the world, whereas now I shall not go thither until the judgment. Now you see if I have cause to weep.

Know, O Barnabas, that for this I must have great persecution, and shall be sold by one of my disciples for thirty pieces of money. Whereupon I am sure that he who shall sell me shall be slain in my name, for that God shall take me up from the earth, and shall change the appearance of the traitor so that every one shall believe him to be me; nevertheless, when he dies an evil death, I shall abide in that dishonour for a long time in the world. But when Muhammad shall come, the sacred Messenger of God, that infamy shall be taken away. And this shall God do because I have confessed the truth of the Messiah who shall give me this reward, that I shall be known to be alive and to be a stranger to that death of infamy."

Then answered he that writes: "O master, tell me who is that wretch, for I fain would choke him to death." "Hold your peace," answered Jesus, "for so God wills, and he cannot do otherwise but see you that when my mother is afflicted at such an event you tell her the truth, in order that she may be comforted." Then answered he who writes: "All this will I do, O master, if God please."

Chapter 113

When the disciples were come they brought pine-cones, and by the will of God they found a good quantity of dates. So after the midday prayer they ate with Jesus. Whereupon the apostles and disciples, seeing him that writes of sad countenance, feared that Jesus needs must quickly depart from the world. Whereupon Jesus consoled them, saying: "Fear not, for my hour is not yet come that I should depart from you. I shall abide with you still for a little while. Therefore must I teach you now, in order that you may go, as I have said, through all Israel to preach penitence; in order that God may have mercy upon the sin of Israel. Let every one therefore beware of sloth, and much more he that does penance; because every tree that bears not good fruit shall be cut down and cast into the fire.

There was a citizen who had a vineyard, and in the midst thereof had a garden, which had a fine fig-tree; whereon for three years when the owner came he found no fruit, and seeing every other tree bare fruit there he said to his vinedresser: "Cut down this bad tree, for it cumbers the ground." The vinedresser answered: "Not so, my lord, for it is a beautiful tree." "Hold your peace," said the owner, "for I care not for useless beauties. You should know that the palm and the balsam are nobler than the fig. But I had planted in the courtyard of my house a plant of palm and one of balsam, which I had surrounded with costly walls, but when these bare no fruit, but leaves which heaped themselves up and putrefied the ground in front of the house, I caused them both to be removed. And how shall I pardon a fig-tree far from the house, which cumbers my garden and my vineyard where every other tree bears fruit? Assuredly I will not suffer it any longer."

Then said the vinedresser: "Lord, the soil is too rich. Wait, therefore, one year more, for I will prune the fig-plant's branches, and take away from it the richness of the soil, putting in poor soil with stones, and so shall it bear fruit." The owner answered: "Now go and do so; for I will wait, and the fig-

plant shall bear fruit." Understand you this parable?" The disciples answered:
"No, Lord, therefore explain it to us."

Chapter 114

Jesus answered: "Truly I say to you, the owner is God, and the vinedresser is
his Law. God, then, had in paradise the palm and the balsam; for Satan is the
palm and the first man the balsam. Then did he cast out because they bare not
fruit of good works, but uttered ungodly words that were the condemnation of
many angels and many men. Now that God has man in the world, in the midst of his
creatures that serve God, all of them, according to his precept: and man, I say,
bearing no fruit, God would cut him down and commit him to hell, seeing he
pardoned not the angel and the first man, punishing the angel eternally, and the
man for a time.

Whereupon the Law of God says that man has too much good in this life, and so it
is necessary that he should suffer tribulation and be deprived of earthly goods,
in order that he may do good works. Therefore our God waits for man to be
penitent. Truly I say to you, that our God has condemned man to work, so that,
as said Job, the friend and prophet of God: "As the bird is born to fly and the
fish to swim, even so is man born to work." So also David our father, a prophet
of God, says: Eating the labours of our hands we shall be blessed, and it shall
be well with us. Wherefore let every one work, according to his quality. Now
tell me, if David our father and Solomon his son worked with their hands, what
ought the sinner to do?"

Said John: "Master, to work is a fitting thing, but this ought the poor to do."
Jesus answered: "Yes, for they cannot do otherwise. But know you not that good,
to be good, must be free from necessity? Thus the sun and the other planets are
strengthened by the precepts of God so that they cannot do otherwise, wherefore
they shall have no merit. Tell me, when God gave the precept to work, he said
not: "A poor man shall live of the sweat of his face"? And Job did not say that:
"As a bird is born to fly, so a poor man is born to work"? But God said to man:
"In the sweat of your countenance shall you eat bread," and Job that "Man is
born to work." Therefore [only] he who is not man is free from this precept.
Assuredly for no other reason are all things costly, but that there are a great
multitude of idle folk: if these were to labour, some attending the ground and
some at fishing the water, there would be the greatest plenty in the world. And
of the lack thereof it will be necessary to render an account in the dreadful
day of judgment.

Chapter 115

Let man say somewhat to me. What has he brought into the world, by reason of
which he would live in idleness? Certain it is that he was born naked, and
incapable of anything. Hence, of all that he has found, he is not the owner, but
the dispenser. And he will have to render an account thereof in that dreadful
day.

The abominable lust, that makes man like the brute beasts, ought greatly to be
feared; for the enemy is of one's own household, so that it is not possible to
go into any place where your enemy may not come. Ah, how many have perished
through lust! Through lust came the deluge, insomuch that the world perished
before the mercy of God and so that there were saved only Noah and eighty-three
human persons. For lust God overwhelmed three wicked cities whence escaped only
Lot and his two children. For lust the tribe of Benjamin was all but
extinguished. And I tell you truly that if I should narrate to you how many have

perished through lust, the space of five days would not suffice." James
answered: "O Master, what signifies lust?"

Jesus answered: "Lust is an unbridled desire of love, which, not being directed
by reason, bursts the bounds of man's intellect and affections; so that the man,
not knowing himself, loves that which he ought to hate. Believe me, when a man
loves a thing, not because God has given him such thing, but as its owner, he is
a fornicator; for that the soul, which ought to abide in union with God its
creator, he has united with the creature. And so God laments by Isaiah the
prophet, saying: You have committed fornication with many lovers; nevertheless,
return to me and I will receive you.

As God lives in whose presence my soul stands, if there were not internal lust
within the heart of man, he would not fall into the external; for if the root be
removed the tree dies speedily. Let a man content himself therefore with the
wife whom his creator has given him, and let him forget every other woman."
Andrew answered: "How shall a man forget the women if he live in the city where
there are so many of them?" Jesus replied: "O Andrew, certain it is he who lives
in the city, it will do him harm; seeing that the city is a sponge that draws in
every iniquity.

Chapter 116

It behoves a man to live in the city, even as the soldier lives when he has
enemies around the fortress, defending himself against every assault and always
fearing treachery on the part of the citizens. Even so, I say, let him repel
every outward enticement of sin, and fear the sense, because it has a supreme
desire for things impure. But how shall he defend himself if he bridle not the
eye, which is the origin of every carnal sin? As God lives in whose presence my
soul stands, he who has not bodily eyes is secure not to receive punishment save
only to the third degree, while he that has eyes receives it to the seventh
degree.

In the time of the prophet Elijah it came to pass that Elijah seeing a blind man
weeping, a man of good life, asked him saying: "Why weep you, O brother?" The
blind man answered: "I weep because I cannot see Elijah the prophet, the holy
one of God.". Then Elijah rebuked him, saying: "Cease from weeping, O man, for
in weeping you sin." The blind man answered: "Now tell me, is it a sin to see a
holy prophet of God, that raises the dead and makes the fire to come down from
heaven?" Elijah answered: "You speak not the truth, for Elijah is not able to do
anything of all that you say, because he is a man as you are. For all the men in
the world cannot make one fly to be born." Said the blind man: "You say this, O
man, because Elijah must have rebuked you for some sin of your, wherefore you
hate him."

Elijah answered: "May it please God that you be speaking the truth; because, O
brother, if I should hate Elijah I should love God, and the more I should hate
Elijah the more I should love God." Hereupon was the blind man greatly angered,
and said: "As God lives, you are an impious fellow! Can God then be loved while
one hates the prophets of God? Begone forthwith, for I will not listen to you
any longer!" Elijah answered: "Brother, now may you see with your intellect how
evil is bodily seeing. For you desire sight to see Elijah, and hate Elijah with
your soul." The blind man answered: "Now begone' for you are the devil, that
would make me sin against the holy one of God."

Then Elijah gave a sigh, and said with tears: "You have spoken the truth, O
brother, for my flesh, which you desire to see, separates you from God." Said

the blind man: "I do not wish to see you; no, if I had my eyes, I would close
them so as not to see you?" Then said Elijah: "Know, brother, that I am Elijah!"
The blind man answered: "You speak not the truth." Then said the disciples of
Elijah: "Brother, he truly is the prophet of God, Elijah." " Let him tell me,"
said the blind man, "if he be the prophet. Of what seed I am, and how I became
blind?"

Chapter 117

Elijah answered: "You are of the tribe of Levi; and because you, in entering the
Temple of God, looks lewdly upon a woman, you being near the sanctuary, our God
took away your sight." Then the blind man weeping said: "Pardon me, O holy
prophet of God, for I have sinned in speaking with you; for if I had seen you I
should not have sinned."

Elijah answered: "May our God pardon you, O brother, because as regards me I
know that you have told me the truth, seeing that the more I hate myself the
more I love God, and if you saw me you would still your desire, which is not
pleasing to God. For Elijah is not your creator, but God; whence, so far as
concerns you, I am the devil," said Elijah weeping, "because I turn you aside
from your creator. Weep then, O brother, because you have not that light which
would make you see the true from the false, for if you had had that you would
not have despised my doctrine. Wherefore I say to you, that many desire to see
me and come from far to see me, who despise my words. Wherefore it were better
for them, for their salvation, that they had no eyes, seeing that everyone that
finds pleasure in the creature, be he who he may, and seeks not to find pleasure
in God, has made an idol in his heart, and forsaken God." Then Jesus said,
sighing: "Have you understood all that Elijah said?" The disciples answered: "In
truth, we have understood, and we are beside ourselves at the knowledge that
here on earth there are very few that are not idolaters."

Chapter 118

Then Jesus said: "You speak the truth, for now was Israel desirous to establish
the idolatry that they have in their hearts, in holding me for God, many of whom
have now despised my teaching, saying that I could make myself lord of all
Judea, if I confessed myself to be God, and that I am mad to wish to live in
poverty among desert places, and not abide continually among princes in delicate
living. Oh hapless man, that prizes the light that is common to flies and ants
and despises the light that is common only to angels and prophets and holy
friends of God!

If, then, the eye shall not be guarded, O Andrew, I tell you that it is
impossible not to fall headlong into lust. Wherefore Jeremiah the prophet,
weeping vehemently, said truly: "My eye is a thief that robs my soul." For
therefore did David our father pray with greatest longing to God our Lord that
he would turn away his eyes in order that he might not behold vanity. For truly
everything which has an end is vain. Tell me, then, if one had two pence to buy
bread, would he spend it to buy smoke? Assuredly not, seeing that smoke does
hurt to the eyes and gives no sustenance to the body. Even so then let man do,
for with the outward sight of his eyes and the inward sight of his mind he
should seek to know God his creator and the good pleasure of his will, and
should not make the creature his end, which causes him to lose the creator.

Chapter 119

For truly every time that a man beholds a thing and forgets God who has made it for man, he has sinned. For if a friend of yours should give you somewhat to keep in memory of him, and you should sell it and forget your friend, you have offended against your friend. Even so does man; for when he beholds the creature and has not in memory the creator, who for love of man has created it, he sins against God his creator by ingratitude.

He therefore who shall behold women and shall forget God who for the good of man created woman, he will love her and desire her. And to such degree will this lust of his break forth, that he will love everything like to the thing loved: so that hence comes that sin of which it is a shame to have memory. If, then, man shall put a bridle upon his eyes, he shall be lord of the sense, which cannot desire that which is not presented to it. For so shall the flesh be subject to the spirit. Because as the ship cannot move without wind, so the flesh without the sense cannot sin.

That thereafter it would be necessary for the penitent to turn story-telling into prayer, reason itself shows, even if it were not also a precept of God. For in every idle word man sins, and our God blots out sin by reason of prayer. For that prayer is the advocate of the soul; prayer is the medicine of the soul; prayer is the defence of the heart; prayer is the weapon of faith, prayer, is the bridle of sense; prayer is the salt of the flesh that suffers it not to be corrupted by sin. I tell you that prayer is the hands of our life, whereby the man that prays shall defend himself in the day of judgment: for he shall keep his soul from sin here on earth, and shall preserve his heart that it be not touched by evil desires; offending Satan because he shall keep his sense within the Law of God, and his flesh shall walk in righteousness;, receiving from God all that he shall ask.

As God lives, in whose presence we are, a man without prayer can no more be a man of good works than a dumb man can plead his cause to a blind one; than fistula can be healed without unguent; a man defend himself without movement; or attack another without weapons, sail without rudder, or preserve dead flesh without salt;. For truly he who has no hand cannot receive. If man could change dung into gold and clay into sugar;, what would he do?

Then, Jesus being silent, the disciples answered: "No one would exercise himself in any way other than in making gold and sugar." Then Jesus said: "Now why does not man change foolish story-telling into prayer? Is time, perhaps, given him by God that he may offend God? For what prince would give a city to his subject in order that the latter might make war upon him? As God lives, if man knew after what manner the soul is transformed by vain talking he would sooner bite off his tongue with his teeth than talk. O wretched world! for today men do not assemble together for prayer, but in the porches of the Temple and in the very Temple ;itself Satan ;has there the sacrifice of vain talk, and that which is worse of things which I cannot talk of without shame.

Chapter 120

The fruit of vain talking is this, that it weakens the intellect in such wise that it is not ready to receive the truth; even as a horse accustomed to carry but one ounce of cottonflock cannot carry an hundred pounds of stone. But what is worse is the man who spends his time in jests. When he is fain to pray, Satan will put into his memory those same jests, insomuch that when he ought to weep over his sins to provoke God to mercy and to win forgiveness for his sins, by laughing he provokes God to anger; who will chastise him, and cast him out.

Woe, therefore, to them that jest and talk vainly! But if our God has in abomination them that jest and talk vainly, how will he hold them that murmur and slander their neighbour, and in what plight will they be who deal with sinning as with a business supremely necessary? Oh impure world, I cannot conceive how grievously you will be punished by God! He, then, who would do penance, he, I say, must give out his words at the price of gold.

His disciples answered: "Now who will buy a man's words at the price of gold? Assuredly no one. And how shall he do penance? It is certain that he will become covetous!" Jesus answered: "You have your heart so heavy that I am not able to lift it up. Hence in every word it is necessary that I should tell you the meaning. But give thanks to God, who has given you grace to know the mysteries of God. I do not say that the penitent should sell his talking, but I say that when he talks he should think that he is casting forth gold. For indeed, so doing, even as gold is spent on necessary things, so he will talk [only] when it is necessary to talk. And just as no one spends gold on a thing which shall cause hurt to his body, so let him not talk of a thing that may cause hurt to his soul.

Chapter 121

When the governor has arrested a prisoner whom he examines while the notary writes down [the case], tell me, how does such a man talk?" The disciples answered: "He talks with fear and to the point, so as not to give suspicion of himself, and he is careful not to say anything that may displease the governor, but seeks to speak somewhat whereby he may be set free." Then answered Jesus: "This ought the penitent to do, then, in order not to lose his soul. For that God has given two angels to every man for notaries, the one writing the good, the other the evil that the man does. If then a man would receive mercy let him measure his talking more than gold is measured.

Chapter 122

As for avarice, that must be changed into almsgiving. truly I say to you, that even as the plummet has for its end the centre, so the avaricious has hell for his end, for it is impossible for the avaricious to possess any good in paradise. Know you wherefore? for I will tell you. As God lives, in whose presence my soul stands, the avaricious, even though he be silent with his tongue, by his works says: "There is no other God than I." Inasmuch as all that he has he is fain to spend at his own pleasure, not regarding his beginning or his end, that he is born naked, and dying leaves all.

Now tell me; if Herod; should give you a garden to keep, and you were fain to bear yourselves as owners, not sending any fruit to Herod, and when Herod sent for fruit you drove away his messengers, tell me, would you be making yourselves kings over that garden? Assuredly you. Now I tell you that even so the avaricious man makes himself god over his riches which God has given him.

Avarice is a thirst of the sense, which having lost God through sin because it lives by pleasure, and being unable to delight itself in God, who is hidden from it, surrounds itself with temporal things which it holds as its good; and it grows the stronger the more it sees itself deprived of God. And so the conversion of the sinner is from God, who gives the grace to repent. As said our father David: This change comes from the right hand of God." It is necessary that I should tell you of what sort man is, if you would know how penitence ought to be done. And so today let us render thanks to God, who has given us the grace to communicate his will by my word."

Whereupon he lifted up his hands and prayed, saying: "Lord God almighty and merciful, who in mercy has created us, giving us the rank of men, your servants, with the faith of your true Messenger, we thank you for all your benefits and would fain adore you only all the days of our life, bewailing our sins praying and giving alms, fasting and studying your word, instructing those that are ignorant of your will, suffering from the world for love of you, and giving up our life to the death to serve you. Do you, O Lord, save us from Satan, from the flesh and from the world, even as you save your elect for love of your own self and for love of your Messenger for whom you did create us, and for love of all your holy ones and prophets." The disciples ever answered: "So be it, so be it, Lord, so be it, O our merciful God."

Chapter 123

When it was day, Friday morning, early, Jesus, after the prayer, assembled his disciples and said to them: "Let us sit down; for even as on this day God created man of the clay of the earth;; even so will I tell you what a thing is man, if God please." When all were seated, Jesus said again: "Our God, to show to his creatures his goodness and mercy and his omnipotence, with his liberality and justice, made a composition of four things contrary the one to the other, and united them in one final object, which is man and this is earth, air, water, and fire in order that each one might temper its opposite.

And he made of these four things a vessel, which is man's body, of flesh, bones, blood, marrow, and skin, with nerves and veins, and with all his inward parts; wherein God placed the soul and the sense, as two hands of this life: giving for lodgement to the sense every part of the body, for it diffused itself there like oil. And to the soul gave he for lodgement the heart, where, united with the sense, it should rule the whole life.

God, having thus created man, put into him a light which is called reason;, which was to unite the flesh, the sense, and the soul in a single end to work for the service of God. Whereupon, he placing this work in paradise, and the reason being seduced of the sense by the operation of Satan, the flesh lost its rest, the sense lost the delight whereby it lives, and the soul lost its beauty. Man having come to such a plight, the sense, which finds not repose in labour, but seeks delight, not being curbed by reason, follows the light which the eyes show it; whence, the eyes not being able to see aught but vanity, it deceives itself, and so, choosing earthly things, sins.

Thus it is necessary that by the mercy of God man's reason be enlightened afresh, to know good from evil and [to distinguish] the true delight: knowing which, the sinner is converted to penitence. Wherefore I say to you truly, that if God our Lord enlighten not the heart of man, the reasonings of men are of no avail." John answered: "Then to what end serves the speech of men?"

Jesus replied "Man as man avails nothing to convert man to penitence; but man as a means which God uses converts man; so that seeing God works by a secret fashion in man for man's salvation, one ought to listen to every man, in order that among all may be received him in whom God speaks to us." James answered: "O Master, if perhaps there shall come a false prophet and lying teacher pretending to instruct us, what ought we to do?

Chapter 124

Jesus answered in parable: "A man goes to fish with a net, and therein he catches many fishes, but those that are bad he throws away.' A man went forth to sow, but only the grain that falls on good ground bears seed.' Even so ought you to do, listening to all and receiving only the truth, seeing that the truth alone bears fruit to eternal life."

Then answered Andrew: "Now how shall the truth be known?" Jesus answered: "Everything that conforms to the Book of Moses, that receive you for true; seeing that God is one, the truth is one; whence it follows that the doctrine is one and the meaning of the doctrine is one; and therefore the faith is one. Truly I say to you that if the truth had not been erased from the Book of Moses, God would not have given to David our father the second. And if the book of David had not been contaminated, God would not have committed the Gospel to me; seeing that the Lord our God is unchangeable, and has spoken but one message to all men. Wherefore, when the Messenger of God shall come, he shall come to cleanse away all wherewith the ungodly have contaminated my book."

Then answered he who writes: "O Master, what shall a man do when the Law shall be found contaminated and the false prophet shall speak?" Jesus answered: "Great is your question, O Barnabas; wherefore I tell you that in such a time few are saved, seeing that men do not consider their end, which is God. As God lives, in whose presence my soul stands, every doctrine that shall turn man aside from his end, which is God, is most evil doctrine. Wherefore there are three things that you shall consider in doctrine namely, love towards God, pity towards one's neighbour, and hatred towards yourself, who had offended God, and offends him every day. Wherefore

every doctrine that is contrary to these three heads do you avoid, because it is most evil.

Chapter 125

I will return now to avarice: and I tell you that when the sense would fain acquire a thing or tenaciously keep it, reason must say: "Such a thing will have its end." It is certain that if it will have an end it is madness to love it. Wherefore it behoves one to love and to keep that which will not have an end. Let avarice then be changed into alms, distributing rightly what [a man] has acquired wrongly.

And let him see to it that what the right hand shall give the left hand shall not know'. Because the hypocrites when they do alms desire to be seen and praised of the world. But truly they are vain, seeing that for whom a man works from him does he receive his wages. If, then, a man would receive anything of God, it behoves him to serve God.

And see that when you do alms, you consider that you are giving to God all that [you give] for love of God. Wherefore be not slow to give, and give of the best of that which you have, for love of God. Tell me, desire you to receive of God anything that is bad? Certainly not, O dust and ashes! Then how have you faith in you if you shall give anything bad for love of God?

It were better to give nothing than to give a bad thing; for in not giving you shall have some excuse according to the world: but in giving a worthless thing, and keeping the best for yourselves, what shall be the excuse? And this is all that I have to say to you concerning penitence." Barnabas answered: "How long ought penitence to last?" Jesus replied: "As long as a man is in a state of sin he ought always to repent and do penance for it. Wherefore as human life always

sins, so ought it always to do penance; unless you would make more account of
your shoes than of your soul, since every time that your shoes are burst you
mend them."

Chapter 126

Jesus having called together his disciples, sent them forth by two and two
through the region of Israel, saying: "Go and preach even as you have heard."
Then they bowed themselves and he laid his hand upon their heads, saying: "In
the name of God, give health to the sick, cast out the demons, and undeceive
Israel concerning me, telling them that which I said before the high priest."

They departed therefore, all of them save him who writes, with James ;and John;;
and they went through all Judea, preaching penitence even as Jesus had told
them, healing every sort of sickness, insomuch that in Israel were confirmed the
words of Jesus that God is one and Jesus is prophet of God, when they saw such a
multitude do that which Jesus did concerning the healing of the sick.

But the sons of the devil found another way to persecute Jesus, and these were
the priests and the scribes. Whereupon they began to say that Jesus aspired to
the monarchy over Israel. But they feared the common people, wherefore they
plotted against Jesus secretly.

Having passed throughout Judea the disciples returned to Jesus, who received
them as a father receives his sons, saying: "Tell me, how has wrought the Lord
our God? Surely I have seen Satan fall under your feet and you trample upon him
even as the vinedresser treads the grapes!" The disciples answered: "O Master,
we have healed numberless sick persons, and cast out many demons which tormented
men."

Jesus said: "God forgive you, O brethren, because you have sinned in saying "We
have healed,' seeing it is God that has done all." Then said they: "We have
talked foolishly; wherefore, teach us how to speak." Jesus answered: "In every
good work say 'God has wrought' and in every bad one say 'I have sinned." "So
will we do," said the disciples to him.

Then Jesus said: "Now what says Israel, having seen God do by the hands of so
many men that which God has done by my hands?" The disciples answered: "They say
that there is one God alone and that you are God's prophet." Jesus answered with
joyful countenance: "Blessed be the holy name of God, who has not despised the
desire of me his servant!" And when he had said this they retired to rest.

Chapter 127

Jesus departed from the desert and entered into Jerusalem; whereupon all the
people ran to the Temple to see him. So after the reading of the psalms Jesus
mounted up on the pinnacle where the scribe used to mount, and, having beckoned
for silence with his hand, he said : "Blessed be the holy name of God, O
brethren, who has created us of the clay of the earth, and not of flaming
spirit. For when we sin we find mercy before God, which Satan will never find,
because through his pride he is incorrigible, saying that he is always noble,
for that he is flaming spirit.

Have you heard, brethren, that which our father David says of our God, that he
remembers that we are dust and that our spirit goes and returns not again,
wherefore he has had mercy upon us? Blessed are they that know these words, for
they will not sin against their Lord eternally, seeing that after the sin they

repent, wherefore their sin abides not. Woe to them that extol themselves, for
they shall be humbled to the burning coals of hell. Tell me, brethren, what is
the cause for self-exaltation? Is there, perhaps, any good here upon earth? No,
assuredly, for as says Solomon, the prophet of God: "Everything that is under
the sun is vanity." But if the things of the world do not give us cause to extol
ourselves in our heart, much less does our life give us cause; for it is
burdened with many miseries, since all the creatures inferior to man fight
against us. O, how many have been slain by the burning heat of summer; how many
have been slain by the frost and cold of winter; how many have been slain by
lightning and by hail; how many have been drowned in the sea by the fury of
winds; how many have died of pestilence, of famine, or because they have been
devoured of wild beasts, bitten of serpents, choked by food!

O hapless man, who extols himself having so much to weigh him down, being laid
wait for by all the creatures in every place! But what shall I say of the flesh
and the sense that desire only iniquity; of the world, that offers nought but
sin; of the wicked, who, serving Satan, persecute whosoever would live according
to the Law of God? Certain it is, brethren, that if man, as says our father
David, with his eyes should consider eternity, he would not sin.

To extol oneself in one's heart is but to lock up the pity and mercy of God,
that he pardon not. For our father David says that our God remembers that we are
but dust and that our spirit goes and returns not again. Whoever extols himself,
then, denies that he is dust, and hence, not knowing his need, he asks not help,
and so angers God his helper. As God lives, in whose presence my soul stands,
God would pardon Satan if Satan should know his own misery, and ask mercy of his
Creator, who is blessed for evermore.

Chapter 128

Accordingly, brethren, I, a man, dust and clay, that walk upon the earth, say to
you: Do penance and know your sins. I say, brethren, that Satan, by means of the
Roman soldiery, deceived you when you said that I was God. Wherefore, beware
that you believe them not, seeing they are fallen under the curse of God,
serving the false and lying gods; even as our father David invokes a curse upon
them, saying: The gods of the nations are silver and gold, the work of their

hands; that have eyes and see not, have ears and hear not, have noses and smell
not, have a mouth and eat not, have a tongue and speak not, have hands and touch
not, have feet and walk not. Wherefore said David our father, praying our living
God, Like to them be they that make them and they that trust in them.

O pride unheard of, this pride of man, who being created by God out of earth
forgets his condition and would fain make God at his own pleasure! Wherein he
silently mocks God, as though he should say: There is no use in serving God. For
so do their works show. To this did Satan desire to reduce you, O brethren, in
making you believe me to be God; because, I not being able to create a fly, and
being passable and mortal, I can give you nothing of use, seeing that I myself
have need of everything. How, then, could I help you in all things, as it is
proper to God to do? Shall we, then, who have for our God the great God who has
created the universe with his word, mock at the Gentiles and their gods?

There were two men who came up here into the Temple to pray: the one was a
Pharisee and the other a publican. The Pharisee drew near to the sanctuary, and
praying with his face uplifted said: "I give you thanks, O Lord my God, because
I am not as other men, sinners, who do every wickedness, and particularly as
this publican; for I fast twice in the week and give tithes of all I possess.'

The publican remained afar off, bowed down to the earth, and beating his breast he said with bent head: 'Lord, I am not worthy to look upon the heaven nor upon your sanctuary, for I have sinned much; have mercy upon me!' Truly I say to you, the publican went down from the Temple in better case than the Pharisee, for that our God justified him, forgiving him his sin. But the Pharisee went down in worse case than the publican, because our God rejected him, having his works in abomination.

Chapter 129

Shall the axe, perhaps, boast itself at having cut down the forest where a man has made a garden? No, assuredly, for the man has done all, yes and [made] the axe, with his hands. And you, O man, shall you boast yourself of having done anything that is good, seeing our God created you of clay and works in you all good that is wrought? And why do you despise your neighbour? Do you not know that if God had not preserved you from Satan you would be worse than Satan?

Do you not know that one single sin changed the fair angel into the most repulsive demon? And that the most perfect man that has come into the world, which was Adam, it changed into a wretched being, subjecting him to what we suffer, together with all his offspring? What decree, then, have you, in virtue whereof you may live at your own pleasure without any fear? Woe to you, O clay, for because you have exalted yourself above God who created you you shall be abased beneath the feet of Satan who lays wait for you."

And having said this, Jesus prayed, lifting up his hands to the Lord, and the people said: "So be it! So be it!" When he had finished his prayer he descended from the pinnacle. Whereupon there were brought to him many sick folk whom he made whole, and he departed from the Temple. Thereupon Simon, a leper whom Jesus had cleansed, invited him to eat bread. The priests and scribes, who hated Jesus, reported to the Roman soldiers that which Jesus had said against their gods. For indeed they were seeking how to kill him, but found it not, because they feared the people.

Jesus, having entered the house of Simon, sat down to the table. And while he was eating, behold a woman named Mary, a public sinner, entered into the house, and flung herself upon the ground behind Jesus' feet, and washed them with her tears, anointed them with precious ointment, and wiped them with the hairs of her head. Simon was scandalized, with all that sat at meat, and they said in their hearts: "If this man were a prophet he would know who and of what sort is this woman, and would not suffer her to touch him." Then Jesus said: "Simon, I have a thing to say to you." Simon answered: "Speak, O Master, for I desire your word."

Chapter 130

Jesus said: "There was a man who had two debtors. The one owed to his creditor fifty pence, the other five hundred. Whereupon, when neither of them had wherewithal to pay, the owner, moved with compassion, forgave the debt to each. Which of them would love his creditor most?" Simon answered: "He to whom was forgiven the greater debt." Jesus said: "You have well said; I say to you, therefore, behold this woman and yourself; for you were both debtors to God, the one for leprosy of the body, the other for leprosy of the soul, which is sin. God our Lord, moved with compassion through my prayers, has willed to heal your body and her soul.

You, therefore, love me little, because you have received little as a gift. And so, when I entered your house you did not kiss me nor anoint my head. But this woman, lo! straightway on entering your house she placed herself at my feet, which she has washed with her tears and anointed with precious ointment. Wherefore truly I say to you, many sins are forgiven her, because she has loved much." And turning to the woman he said: "Go your way in peace, for the Lord our God has pardoned your sins; but see you sin no more. Your faith has saved you."

Chapter 131

His disciples drew near to Jesus after the nightly prayer, and said: "O Master, how must we do to escape pride?" Jesus answered: "Have you seen a poor man invited to a prince's house to eat bread?" John answered: "I have eaten bread in Herod's house. For before I knew you I went to fish, and used to sell the fish to the family of Herod. Whereupon, one day when he was feasting, I having brought thither a fine fish, he made me stay and eat there." Then Jesus said: "Now how did you eat bread with infidels? God pardon you, O John! But tell me, how did you bear yourself at the table? Did you seek to have the most honourable place? Did you ask for the most delicate food? Did you speak when you were not questioned at the table? Did you account yourself more worthy than the others to sit at table?"

John answered: "As God lives, I did not dare to lift up my eyes, seeing myself, a poor fisherman, ill-clad, sitting among the king's barons. Whereupon, when the king gave me a little piece of flesh, I thought that the world had fallen upon my head, for the greatness of the favour that the king did to me. And truly I say that, if the king had been of our Law, I should have been fain to serve him all the days of my life." Jesus cried out: "Hold your peace, John, for I fear lest God should cast us into the abyss, even like Abiram, for our pride!"

The disciples trembled with fear at the words of Jesus; when he said again: "Let us fear God, that He cast us not into the abyss for our pride. O brethren, have you heard of John what is done in the house of a prince? Woe to the men that come into the world, for as they live in pride they shall die in contempt and shall go into confusion. For this world is a house where God feasts men, wherein have eaten all the holy ones and prophets of God. And truly I say to you, everything that a man receives, he receives it from God. Wherefore man ought to bear himself with deepest humility; knowing his own vileness and the greatness of God, with the great bounty by which he nourishes us. Therefore it is not lawful for man to say: 'Ah, why is this done and this said in the world?' but rather to account himself, as in truth he is, unworthy to stand in the world at God's board. As God lives, in whose presence my soul stands, there is nothing so small received here in the world from [the hand of] God, but that in return man ought to spend his life for love of God.

As God lives, you sinned not, O John, in eating with Herod, for it was of God's disposition you did so, in order that you might be our teacher and [the teacher] of every one that fears God. So do," said Jesus to his disciples, "that you may live in the world as John lived in the house of Herod when he ate bread with him, for so shall you be in truth free from all pride."

Chapter 132

Jesus walking along the sea of Galilee was surrounded by a great multitude of folk, wherefore he went into a little boat which lay a little off from the shore by itself, and anchored so near the land that the voice of Jesus might be heard.

Whereupon they all drew near to the sea, and sitting down awaited his word. He
then opened his mouth and said:

"Behold, the sower went out to sow, whereupon as he sowed some of the seed fell
upon the road, and this was trodden under foot of men and eaten up of birds;
some fell upon the stones, whereupon when it sprang up, because it had no
moisture, it was burnt up by the sun; some fell in the hedges, whereupon when it
grew up the thorns chocked the seed; and some fell on good ground, whereupon it.
bare fruit, even to thirty, sixty, and an one hundredfold."

Again Jesus said: "Behold, the father of a family sowed good seed in his field:
whereupon, as the servants of the good man slept, the enemy of the man their
master came and sowed tares over the good seed. Whereupon, when the corn sprang
up, there was seen sprung up among the corn a great quantity of tares. The
servants came to their master and said: "O Sir, did you not sow good seed in
your field? Wherefore then is there sprung up therein a great quantity of
tares?" The master answered: 'Good seed did I sow, but while men slept the enemy
of man came and sowed tares over the corn.'

Said the servants: "Will you that we go and pull up the tares from among the
corn?" The master answered: "Do not so, for you would pull up the corn
therewith; but wait till the time of harvest comes. For then shall you go and
pull up the tares from among the corn and cast them into the fire to be burned,
but the corn you shall put into my granary.' "

Again Jesus said: "There went forth many men to sell figs. But when they arrived
at the market-place, behold, men sought not good figs but fair leaves. Therefore
the men were not able to sell their figs. And seeing this, an evil citizen said:
'Surely I may become rich.' Whereupon he called together his two sons and
[said]: 'Go you and gather a great quantity of leaves with bad figs.' And these
they sold for their weight in gold, for the men were mightily pleased with
leaves. Whereupon the men, eating the figs, became sick with a grievous
sickness."

Again Jesus said: "Behold a citizen has a fountain, from which all the
neighbouring citizens take water to wash off their uncleanness; but the citizen
suffers his own clothes to putrefy."

Again Jesus said: "There went forth two men to sell apples. The one chose to
sell the peel of the apple for its weight in gold, not caring for the substance
of the apples. The other desired to give the apples away, receiving only a
little bread for his journey. But men bought the peel of the apples for its
weight in gold, not caring for him who was fain to give them, no even despising
him."

And thus on that day Jesus spoke to the crowd in parables. Then having dismissed
them, he went with his disciples to Nain, where he had raised to life the
widow's son; who, with his mother, received him into his house and ministered to
him.

Chapter 133

His disciples drew near to Jesus and asked him, saying: "O Master, tell us the
meaning of the parables which you spoke to the people." Jesus answered: "The
hour of prayer draws near; wherefore when the evening prayer is ended I will
tell you the meaning of the parables." When the prayer was ended, the disciples
came near to Jesus and he said to them: 'The man who sows seed upon the road,

upon the stones, upon the thorns, upon the good ground, is he who teaches the word of God, which falls upon a great number of men.

It falls upon the road when it comes to the ears of sailors and merchants, who by reason of the long journeys which they make, and the variety of nations with whom they have dealings, have the word of God removed from their memory by Satan. It falls upon the stones when it comes to the ears of courtiers, for by reason of the great anxiety these have to serve the body of a prince the word of God to does not sink into them. Wherefore, albeit they have some memory thereof, as soon as they have any tribulation the word of God goes out of their memory: for, seeing they serve not God, they cannot hope for help from God.

It falls among the thorns when it comes to the ears of them that love their own life, whereupon, though the word of God grow upon them, when carnal desires grow up they choke the good seed of the word of God, for carnal comforts cause [men] to forsake the word of God. That which falls on good ground is when the word of God comes to the ears of him who fears God, whereupon it brings forth fruit of eternal life. Truly I say to you, that in every condition when man fears God the word of God will bear fruit in him.

'Of that father of a family, I tell you truly that he is God our Lord; father of all things, for that he has created all things. But he is not a father after the manner of nature, for that he is incapable of motion, without which generation is impossible. It is, then, our God, whose is this world; and the field where he sows is mankind, and the seed is the word of God. So when the teachers are negligent in preaching the word of God, through being occupied in the business of the world, Satan sows error in the heart of men, whence are come countless sects of wicked doctrine.

'The holy ones and prophets cry: "O Sir, gave you not, then, good doctrine to men? Wherefore, then, be there so many errors?" God answers: 'I have given good doctrine to men, but while men have been given up to vanity Satan has sowed errors to bring to nothing my Law.' The holy ones say: 'O Sir, we will disperse these errors by destroying men."

God answers: 'Do not so, for the faithful are so closely joined to the infidels by kinship that the faithful will be lost with the infidel. But wait until the Judgment, for at that time shall the infidels be gathered by my angels and shall be cast out with Satan into hell, while the good faithful ones shall come to my kingdom.' Surely, many infidel fathers shall beget faithful sons, for whose sake God waits for the world to repent.

Chapter 134

They that bear good figs are the true teachers who preach good doctrine, but the world, which takes pleasure in lies, seeks from the teachers leaves of fine words and flattery. The which seeing, Satan joins himself with the flesh and the sense, and brings a large supply of leaves; that is, a quantity of earthly things, in which he covers up sin; the which receiving, man becomes sick and ready for eternal death. The citizen who has the water and gives his water to others to wash off their uncleanness, but suffers his own garments to become putrefied, is the teacher who to others preaches penitence and himself abides still in sin. O wretched man, because not the angels but his own tongue writes upon the air the punishment that is fitting for him!

If one had the tongue of an elephant, and the rest of his body were as small as an ant, would not this thing be monstrous? Yes, surely. Now I say to you, truly, that he is more monstrous who preaches penitence to others, but himself repents not of his sins. Those two men that sell apples are the one, he who preaches for love of God, wherefore he flatters none, but' preaches in truth, seeking only a poor man's livelihood. As God lives, in whose presence my soul stands, such a man is not received by the world, but rather despised. But he who sells the peel for its weight in gold, and gives the apple away, he it is who preaches to please men: and, so flattering the world, he ruins the soul that follows his flattery. Ah! how many have perished for this cause!' Then answered he who writes and said: "How should one listen to the word of God; and how should one know him that preaches for love of God?"

Jesus answered: "He that preaches should be listened to as though God were speaking when he preaches good doctrine; because God is speaking through his mouth. But he that reproves not sins, having respect of persons, flattering particular men, should be avoided as an horrible serpent, for in truth he poisons the human ear." Understand you? Truly I say to you, even as a wounded man has no need of fine bandages to bind up his wounds, but rather of a good ointment, so also has a sinner no need of fine words, but rather of good reproofs, in order that he may cease to sin.'

Chapter 135

Then said Peter: "O Master, tell us how the lost shall be tormented, and how long they shall be in hell, in order that man may flee from sin." Jesus answered: 'O Peter, it is a great thing that you have asked, nevertheless, if God please, I will answer you. Know you, therefore, that hell is one, yet has seven centres one below another;. Hence, even as sin is of seven kinds, for as seven gates of hell has Satan generated it: so are there seven punishments therein.

For the proud, that is the loftiest in heart, shall be plunged into the lowest centre, passing through all the centres above it, and suffering in them all the pains that are therein. And as here he seeks to be higher than God, in wishing to do after his own manner, contrary to that which God commands, and not wishing to recognize anyone above him: even so there shall he be put under the feet of Satan and his devils, who shall trample him down as the grapes are trampled when wine is made, and he shall be ever derided and scorned of devils.

'The envious, who here chaffs at the good of his neighbour and rejoices at his misfortune, shall go down to the sixth Centre, and there shall be chafed by the fangs of a great number of infernal serpents. And it shall seem to him that all things in hell rejoice at his torment, and mourn that he be not gone down to the seventh centre. For although the damned are incapable of any joy, yet the justice of God shall cause that it shall so seem to the wretched envious man, as when one seems in a dream to be spurned by some one and feels torment thereby even so shall be the object set before the wretched envious man. For where there is no gladness at all it shall seem to him that every one rejoices at his misfortune, and mourns that he has no worse.

The covetous shall go down to the fifth Centre, where he shall suffer extreme poverty, as the rich feast suffered. And the demons, for greater torment, shall offer him that which he desires, and when he shall have it in his hands other devils with violence shall snatch it from his hands with these words: "Remember that you would not give for love of God; so God wills not that you now receive. Oh unhappy man! Now shall he find himself in that condition when he shall remember past abundance and behold the penury of the present; and that with the goods that then he may not have he could have acquired eternal delights!

To the fourth centre shall go the lustful, where they that have transformed the way given them by God shall be as corn that is cooked in the burning dung of the devil. And there shall they be embraced by horrible infernal serpents. And they that shall have sinned with harlots, all these acts of impurity shall be transformed for them into union with the infernal furies; which are demons like women, whose hair is serpents, whose eyes are flaming sulphur, whose mouth is poisonous, whose tongue is gull whose body is all girt with barbed hooks like those wherewith they catch the silly fish, whose claws are like those of gryphons, whose nails are razors, the nature of whose generative organs is fire. Now with these shall all the lustful enjoy the infernal embers which shall be their bed.

To the third centre shall go down the slothful who will not work now. Here are built cities and immense palaces, which as soon as they are finished must needs be pulled down straightway, because a single stone is not placed aright. And these enormous stones are laid upon the shoulders of the slothful, who has not his hands free to cool his body as he walks and to ease the burden, seeing that sloth has taken away the power of his arms. and his legs are fettered with infernal serpents. And, what is worse, behind him are the demons, who push him, and make him fall to earth many times beneath the weight; nor does any help him to lift it up: no, it being too much to lift, a double amount is laid upon him.

To the second centre shall go down the gluttonous. Now here there is dearth of food, to such a degree that there shall be nought to eat but live scorpions and live serpents, which give such torment that it would be better never to have been born than to eat such food. There are offered to them indeed by the demons, in appearance, delicate meats; but for that they have their hands and feet bound with fetters of fire, they cannot put out a hand on the occasion when the meat appears to them. But what is worse, those very scorpions which he eats that they may devour his belly, not being able to come forth speedily, rend the secret parts of the glutton. And when they are come forth foul and unclean, filthy as they are, they are eaten over again.

The wrathful goes down to the first centre, where he is insulted by all the devils and by as many of the damned as go down lower than he. They spurn him and smite him, making him lie down upon the road where they pass, planting their feet upon his throat. Yet is he not able to defend himself, for that he has his hands and feet bound. And what is worse, he is not able to give vent to his wrath by insulting others, seeing that his tongue is fastened by a hook, like that which he uses who sells flesh. In this accursed place shall there be a general punishment, common to all the centres, like the mixture of various grains make a loaf. For fire, ice, thunderstorms, lightning,

sulphur, heat, cold, wind, frenzy, terror, shall all be united by the justice of God, and in such wise that the cold shall not temper, the heat nor the fire the ice, but each shall give torment to the wretched sinner.

Chapter 136

In this accursed spot shall abide the infidels for evermore: insomuch that if the world were filled with grains of millet, and a single bird once in a hundred years should take away a single grain to empty the world if when it should be empty the infidels were to go into paradise, they would rest delighted. But there is not this hope, because their torment cannot have an end, seeing that they were not willing for the love of God to put an end to their sin. But the faithful shall have comfort, because their torment shall have an end.' The

disciples were affrighted, hearing this, and said: 'So then the faithful must go
into hell?'

Jesus answered: 'Every one, be he who he may, must go into hell. It is true,
however, that the holy ones and prophets of God shall go there to behold, not
suffering any punishment and the righteous, only suffering fear. And what shall
I say? I tell you that thither shall come [even] the Messenger of God, to behold
the justice of God. Thereupon hell shall tremble at his presence. And because he
has human flesh, all those that have human flesh and shall be under punishment,
so long as the Messenger of God shall abide to behold hell, so long shall they
abide without punishment. But he shall abide there [only] so long as it takes to
shut and open the eyes. And this shall God do in order that every creature may
know that he has received benefit from the Messenger of God.

When he shall go there all the devils shall shriek, and seek to hide themselves
beneath the burning embers, saying one to another: "Fly, fly, for here comes
Muhammad ;our enemy!" Hearing which, Satan shall smite himself upon the face
with both his hands, and screaming shall say: "You are more noble than I, in my
despite, and this is unjustly done!" As for the faithful, who are in seventy-two
grades, those of the two last grades, who shall have had the faith without good
works, the one being sad at good works, and the other delighting in evil, they
shall abide in hell seventy thousand years.

After those years shall the angel Gabriel ;come into hell, and shall hear them
say: "O Muhammad, where are your promises made to us, saying that those who have
your faith shall not abide in hell for evermore?" Then the angel of God shall
return to paradise, and having approached with reverence the Messenger of God
shall narrate to him what he has heard. Then shall his Messenger speak to God
and say: "Lord, my God, remember the promise made to me your servant, concerning
them that have received my faith, that they shall not abide for evermore in
hell." God shall answer: "Ask what you will, O my friend, for I will give you
all that you ask."

Chapter 137

Then shall the Messenger of God say: "O Lord, there are of the faithful who have
been in hell seventy thousand years. Where, O Lord, is your mercy? I pray you,
Lord, to free them from those bitter punishments."

Then shall God command the four favourite angels of God; that they go to hell
and take out every one that has the faith of his Messenger, and lead him into
paradise. And this they shall do.

And such shall be the advantage of the faith of God's Messenger;, that those
that shall have believed in him, even though they have not done any good works,
seeing they died in this faith, shall go into paradise after the punishment of
which I have spoken.'

Chapter 138

When morning was come, early, all the men of the city, with the women and
children, came to the house where Jesus was with his disciples, and sought him
saying: "Sir, have mercy upon us, because this year the worms have eaten the
corn, and we shall not receive any bread this year in our land." 2. Jesus
answered: "O what fear is yours! Do you not know that Elijah, the servant of
God, while the persecution of Ahab continued for three years, did not see bread,
nourishing himself only with herbs and wild fruits? David our father, the

prophet of God, ate wild fruits and herbs for two years, [while] being
persecuted [by] Saul, [and] twice only did he eat bread." 3. The men answered:
"Sir, they were prophets of God, nourished with spiritual delight, and therefore
they endured well; but how shall these little ones fare?" and they showed him
the multitude of their children. Then Jesus had compassion on their misery, and
said: "How long is it until harvest?" They answered: "Twenty days." 4. Then
Jesus said: "See that for these twenty days we give ourselves to fasting and
prayer; for God will have mercy upon you. Truly I say to you, God has caused
this dearth because here began the madness of men and the sin of Israel when
they said that I was God, or Son of God." 5. When they had fasted for nineteen
days, on the morning of the twentieth day, they beheld the fields and hills
covered with ripe corn. They ran to Jesus, and recounted everything to him. And
when he had heard it Jesus gave thanks to God, and said: "Go, brethren, gather
the bread which God has given." They gathered so much corn that they did not
know where to store it; and this thing was cause of plenty in Israel.

The citizens took council to set up Jesus as their king knowing which he fled
from them and the disciples strove fifteen days to find him.

Chapter 139

Jesus was found by him who writes, and by James with John. And they, weeping,
said: "O Master, why did you flee from us? We have sought you mourning; yes, all
the disciples seek you weeping." Jesus answered: "I fled because I knew that a
host of devils is preparing for me that which in a short time you shall see.
For, the chief priests with the elders of the people shall rise against me and
[they] shall wrest authority to kill me from the Roman governor, because they
shall fear that I wish to usurp kingship over Israel. Moreover, I shall be sold
and betrayed by one of my disciples, as Joseph was sold into Egypt. 2. But the
just God shall make him fall, as says the prophet David: He shall make him fall
into the pit who spreads a snare for his neighbour. For God shall save me from
their hands, and shall take me out of the world." The three disciples were
afraid; but Jesus comforted them saying: "Do not be afraid, for none of you
shall betray me." [And the three disciples] received some consolation [from
this].

The day following there came, two by two, thirty-six of Jesus' disciples; and he
abode in Damascus awaiting the others. And they mourned every one, for they knew
that Jesus must depart from the world. Wherefore he opened his mouth and said:
"He who walks without knowing where he goes is surely unhappy; but more unhappy
is he who is able and knows how to reach a good hostelry, yet desires and wills
to abide on the miry road, in the rain, and in peril of robbers.

Tell me, brethren, is this world our native country? Surely not, seeing that the
first man was cast out into the world into exile and there he suffers the
punishment of his error. [Is there] an exile who does not aspire to return to
his own rich country when he finds himself in poverty? Assuredly reason denies
it, but experience proves it, because the lovers of the world will not think
upon death. No, when one speaks to them [of death] they will not [heed] his
speech.

Chapter 140

Believe, O men, that I [have] come into the world with a privilege which no man
has had, nor will even the Messenger of God have it; seeing that our God did not
create man to set him in the world, but rather to place him in paradise. It is
certain that he who has no hope of receiving anything from the Romans, because

they are of a law that is foreign to him, is not willing to leave his own country with all that he has, never to return, and go to live in Rome. And much less would he do so when he found himself to have offended Caesar. Even so I tell you truly, and Solomon, God's prophet, cries with me: O death, how bitter is the remembrance of you to them that have rest in their riches! 2. I do not say this because I have to die now, for I am sure that I shall live even near to the end of the world. But I will speak to you of this [matter] in order that you may learn to die. As God lives, everything that is done amiss, even once, shows that to work a thing well it is necessary to exercise oneself in that [thing]. Have you seen the soldiers, how in time of peace they exercise themselves with one another as if they were at war? How shall a man who has not learned to die well die a good death? 3. The death of the holy is precious in the sight of the Lord, said the prophet David. Do you know why [such a death is precious]? I will tell you. It is because, even as all rare things are precious, so the death of them that die well, being rare, is precious in the sight of God our creator. Whenever a man begins anything, not only is he [aiming] to finish [it], but he takes pains that his design may have a good conclusion. 4. O miserable man, that prizes his [clothes] more than himself; for when he cuts the cloth he measures it carefully before he cuts it; and when it is cut he sews it with care. But his life - which is born to die, since [only he] who is not born does not die - [why] will men not measure their life by death? 5. Have you seen them that build [and] how they lay every stone with the foundation in view, measuring if it is straight [so] that the wall will not fall down? O wretched man! for the building of his life will fall with great ruin because he does not look not to the foundation of death!

Chapter 141

Tell me: when a man is born, how is he born? Surely, he is born naked. And when he is laid dead beneath the ground, what advantage has he? A mean linen cloth in which he is wound: and this is the reward which the world gives him. If the means in every work must be proportionate to the beginning and the end in order that the work is brought to a good end, what end shall the man have who desires earthly riches? He shall die, as says David, prophet of God: "The sinner shall die a most evil death."

If a man sewing cloth should thread beams instead of thread in the needle, how would the work attain [its end]? Surely he would work in vain, and be despised of his neighbours. Now man sees not that he is doing this continually when he gathered earthly goods. For death is the needle, wherein the beams of earthly goods cannot be threaded. Nevertheless in his madness he strives continually to make the work succeed, but in vain.

And whoever believes not this at my word, let him gaze upon the tombs, for there shall he find the truth. He who would fain become wise beyond all others in the fear of God, let him study the book of the tomb, for there shall he find the true doctrine for his salvation. For he will know to beware of the world, the flesh, and the sense, when he sees that man's flesh is reserved to be food of worms. Tell me, if there were a road which was of such condition that walking in the midst thereof a man should go safely, but walking on the edges he would break his head; what would you say if you saw men opposing one another, and striving in emulation to get nearest to the edge and kill themselves? What amazement would be yours! Assuredly you would say: "They are mad and frenzied, and if they are not frenzied they are desperate." 'Even so is it true,' answered the disciples.

Then Jesus wept and said: 'Even so, truly, are the lovers of the world. For if
they lived according to reason, which holds a middle place in man, they would
follow the Law of God, and would be saved from eternal death. But because they
follow the flesh and the world they are frenzied, and cruel enemies of their own
selves, striving to live more arrogantly and more lasciviously than one
another.'

Chapter 142

Judas, the traitor, when he saw that Jesus was fled, lost the hope of becoming
powerful in the world, for he carried Jesus' purse, wherein was kept all that
was given him for love of God. He hoped that Jesus would become king of Israel,
and so he himself would be a powerful man. Wherefore, having lost this hope, he
said within himself: 'If this man were a prophet, he would know that I steal his
money; and so he would lose patience and cast me out of his service, knowing
that I believe not in him. And if he were a wise man he would not flee from the
honour that God wills to give him. Wherefore it will be better that I make
arrangement with the chief priests and with the scribes and Pharisees, and see
how to give him up into their hands, for so shall I be able to obtain something
good.'

Whereupon, having made his resolution, he gave notice to the scribes and
Pharisees how the matter had passed in Nain. And they took counsel with the high
priest, saying: 'What shall we do if this man become king? Surely we shall fare
badly; because he is fain to reform the worship of God after the ancient custom,
for he cannot away with our traditions. Now how shall we fare under the
sovereignty of such a man? Surely we shall all perish with our children: for
being cast out of our office we shall have to beg our bread.

We now, praised be God, have a king and a governor that are alien to our Law,
who care not for our Law, even as we care not for theirs. And so we are able to
do whatsoever we list; for, even though we sin, our God is so merciful that he
is appeased with sacrifice and fasting. But if this man become king he will not
be appeased unless he shall see the worship of God according as Moses wrote; and
what is worse, he says that the Messiah shall not come of the seed of David (as
one of his chief disciples has told us), but says that he shall come of the seed
of Ishmael, and that the promise was made in Ishmael and not in Isaac.

What then shall the fruit be if this man be suffered to live? Assuredly the
Ishmaelites shall come into repute with the Romans, and they shall give them our
country in possession; and so shall Israel again be subjected to slavery as it
was aforetime.' Wherefore, having heard the proposal, the high priest gave
answer that he must needs treat with Herod and with the governor, 'because the
people are so inclined towards him that without the soldiery we shall not be
able to do anything; and may it please God that with the soldiery we may
accomplish this business.' Wherefore, having taken counsel among themselves,
they plotted to seize him by night, when the governor and Herod should agree
thereto.

Chapter 143

Then all the disciples came to Damascus, by the will of God. And on that day
Judas the traitor, more than any other, made show of having suffered grief at
Jesus' absence, at which Jesus said: "Let every one beware of him who without
occasion labours to give you tokens of love." And God took away our
understanding, that we might not know to what end he said this. After the coming

of all the disciples, Jesus said: "Let us return into Galilee, for the angel of
God has said to me that I must go there."

So one sabbath morning, Jesus came to Nazareth. When the citizens recognized
Jesus, everyone desired to see him. A publican named Zacchaeus, who was of small
stature, not being able to see Jesus because of the great multitude, climbed to
the top of a sycamore, and there waited for Jesus to pass that place when he
went to the synagogue. Jesus then, having come to that place, lifted up his eyes
and said: "Come down, Zacchaeus, for today I will abide in your house." The man
came down and received him with gladness, making a splendid feast.

The Pharisees murmured, saying to Jesus' disciples: "Why [has] your master gone
in to eat with publicans and sinners?" Jesus answered: "Why does the physician
[enter] into a house? Tell me, and I will tell you why I am come in here." They
answered: "To heal the sick." "You say the truth," said Jesus, "for [those who
are] whole have no need of medicine, only the sick.

Chapter 144

As God lives, in whose presence my soul stands, God sends his prophets and
servants into the world in order that sinners may repent; and he sends [them]
not for the sake of the righteous, because they had no need of repentance, even
as he that is clean has no need of the bath. But truly I say to you, if you were
true Pharisees you would be glad that I should have gone in to sinners for their
salvation. Tell me, do you know your origin and how the world began to receive

Pharisees? I will tell you, seeing that you do not know it, so hearken to my
words.

Enoch, a friend of God, who walked with God in truth, making no account of the
world, was translated into paradise; and there he abides until the Judgment (for
when the end of the world draws near he shall return to help the world with
Elijah and one other). And so men, having knowledge of this, through desire of
paradise, began to seek God their creator. For 'Pharisee' strictly means 'seeks
God' in the language of Canaan, for there did this name begin [as a] way of
deriding good men, since the Canaanites were given up to idolatry, which is the
worship of human hands.

Whereupon the Canaanites, beholding those of our people that were separated from
the world to serve God, when they saw such an one, said in derision 'Pharisee!'
that is, 'He seeks God'; as much as to say: 'O madman, you have no statues of
idols and adore the wind; look to your fate and come and serve our gods.' Truly
I say to you," said Jesus, "all the saints and prophets of God have been
Pharisees not in name, as you are, but in very deed. For in all their acts they
sought God their creator, and for love of God they forsook cities and their own
goods, selling [their goods] and giving to the poor for love of God."

Chapter 145

As God lives, in the time of Elijah, friend and prophet of God, there were
twelve mountains inhabited by seventeen thousand Pharisees; and so it was that
[even] in so great a number there was not found a single reprobate, but all were
elect of God. But now, when Israel has more than a hundred thousand Pharisees,
may it please God that out of every thousand there be one elect!"

The Pharisees answered in indignation: "So then we are all reprobate, and you
hold our religion in reprobation!" Jesus answered: "I do not hold the religion

of the true Pharisees in reprobation but in approbation and for that I am ready to die. But come, let us see if you are [true] Pharisees. Elijah, the friend of God, at the prayer of his disciple Elisha, wrote a little book in which he included all human wisdom with the Law of God our Lord."

The Pharisees were confounded when they heard the name of the book of Elijah, because they knew that, through their traditions, no one observed such doctrine. They [claimed they had] to depart under pretext of business to be done. Then Jesus said: "If you were [true] Pharisees you would forsake all other business to attend to this; for the Pharisee seeks God alone." So they tarried in confusion to listen to Jesus, who said again.:

"Elijah, servant of God" (for so begins the little Book), "to all them that desire to walk with God their creator, writes this:

Whoever desires to learn much, they (sic) fear God little, because he who fears God is content to know only that which God wills. They that seek fair words do not seek God, who does nothing but reprove our sins.

They that desire to seek God, let them shut fast the doors and windows of their house, for the master does not suffer himself to be found outside his house [in a place] where he is not loved.

Therefore guard your senses and guard your heart, because God is not found outside of us, in this world in which he is hated.

They that wish to do good works, let them attend to their own selves, for [there is no profit] in gaining the whole world and losing one's own soul.

They that wish to teach others, let them live better than others, because nothing can be learned from him who knows less than ourselves. How shall the sinner amend his life when he hears one worse than he teaching him?

They that seek God, let him (sic) flee the conversation of men; because Moses being alone upon Mount Sinai found him and spoke with God, as does a friend who speaks with a friend.

They that seek God, shall come forth [to where] there are men of the world only once in [every] thirty days for in respect of the business of him that seeks God works for two years can be done in one day.

When he walks, let him not look save at his own feet.

When he speaks, let him not speak save that which is necessary.

When they eat, let them rise from the table still hungry; thinking every day not to attain to the next; spending their time as one draws his breath.

Let one garment, of the skin of beasts, suffice.

Let the lump of earth sleep on the naked earth [and] for every night let two hours of sleep suffice.

Let him hate no one save himself; condemn no one save himself.

In prayer, let them stand in such fear as if they were at the Judgment to come.

Now do this in the service of God, with the Law that God has given you through Moses, for in this way you shall find God [so] that in every time and place you shall feel that you are in God and God [is] in you."

This is the little book of Elijah, O Pharisees. Again I say to you that if you were [true] Pharisees you would have had joy that I [have] entered in here, because God has mercy upon sinners."

Chapter 146

Then Zacchaeus said: "Sir, behold I will give, for love of God, fourfold all that I have received by usury." Then Jesus said: "This day has salvation come to this house. Truly, truly, many publicans, harlots, and sinners shall go into the kingdom of God, and they that account themselves righteous shall go into eternal flames." Hearing this, the Pharisees departed in indignation.

Then Jesus said to them that were converted to repentance, and to his disciples: "* There was a father who had two sons, and the younger said: 'Father, give me my portion of goods'; and his father gave it [to] him. And he, having received his portion, departed and went into a far country, where he wasted all his substance with harlots, living luxuriously. After this there arose a mighty famine in that country, such that the wretched man went to serve a citizen, who set him to feed swine in his property. And while feeding them he assuaged his hunger in company with the swine, eating acorns.

But when he came to himself he said: 'Oh, how many in my father's house [are] feasting in abundance, and I perish here with hunger! I will arise, therefore, and will go to my father, and will say to him: 'Father, I have sinned in heaven against you; do with me as you do to one of your servants.' The poor man went, and it came to pass that his father saw him coming from afar off, and was moved to compassion over him. So he went forth to meet him, and having come up to him he embraced him and kissed him.

The son bowed himself down, saying: 'Father, I have sinned in heaven against you, do to me as to one of your servants, for I am not worthy to be called your son.' The father answered: 'Son,do not say so, for you are my son, and I will not suffer you to be in the condition of my slave.' And he called his servants and said: 'Bring new robes here and clothe my son, and give him new [garments]; give him the ring on his finger, and kill the fatted calf and we will make merry. For [this] son [of mine] was dead but has now come to life again; he was lost and now is found.'

Chapter 147

While they were making merry in the house, the elder son came home, and hearing that they were making merry within, he marvelled and called one of the servants, asking him why they were making merry in this way. The servant answered him: 'Your brother [has] come [home] and your father has killed the fatted calf, and they are feasting.' The elder son was greatly angered when he heard this, and would not go into the house. Therefore his father came out to him and

said to him: 'Son, your brother [has] come. Come therefore and rejoice with him.'

The [elder] son answered with indignation: 'I have always served you with good service, and you never gave me a lamb to eat with my friends. But as for this worthless fellow that departed from you, wasting all his portion with harlots, now that he is come you have killed the fatted calf!" The father answered: 'Son, you are always with me and everything is yours; but this one was dead and is alive again, was lost and now is found; [that is why] we must rejoice.' The elder son was more angry, and said: 'You can go and triumph [but] I will not eat at the table of fornicators." And he departed from his father without receiving even a piece of money. As God lives," said Jesus, "even so is there rejoicing among the angels of God over one sinner that repents."

And when they had eaten he departed for he [was going] to Judea. The disciples said: "Master, do not go to Judea, for we know that the Pharisees have taken counsel with the high priest against you." Jesus answered: "I knew it before they did it, but I do not fear, for they cannot do anything contrary to the will of God. Let them do all that they desire, for I do not fear them but [rather] fear God.

Chapter 148

'Tell me now: the Pharisees of today, are they [really] Pharisees? are they servants of God? Surely not! Yes, and I say to you truly, that there is nothing worse here upon earth than [when] a man covers himself with [the] profession and garb of religion [in order] to cover his wickedness. I will tell you one single example of the Pharisees of old time, in order that you may know the present ones. After the departure of Elijah, because of the great persecution by idolaters, that holy congregation of Pharisees was dispersed. For in that same time of Elijah more than ten thousand prophets who were true Pharisees were slain in one year.

Two Pharisees went into the mountains to dwell there, and one [of them] abode fifteen years knowing nothing of his neighbour, although they were but one hour's journey apart. See then if they were inquisitive! It came to pass that there arose a drought on those mountains, and so both set themselves to search for water, and so they found each other. The more aged [one] said - for it was their custom that the eldest should speak before every other, and they held it a great sin for a young man to speak before an old one - the elder, therefore, said: 'Where do you dwell, brother?' He answered, pointing out the dwelling with his finger: 'I dwell here' (for they were near to the dwelling of the younger.)

The elder said: 'How long [have] you dwelt here, brother?' The younger answered: 'Fifteen years.' The elder said: 'Perhaps you came [here] when Ahab slew the servants of God?' 'Even so,' replied the younger. The elder said: 'O brother, do you know who is now king of Israel?' The younger answered: 'It is God that is King of Israel, for the idolaters are not kings but persecutors of Israel.' 'It is true,' said the elder, "but I meant to say, who is it that now persecutes Israel?'

The younger answered: 'The sins of Israel persecute Israel, because, if they had not sinned, [God] would not have raised the idolatrous princes up against Israel.' Then the elder said: 'Who is that infidel prince whom God has sent for the chastisement of Israel?' The younger answered: 'How should I know, seeing [that for] these fifteen years I have not seen any man except you, and I do not know how to read so no letters are sent to me?' The elder said: '[But] how new are your sheepskins! Who has given them to you, if you have not seen any man?'

Chapter 149

The younger answered: 'He who kept the raiment of the people of Israel good for forty years in the wilderness has kept my skins even as you see [them].' Then the elder perceived that the younger was more perfect than he, for every year he had had dealings with men. So, in order that he might have [the benefit of] his conversation, he said: 'Brother, you do not know how to read, [but] I know how to read, and I have in my house the psalms of David. Come, then, that I may give you a reading each day and make plain to you what David says.' The younger answered: 'Let us go now.'

The elder said: 'O brother, it is now two days since I have drunk water; therefore let us seek a little water.' The younger replied: 'O brother, it is now two months since I have drunk water. Let us go, therefore, and see what God says by his prophet David: the Lord is able to give us water.' [And so] they returned to the dwellings of the elder, at the door of which they found a spring of fresh water. The elder said: 'O brother, you are a holy one of God; God has given this spring for your sake.'

The younger answered: 'O brother, you say this in humility; but it is certain that if God had done this for my sake he would have made a spring close to my dwelling [so] that I should not [have to] depart [in search of it]. For I confess to you that I sinned against you. When you said that for two days you did not drink [and that] you sought water, and I had been for two months without drinking, I felt an exaltation within me, as though I were better than you.' Then the elder said: 'O brother, you said the truth, therefore you did not sin.'

The younger said: 'O brother, you have forgotten what our father Elijah said, that he who seeks God ought to condemn himself alone. Surely he did not write it that we might [only] know it, but rather that we might observe it.' The more aged [of the two], perceiving the truth and righteousness of his companion, said: 'It is true; and our God has pardoned you.' And having said this he took the Psalms, and read that which our father David says: I will set a watch over my mouth that my tongue decline not to words of iniquity, excusing with excuse my sin. And here the aged man made a discourse upon the tongue, and the younger departed. [After this] there were fifteen more years before they found one another, because the younger changed his dwelling.

Accordingly, when he had found him again, the elder [Pharisee] said: 'O brother, why have you not returned to any dwelling?' The younger answered: 'Because I have not yet learned well what you said to me.' Then the elder said: 'How can this be, seeing [that] fifteen years have past?' The younger replied: 'As for the words, I learned them in a single hour and have never forgotten them; but I have not yet observed them. To what purpose is it, then, to learn too much, and not to observe it? Our God does not seek that our intellect should be good, but rather our heart. So, on the Day of Judgment, he will not ask us what we have learned, but what we have done.'

Chapter 150

'The elder answered: "O brother, say not so, for you despise knowledge, which our God wills to be prized." The younger replied: "Now, how shall I speak now so as not to fall into sin: for your word is true, and mine also. I say, then, that they who know the commandments of God written in the Law ought to observe those [first] if they would afterwards learn more. And all that a man learns, let it be observe it, and not [merely] to know it." Said the elder: "O brother, tell me, with whom have you spoken, that you know you have not learned all that I said?"

'The younger answered: "O brother, I speak with myself. Every day I place myself before the judgment of God, to give account of myself. And ever do I feel within myself one that excuses my faults." 'Said the elder: "O brother, what faults have you, who are perfect ? The younger answered: "O brother, say not so, for that I stand between two great faults: the one is that I do not know myself to be the greatest of sinners, the other that I do not desire to do penance for it more than other men." 'The elder answered: "Now, how shouldst you know yourself to be the greatest of sinners, if you are the most perfect [of men]?"

'The younger replied: "The first word that my master said to me when I took the habit of a Pharisee was this: that I ought to consider the goodness of others and my own iniquity for if I should do so I should perceive myself to be the greatest of sinners. 'Said the elder: "O brother, whose goodness or whose faults consider you on these mountains, seeing there are no men here?" The younger answered: "I ought to consider the obedience of the sun and the planets, for they serve their Creator better than I. But them I condemn, either because they give not light as I desire, or because their heat is too great, or there is too much or too little rain upon the ground."

'Whereupon, hearing this, the elder said: "Brother, where have you learned this doctrine, for I am now ninety years old, for seventy-five years whereof I have been a Pharisee?" The younger answered: "O brother, you say this in humility, for you are a holy one of God. Yet I answer you that God our creator looks not on time, but looks on the heart: wherefore David, being fifteen years; old, younger than six other his brethren, was chosen king of Israel, and became a prophet of God our Lord."

Chapter 151

'This man was a true Pharisee,' said Jesus to his disciples; and may it please God that we be able on the day of judgment to have him for our friend.'

Jesus then embarked on a ship, and the disciples were sorry that they had forgotten to bring bread. Jesus rebuked them, saying: "Beware of the leaven of the Pharisees of our day, for a little leaven mars a mass of meal." Then said the disciples one to another: 'Now what leaven have we, if we have not even any bread?' * Then Jesus said: 'O men of little faith, have you then forgotten what God wrought in Nain, where there was no sign of corn? And how many ate and were satisfied with five loaves and two fishes? The leaven of the Pharisee is want of faith in God, and thought of self, which has corrupted not only the Pharisees of this day, but has corrupted Israel.

For the simple folk, not knowing how to read, do that which they see the Pharisees do, because they hold them for holy ones.

Know you what is the true Pharisee? He is the oil of human nature. For even as oil rests at the top of every liquor, so the goodness of the true Pharisee rests at the top of all human goodness. He is a living book, which God gives to the world; for everything that he says and does is according to the Law of God. Wherefore, who does as he does observes the Law of God. The true Pharisee is salt that suffers not human flesh to be putrefied by sin; for every one who sees him is brought to repentance. He is a light that lightens the pilgrims' way, for every one that considers his poverty with his penitence perceives that in this world we ought not to shut up our heart. But he that makes the oil rancid, corrupts the book, putrefies the salt, extinguishes the light - this man is a false Pharisee. If, therefore, you would not perish, beware that you do not as does the Pharisee today.?

Chapter 152

Jesus having come to Jerusalem, and having entered one sabbath day into the Temple, the soldiers drew near to tempt him and take him, and they said: "Master, is it lawful to wage war?" Jesus answered: "Our faith tells us that our life is a continual warfare upon the earth." Said the soldiers: "So would you convert us to your faith, and wish that we should forsake the multitude of gods (for Rome alone has twenty-eight thousand gods that are seen) and should follow your God who is one only and for that he cannot be seen, it is not known where he is, and perhaps he is but vanity."

Jesus answered: "If I had created you, as our God has created you, I would seek to convert you." They answered: "Now how has your God created us, seeing it is not known where he is? Show us your God, and we will become Jews." Then Jesus said: "If you had eyes to see him I would show him to you, but since you are blind, I cannot show you him." The soldiers answered: "Surely, the honour which this people pays you must have taken away your understanding. For every one of us has two eyes in his head, and you say we are blind."

Jesus answered: "The carnal eyes can only see things gross and external: you therefore will only be able to see your gods of wood and silver and gold that cannot do anything. But we of Judah have spiritual eyesight which are the fear and the faith of our God, wherefore we can see our God in every place." The soldiers answered: "Beware how you speak, for if you pour contempt on our gods we will give you into the hand of Herod, who will take vengeance for our gods, who are omnipotent."

Jesus answered: "If they are omnipotent as you say, pardon me, for I will worship them." The soldiers rejoiced at hearing this, and began to extol their idols. Then Jesus said: "[In this matter] we need not words but deeds; cause therefore that your gods create one fly, and I will worship them." The soldiers were dismayed at hearing this, and knew not what to say, wherefore Jesus said: "Assuredly, seeing they make not a single fly afresh, I will not for them forsake that God who has created everything with a single word; whose name alone affrights armies." The soldiers answered: "Now let us see this; for we are fain to take you," and they were fain to stretch forth their hands against Jesus.

Then Jesus said: "Adonai Sabaoth!" Whereupon straightway the soldiers were rolled out of the Temple as one rolls casks of wood when they are washed to refill them with wine; insomuch that now their head and now their feet struck the ground, and that without any one touching them. And they were so affrighted and fled in such wise that they were never more seen in Judea.

Chapter 153

The priests and Pharisees murmured among themselves and said: "He has the wisdom of Baal and Ashtaroth, and so in the power of Satan has he done this." Jesus opened his mouth and said: "Our God commanded that we should not steal our neighbour's goods. But this single precept has been so violated and abused that it has filled the world with sin, and such [sin] as shall never be remitted as other sins are remitted: seeing that for every other sin, if a man bewail it and commit it no more, and fast with prayer and almsgiving, our God, mighty and merciful, forgives. But this sin is of such a kind that it shall never be remitted,, except that which is wrongly taken be restored.

Then said a scribe: 'O master, how has robbery filled all the world with sin? Assuredly now, by the grace of God, there are but few robbers, and they cannot show themselves but they are immediately hanged by the soldiery.' Jesus

answered: 'Whoso knows not the goods, they (sic) cannot know the robbers;. No, I
say to you truly that many rob who know not what they do, and therefore their
sin is greater than that of the others, for the disease that is not known is not
healed.' Then the Pharisees drew near to Jesus and said: 'O master, since you
alone in Israel know the truth, teach you us.'

Jesus answered: 'I say not that I alone in Israel know the truth, for this word
"alone" appertains to God alone and not to others. For he is the truth, who
alone knows the truth. Wherefore, I should say so I should be a greater robber,
for I should be stealing the honour of God. And in saying that I alone knew God
I should be falling into greater ignorance than all. You, therefore, committed a
grievous sin in saying that I alone know the truth. And I tell you that, if you
said this to tempt me, your sin is greater still.'

Then Jesus, seeing that all held their peace, said again: 'Though I be not alone
in Israel knowing the truth, I alone will speak; wherefore hearken to me, since
you have asked me. All things created belong to the Creator, in such wise that
nothing can lay claim to anything. Thus soul, sense, flesh, time, goods, and
honour, all are God's possessions, so that if a man receive them not as God
wills he becomes a robber. And in like manner, if he spend them contrary to that
which God wills, he is likewise a robber. I say, therefore, to you that, as God
lives, in whose presence my soul stands, when you take time, saying: "Tomorrow I
will do thus, I will say such a thing, I will go to such a place," and not
saying: "If God will," you are robbers: And you are greater robbers when you
spend the better part of your time in pleasing yourselves and not in pleasing
God, and spend the worse part in God's service: then are you robbers indeed.
Whoever commits sin, be he of what fashion he will, is a robber; for he steals
time and the soul and his own life, which ought to serve God, and gives it to
Satan, the enemy of God.'

Chapter 154

'The man, therefore, who has honour, and life, and goods - when his possessions
are stolen, the robber shall be hanged; when his life is taken, the murderer
shall be beheaded. And this is just, for God has so commanded. But when a
neighbour's honour is taken away, why is not the robber crucified? Are goods,
forsooth, better than honour? Has God, perhaps, commanded that he who takes
goods shall be punished and he that takes life with goods shall be punished, but
he that takes away honour shall go free? Surely not; for by reason of their
murmuring our fathers entered not into the land of promise, but only their
children. And for this sin the serpents slew about seventy thousand of our
people.

As God lives, in whose presence my soul stands, he that steals honour is worthy
of greater punishment than he that robs a man of goods and of life. And he that
hearkens to the murmurer is likewise guilty, for the one receives Satan on his
tongue and the other in his ears." The Pharisees were consumed [with rage] at
hearing this, because they were not able to condemn his speech. Then there drew
near to Jesus a doctor, and said to him: 'Good master, tell me, wherefore God
did not grant corn and fruit to our fathers? Knowing that they must needs fall,
surely he should have allowed them corn, or not have suffered men to see it.'

Jesus answered: 'Man, you call me good, but you err, for God alone is good. And
much more do you err in asking why God has not done according to your brain. Yet
I will answer you all. I tell you, then, that God our creator in his working
conforms not himself to us, wherefore it is not lawful for the creature to seek
his own way and convenience, but rather the honour of God his creator, in order

that the creature may depend on the Creator and not the Creator on the creature. As God lives, in whose presence my soul stands, if God had granted everything to man, man would not have known himself to be God's servant; and so he would have accounted himself lord of paradise. Wherefore the Creator, who is blessed for evermore, forbade him the food, in order that man might remain subject to him.

And truly I say to you, that whoever has the light of his eyes clear sees everything clear, and draws light even out of darkness itself; but the blind does not so. Wherefore I say that, if man had not sinned, neither I nor you would have known the mercy of God and his righteousness. And if God had made man incapable of sin he would have been equal to God in that matter; wherefore the blessed God created man good and righteous, but free to do that which he pleases in regard to his own life and salvation or damnation.' The doctor was astounded when he heard this, and departed in confusion.

Chapter 155

Then the high-priest called two old priests secretly and sent them to Jesus, who was gone out of the Temple, and was sitting in Solomon's porch, waiting to pray the midday prayer. And near him he had his disciples with a great multitude of people. The priests drew near to Jesus and said: 'Master, wherefore did man eat corn and fruit? Did God will that he should eat it, or no?' And this they said tempting him; for if he said: 'God willed it,' they would answer: 'Why did he forbid it?' and if he said: 'God willed it not,' they would say: 'Then man has more power than God, since he works contrary to the will of God.'

Jesus answered: 'Your question is like a road over a mountain, which has a precipice on the right hand and on the left: but I will walk in the middle.' When they heard this the priests were confounded, perceiving that he knew their heart. Then Jesus said: 'Every man, for that he has need, works everything for his own use. But God, who has no need of anything, wrought according to his good pleasure. Wherefore in creating man he created him free in order that he might know that God had no need of him; Verbi gratia, as does a King, who to display his riches, and in order that his slaves may love him more, gives freedom to his slaves.

God, then, created man free in order that he might love his Creator much the more and might know his bounty. For although God is omnipotent, not having need of man, having created him by his omnipotence, he left him free by his bounty, in such wise that he could resist evil and do good. For although God had power to hinder sin, he would not contradict his own bounty (for God has no contradiction) in order that, his omnipotence and bounty having wrought in man, he should not contradict sin in man, I say, in order that in man might work the mercy of God and his righteousness. And in token that I speak the truth, I tell you that the high-priest has sent you to tempt me, and this is the fruit of his priesthood.' The old men departed and recounted all to the high-priest, who said: 'This fellow has the devil at his back, who recounts everything to him; for he aspires to the kingship over Israel; but God will see to that.'

Chapter 156

When he had made the midday prayer, Jesus, as he went out of the Temple, found one blind from his mother's womb. His disciples asked him saying: "Master, who sinned in this man, his father or his mother, that he was born blind?' Jesus answered: "Neither his father nor his mother sinned in him, but God created him so, for a testimony of the Gospel. And having called the blind man up to him he spat on the ground and made clay and placed it upon the eyes of the blind man and said to him: 'Go to the pool of Siloam and wash you!'

The blind man went, and having washed received light; whereupon, as he returned home, many who met him said: 'If this man were blind I should say for certain that it was he who was wont to sit at the beautiful gate of the Temple;.' Others said: 'It is he, but how has he received light?' And they accosted him saying: 'Are you the blind man that was wont to sit at the beautiful gate of the Temple;?' He answered: 'I am he and wherefore?' They said: 'Now how did you receive your sight?'

He answered:, 'A man made clay, spitting on the ground, and this clay he placed upon my eyes and said to me: "Go and wash you in the pool of Siloam;." I went and washed, and now I see: blessed be the God of Israel!' When the man born blind was come again to the beautiful gate of the Temple, all Jerusalem was filled with the matter. Wherefore he was brought to the chief of the priests, who was conferring with the priests and the Pharisees against Jesus. The high priest asked him, saying: 'Man, wast you born blind?' 'Yes,' he replied. 'Now give glory of God,' said the high-priest, 'and tell us what prophet has appeared to you in a dream and given you light. Was it our father Abraham;, or Moses ;the servant of God, or some other prophet? For others could not do such a thing.

The man born blind replied: 'Neither Abraham nor Moses, nor any prophet have I seen in a dream and been healed by him, but as I sat at the gate of the Temple a man made me come near to him and, having made clay of earth with his spittle, put some of that clay upon my eyes and sent me to the pool of Siloam to wash; whereupon I went, and washed me, and returned with the light of my eyes.' The high-priest asked him the name of that man. The man born blind answered: 'He told me not his name, but a man who saw him called me and said: "Go and wash you as that man has said, for he is Jesus the Nazarene;, a prophet and an holy one of the God of Israel."' Then said the high-priest: 'Did he heal you perhaps today, that is, the Sabbath;?' The blind man answered: 'Today he healed me.' Said the high-priest: 'Behold now, how that this fellow is a sinner, seeing he keeps not the Sabbath!'

Chapter 157

The blind man answered: 'Whether he is a sinner I know not; but this I know, that whereas I was blind, he has enlightened me.' The Pharisees did not believe this; so they said to the high priest: 'Send for his father and mother, for they will tell us the truth.' They sent, therefore, for the father and mother of the blind man, and when they were come the high-priest questioned them saying: 'Is this man your son?' They answered: 'He is truly our son.' Then said the high-priest: 'He says that he was born blind, and now he sees; how has this thing befallen?'

The father and mother of the man born blind replied: 'Truly he was born blind, but how he may have received the light, we know not; he is of age, ask him and he will tell you the truth.' Thereupon they were dismissed, and the high-priest said again to the man born blind: 'Give glory to God, and speak the truth.' (Now the father and mother of the blind man were afraid to speak, because a decree had gone forth from the Roman senate that no man might contend for Jesus, the prophet of the Jews, under pain of death: this decree had the governor obtained wherefore they said: 'He is of age, ask him.')

The high-priest, then, said to the man born blind: 'Give glory to God and speak the truth, for we know this man, whom you say to have healed you, that he is a

sinner.' The man born blind answered: 'Whether he be a sinner, I know not; but
this I know, that I saw not and he has enlightened me. Surely, from the
beginning of the world to this hour, there has never yet been enlightened one
who was born blind; and God would not hearken to sinners.' Said the Pharisees:
'Now what did he when he enlightened you?' Then the man born blind marvelled at
their unbelief, and said: 'I have told you, and wherefore ask you me again?
Would you also become his disciples?'

The high-priest then reviled him saying: 'You were altogether born in sin, and
would you teach us? Begone, and become you disciple of such a man! for we are
disciples of Moses;, and we know that God has spoken to Moses, but as for this
man, we know not whence he is.' And they cast him out of the synagogue ;and
Temple;, forbidding him to make prayer with the clean among Israel.

Chapter 158

The man born blind went to find Jesus, who comforted him saying: 'At no time
have you been so blessed as you are now, for you are blest of our God who spoke
through David, our father and his prophet, against the friends of the world,
saying: "They curse and I bless"; and by Micah the prophet he said: "I curse
your blessing." For earth is not so contrary to air, water to fire, light to
darkness, cold to heat, or love to hate, as is the will that God has contrary to
the will of the world.'

The disciples accordingly asked him, saying: 'Lord, great are your words; tell
us, therefore, the meaning, for as yet we understand not." Jesus answered: "When
you shall know the world, you shall see that I have spoken the truth, and so
shall you know the truth in every prophet. Know you, then, that there be three
kinds of worlds comprehended in a single name;: the one stands for the heavens
and the earth, with water, air and fire, and all the things that are inferior to
man. Now this world in all things follows the will of God, for, as says David;,
prophet of God: "God has given them a precept which they transgress not."

The second stands for all men, even as the "house of such an one" stands not for
the walls, but for the family. Now this world, again, loves God; because by
nature they long after God, forasmuch as according to nature every one longs
after God, even though they err in seeking God. And know you wherefore all long
after God? Because they long every one after an infinite good without any evil,
and this is God alone. Therefore the merciful God has sent his prophets to this
world for its salvation.

'The third world is men's fallen condition of sinning, which has transformed
itself into a law contrary to God, the creator of the world. This makes man
become like to the demons, God's enemies. And this world our God hates so sore
that if the prophets had loved this world what think you? - assuredly God would
have taken from them their prophecy. And what shall I say As God lives, in whose
presence my soul stands, when the Messenger of God shall come to the world, if
he should conceive love towards this evil world, assuredly God would take away
from him all that he gave him when he created him, and would make him reprobate:
so greatly is God contrary to this world."

Chapter 159

The disciples answered: "O master, exceeding great are your words, therefore
have mercy upon us, for we understand them not." Jesus said: "Think you perhaps
that God has created his Messenger to be a rival, who should be fain to make
himself equal with God? Assuredly not, but rather as his good slave, who should

not will that which his Lord wills not. You are not able to understand this because you know not what a thing is sin. Wherefore hearken to my words. Truly, truly, I say to you, sin cannot arise in man save as a contradiction of God, seeing that only is sin which God wills not: insomuch that all that God wills is most alien from sin.

Accordingly, if our high-priests and priests, with the Pharisees, persecuted me because the people of Israel has called me God, they would be doing a thing pleasing to God, and God would reward them; but because they persecute me for a contrary reason, since they will not have me say the truth, how they have contaminated the Book of Moses; and that of David;, prophets and friends of God, by their traditions, and therefore hate me and desire my death therefore God has them in abomination. Tell me, Moses slew men and Ahab slew men, is this in each case murder? Assuredly not; for Moses slew the men to destroy idolatry and to preserve the worship of the true God, but Ahab slew the men to destroy the worship of the true God and to preserve idolatry. Wherefore to Moses the slaying of men was converted into sacrifice, while to Ahab it was converted into sacrilege: insomuch that one and the same work produced these two contrary effects.

"As God lives, in whose presence my soul stands, if Satan had spoken to the angels in order to see how they loved God, he would not have been rejected of God, but because he sought to turn them away from God, therefore is he reprobate." Then answered he who writes : "How, then, is to be understood that which was said in Micaiah the prophet, concerning the lie which God ordained to be spoken by the mouth of false prophets, as is written in the book of the kings of Israel?" Jesus answered: "O Barnabas, recite briefly all that befell, that we may see the truth clearly."

Chapter 160

Then said he who writes: "Daniel the prophet, describing the history of the kings of Israel and their tyrants, writes thus: "The king of Israel joined himself with the king of Judah to fight against the sons of Belial (that is, reprobates) who were the Ammonites. Now Jehoshaphat, king of Judah, and Ahab, king of Israel, being seated both on a throne in Samaria, there stood before them four hundred false prophets, who said to the king of Israel: "Go up against the Ammonites, for God will give them into your hands, and you shall scatter Ammon."

Then said Jehoshaphat: "Is there here any prophet of the God of our fathers?" Ahab answered: "There is one only, and he is evil, for he always predicts evil concerning me; and him I hold in prison." And this he said, to wit, "there is only one," because as many as were found had been slain by decree of Ahab;, so that the prophets, even as you have said, O Master, were fled to the mountain tops where men dwelt not. Then said Jehoshaphat: "Send for him here, and let us see what he says." Ahab therefore commanded that Micaiah be sent for hither, who came with fetters on his feet, and his face bewildered like a man that lives between life and death. Ahab asked him, saying: "Speak, Micaiah;, in the name of God. Shall we go up against the Ammonites? Will God give their cities into our hands?"

Micaiah answered: "Go up, go up, for prosperously shall you go up, and still more prosperously come down!" Then the false prophets praised Micaiah as a true prophet of God, and broke off the fetters from his feet. Jehoshaphat, who feared our God, and had never bowed his knees before the idols, asked Micaiah, saying: "For the love of the God of our fathers, speak the truth, as you have seen the

issue of this war." Micaiah ;answered: "O Jehoshaphat, I fear your face where.
fore I tell you that I have seen the people of Israel as sheep without a
shepherd." Then Ahab, smiling, said to Jehoshaphat;: "I told you that this
fellow predicts only evil, but you did not believe it..

Then said they both: "Now how know you this, O Micaiah?"

"Micaiah answered: "Methought there assembled a council of the angels in the
presence of God, and I heard God say thus: "Who will deceive Ahab that he may go
up against Ammon and be slain?" Whereupon one said one thing and another said
another. Then came an angel and said: "Lord, I will fight against Ahab, and will
go to his false prophets and will put the lie into their mouth, and so shall he
go up and be slain." And hearing this, God said: "Now go and do so, for you
shall prevail". Then were the false prophets enraged, and their chief smote
Micaiah's cheek, saying: "O reprobate of God, when did the angel of truth depart
from us and come to you? Tell us, when came to us the angel that brought the
lie?"

'Micaiah answered: "You shall know when you shall flee from house to house for
fear of being slain, having deceived your king." Then Ahab was wroth, and said:
"Seize Micaiah, and the fetters which he had upon his feet place on his neck,
and keep him on barley bread and water until my return, for now I know not what
death I would inflict on him"., They went up, then, and according to the word of
Micaiah the matter befell. For the king of the Ammonites ;said to his servants:
"See that you fight not against the king of Judah, nor against the princes of
Israel, but slay the king of Israel, Ahab, my enemy."' Then Jesus said: "Stop
there, Barnabas; for it is enough for our purpose."

Chapter 161

"Have you heard all?" said Jesus. The disciples answered: "Yes, Lord." Whereupon
Jesus said: "Lying is indeed a sin, but murder is a greater, because the lie is
a sin that appertains to him that speaks, but the murder, while it appertains to
him that commits it, is such that it destroys also the dearest thing that God
has here upon earth, that is, man. And lying can be remedied by saying the
contrary of that which has been said; whereas murder has no remedy, seeing it is
not possible to give life again to the dead. Tell me, then, did Moses the
servant of God sin in slaying all whom he slew?"

The disciples answered: "God forbid; God forbid that Moses should have sinned in
obeying God who commanded him!" Then Jesus said: "And I say, God forbid that
that angel should have sinned who deceived Ahab's false prophets with the lie;
for even as God receives the slaughter of men as sacrifice, so received he the
lie for praise. Truly, truly, I say to you, that even as the child errs which
causes its shoes to be made by the measure of a giant, even so errs he who would
subject God to the law, as he himself as man is subject to the law. When,
therefore, you shall believe that only to be sin which God wills not, you will
find the truth, even as I have told you. Wherefore, because God is not composite
nor changeable, so also is he unable to will and not will a single thing; for so
would he have contradiction in himself, and consequently pain, and would not be
infinitely blessed."

Philip answered: 'But how is that saying of the prophet Amos to be understood,
that "there is not evil in the city that God has not done?" Jesus answered: 'Now
here see, Philip, how great is the danger of resting in the letter, as do the
Pharisees, who have invented for themselves the "predestination of God in the

elect," in such wise that they come to say in fact that God is unrighteous, a deceiver and a liar and a hater of judgment (which shall fall upon them).

Wherefore I say that here Amos the prophet of God speaks of the evil which the world calls evil: for if he had used the language of the righteous he would not have been understood by the world. For all tribulations are good, either for that they purge the evil that we have done, or are good because they restrain us from doing evil, or are good because they make man to know the condition of this life, in order that we may love and long for life eternal. Accordingly, had the prophet Amos said: "There is no good in the city but what God has wrought it," he had given occasion for despair to the afflicted, as they beheld themselves in tribulation and sinners living in prosperity. And, what is worse, many, believing Satan to have such sovereignty over man, would have feared Satan and done him service, so as not to suffer tribulation. Amos therefore did as does the Roman interpreter, who considers not his words [as one] speaking in the presence of the high-priest, but consider the will and the business of the Jew that knows not to speak the Hebrew tongue.

Chapter 162

If Amos had said: "There is no good in the city but what God has done it," as God lives, in whose presence my soul stands, he would have made a grievous error, for the world holdsnothing good save the iniquities and sins that are done in the way of vanity. Whereupon men would have wrought much more iniquitously, believing that there is not any sin or wickedness which God has not done, at hearing whereof the earth trembles." And when Jesus had said this, straightway there arose a great earthquake, in so much that every one fell as dead. Jesus raised them up, saying: 'Now see if I have told you the truth. Let this, then, suffice you, that Amos, when he said that "God has done evil in the city talking with the world," spoke of tribulations, which sinners alone call evil. Let us come now to predestination, of which you desire to know, and whereof I will speak to you near Jordan on the other side, tomorrow, if God will.'

Chapter 163

Jesus went into the wilderness beyond Jordan with his disciples, and when the midday prayer was done he sat down near to a palm-tree, and under the shadow of the palm-tree his disciples sat down. Then Jesus said: 'So secret is predestination, O brethren, that I say to you, truly, only to one man shall it be clearly known. He it is whom the nations look for, to whom the secrets of God are so clear that, when he comes into the world, blessed shall they be that shall listen to his words, because God shall overshadow them with his mercy even as this palm-tree overshadows us. Yes, even as this tree protects us from the burning heat of the sun, even so the mercy of God will protect from Satan them that believe in that man.'

The disciples answered, "O Master, who shall that man be of whom you speak, who shall come into the world?" Jesus answered with joy of heart: 'He is Muhammad;, Messenger of God, and when he comes into the world, even as the rain makes the earth to bear fruit when for a long time it has not rained, even so shall he be occasion of good works among men, through the abundant mercy which he shall bring. For he is a white cloud full of the mercy of God, which mercy God shall sprinkle upon the faithful like rain.'

Chapter 164

I will accordingly tell you now [what] little God has granted me to know concerning this same predestination. The Pharisees say that everything has been so predestined that he who is elect cannot become reprobate, and he who is reprobate cannot by any means become elect; and that, even as God has predestined well-doing as the road by which the elect shall walk to salvation, even so has he predestined sin as the road by which the reprobate shall walk into damnation. Cursed be the tongue that said this, with the hand that wrote it, for this is the faith of Satan. Wherefore one may know of what manner are the Pharisees of the present day, for they are faithful servants of Satan.

What can predestination mean but an absolute will to give an end to a thing [of which] one has the means in hand? for without the means one cannot destine an end. How, then, shall he who not only lacks stone and money to spend, but has not even so much land as to place one foot upon, destine to build a house? Surely, none [could do so]. No more, then, I tell you, is predestination, taking away the free will that God has given to man of his pure bounty, the Law of God. Surely it is not predestination but abomination we shall be establishing.

That man is free the Book of Moses shows, where, when our God gave the Law upon Mount Sinai, he spoke thus: My commandment is not in the heaven that you should excuse yourself, saying: Now, who shall go to bring us the commandment of God? and who perhaps shall give us strength to observe it? Neither is it beyond the sea, that in like manner you should excuse yourself. But my commandment is near to your heart, that when you will you may observe it..

Tell me, if King Herod should command an old man to become young and a sick man that he should become whole, and when they did not [do] iti should cause them to be killed, would this be just? The disciples answered: "If Herod gave this command, he would be most unjust and impious."

Then Jesus, sighing, said: "These are the fruits of human traditions, O brethren; for in saying that God has predestinated the reprobate such that he cannot become elect they blaspheme God as impious and unjust. For he commands the sinner not to sin, and when he sins to repent; while such predestination takes away from the sinner the power not to sin, and entirely deprives him of repentance."

Chapter 165

But hear what says God by Joel the prophet: "As I live, [says] your God, I will not the death of a sinner, but I seek that he should be converted to penitence." Will God then predestinate that which he [does] not will? Consider that which God says, and that which the Pharisees of this present time say. Further, God says by the prophet Isaiah: "I have called, and you would not hearken to me." And how much God has called, hear how he says by the same prophet: All the day have I spread out my hands to a people that believe me not, but contradict me."

And our Pharisees, when they say that the reprobate cannot become elect, what [do] they say, then, but that God mocks men even as he would mock a blind man who should show him something white, and as he would mock a deaf man who should speak into his ears? And that the elect can be reprobated, consider what our God says by Ezekiel the prophet: "As I live, says God, if the righteous shall forsake his righteousness and shall do abominations, he shall perish, and I will not remember any more any of his righteousness; for trusting therein it shall forsake him before me and it shall not save him." And of the calling of the reprobate, what says God by the prophet Hosea but this: I will call a people not elect, I will call them elect." God is true, and cannot tell a lie: for God being truth speaks truth. But the Pharisees of this present time with their doctrine contradict God altogether.

Chapter 166

Andrew replied: "But how is that to be understood which God said to Moses, that he will have mercy on whom he wills to have mercy and will harden whom he wills to harden." Jesus answered: "God says this in order that man may not believe that he is saved by his own virtue, but may perceive that life and the mercy of God have been granted him by God of his bounty. And he says it in order that men may shun the opinion that there be other gods than he.

If, therefore, he hardened Pharaoh he did it because he had afflicted our people and essayed to bring it to nought by destroying all the male children in Israel: whereby Moses was near to losing his life. Accordingly, I say to you truly, that predestination has for its foundation the Law of God and human free will. Yes, and even if God could save the whole world so that none should perish he would not will to do so lest thus he should deprive man of freedom, which he preserves to him in order to do despite to Satan, in order that this [lump of] clay, scorned of the spirit, even though it shall sin as the spirit did, may have power to repent and go to dwell in that place whence the spirit was cast out. Our God wills, I say, to pursue with his mercy man's free will, and wills not to forsake the creature with his omnipotence. And so on the day of judgment none will be able to make any excuse for their sins, seeing that it will then be manifest to them how much God has done for their conversion, and how often he has called them to repentance.

Chapter 167

Accordingly, if your mind will not rest content in this, and you be fain to say again: "Why so?" I will disclose to you a wherefore." It is this. Tell me, wherefore cannot a [single] stone rest on the top of the water, yet the whole earth rests on the top of the water? Tell me, why is it that, while water extinguishes fire, and earth flees from air, so that none can unite earth, air, water, and fire in harmony, nevertheless they are united in man and are preserved harmoniously?

If, then, you know not this no, all men, as men, cannot know it how shall they understand that God created the universe out of nothing with a single word? How shall they understand the eternity of God? Assuredly they shall by no means be able to understand this, because, man being finite and composite with the body, which, as says the prophet Solomon, being corruptible, presses down the soul, and the works of God being proportionate to God, how shall they be able to comprehend them?

Isaiah, prophet of God, seeing [it to be] thus, exclaimed, saying: Truly you are a hidden God! And of the Messenger of God, how God has created him, he says: His generation, who shall narrate? And of the working of God he says: Who has been his counsellor? Wherefore God says to human nature: Even as the heaven is exalted above the earth, so are my ways exalted above your ways and my thoughts above your thoughts. Therefore I say to you, the manner of predestination is not manifest to men, albeit the fact is true, as I have told you. Ought man then, because he cannot find out the mode, to deny the fact? Assuredly, I have never yet seen any one refuse health, though the manner of it be not understood. For I know not even now how God by my touch heals the sick."

Chapter 168

Then said the disciples: "Truly God speaks in you, for never has man spoken as you speak." Jesus answered: "Believe me when God chose me to send me to the House of Israel, he gave me a book like to a clear mirror; which came down into my heart in such wise that all that I speak comes forth from that book. And when that book shall have finished coming forth from my mouth, I shall be taken up from the world." Peter answered: "O master, is that which you now speak written in that book?" Jesus replied: "All that I say for the knowledge of God and the service of God, for the knowledge of man and for the salvation of mankind all this comes forth from that book, which is my gospel;." Said Peter: "Is there written therein the glory of paradise?"

Chapter 169

Jesus answered: ."Hearken, and I will tell you of what manner is paradise, and how the holy and the faithful shall abide there without end, for this is one of the greatest blessings of paradise seeing that everything, however great, if it have an end, becomes small, yes nought. 'Paradise is the home where God stores his delights, which are so great that the ground which is trodden by the feet of the holy and blessed ones is so precious that one drachma of it is more precious than a thousand worlds.

These delights were seen by our, father, David, prophet of God, for God showed them to him, seeing he caused him to behold the glories of paradise: whereupon, when he returned to himself, he closed his eyes with both his hands, and weeping said: "Look not any more upon this world, O my eyes, for all is vain, and there is no good!". Of these delights said Isaiah ;the prophet: "The eyes of man have not seen, his ears have not heard, nor has the human heart conceived, that which God has prepared for them that love him." Know you wherefore they have not seen, heard, conceived such delights? It is because while they live here below they are not worthy to behold

such things. Wherefore, albeit our father David ;truly saw them, I tell you that he saw them not with human eyes, for God took his soul to himself, and thus, united with God, he saw them with light divine. As God lives, in whose presence my soul stands, seeing that the delights of paradise are infinite and man is finite, man cannot contain them; even as a little earthen jar cannot contain the sea.

Behold, then, how beautiful is the world in summer-time, when all things bear fruit! The very peasant, intoxicated with gladness by reason of the harvest that is come, makes the valleys and mountains resound with his singing, for that he loves his labours supremely. Now lift up even so your heart to paradise, where all things are fruitful with fruits proportionate to him who has cultivated it. As God lives, this is sufficient for the knowledge of paradise, forasmuch as God has created paradise for the home of his own delights. Now think you that immeasurable goodness would not have things immeasurably good? Or that immeasurable beauty would not have things immeasurably beautiful? Beware, for you err greatly if you think he have them not.

Chapter 170

God says thus to the man who shall faithfully serve him: "I know your works, that you work for me. As I live eternally, your love shall not exceed my bounty. Because you serve me as God your creator, knowing yourself to be my work, and ask nought of me save grace and mercy to serve me faithfully; because you set no end to my service, seeing you desire to serve me eternally: even so will I do,

for I will reward you as if you were God, my equal. For not only will I place in
your hands the abundance of paradise, but I will give you myself as a gift, so
that, even as you are fain to be my servant for ever, even so will I make your
wages forever."'

Chapter 171

What think you," said Jesus to his disciples, "of paradise? Is there a mind that
could comprehend such riches and delights? Man must needs have a knowledge as
great as God's if he would know what God wills to give to his servants. Have you
seen, when Herod; makes a present to one of his favourite barons, in what sort
he presents it?" John answered: "I have seen it twice; and assuredly the tenth
part of that which he gives would be sufficient for a poor man." Jesus said:
"But if a poor man shall be presented to Herod what will he give to him" John
answered: "One or two mites." Now let this be your book wherein to study the
knowledge of paradise," [said Jesus]: "because all that God has given to man in
this present world for his body is as though Herod should give a mite to a poor
man;; but what God will give to the body and soul in paradise is as though Herod
should give all that he has, yes and his own life, to one of his servants."

Chapter 172

God says thus to him that loves him, and serves him faithfully: "Go and consider
the sands of the sea, O my servant, how many they are. Wherefore, if the sea
should give you one single grain of sand, would it appear small to you?
Assuredly, yes. As I, your creator, live, all that I have given in this world to
all the princes and kings of the earth is less than a grain of sand that the sea
would give you, in comparison of that which I will give you in my paradise."

Chapter 173

'Consider, then," said Jesus, "the abundance of paradise. For if God has given
to man in this world an ounce of welling, in paradise he will give him ten
hundred thousand loads. Consider the quantity of fruits that are in this world,
the quantity of food, the quantity of flowers, and the quantity of things that
minister to man. As God lives, in whose presence my soul stands, as the sea has
still sand over and above when one receives a grain thereof, even so will the
quality and

quantity of figs [in paradise] excel the sort of figs we eat here. And in like
manner every other thing in paradise. But furthermore, I say to you that truly,
as a mountain of gold and pearls is more precious than the shadow of an ant,
even so are the delights of paradise more precious than all the delights of the
princes of the world which they have had and shall have even to the judgment of
God when the world shall have an end."

Peter answered: "Shall, then, our body which we now have go into paradise?"
Jesus answered: "Beware, Peter; lest you become a Sadducee; for the Sadducees
say that the flesh shall not rise again, and that there be no angels. 'Wherefore
their body and soul are deprived of entrance into paradise, and they are
deprived of all ministry of angels in this world. Have you perhaps forgotten
Job, prophet and friend of God, how he says: "I know that my God lives; and in
the last day I shall rise again in my flesh, and with my eyes I shall see God my
Saviour"?

But believe me, this flesh of ours shall be so purified that it shall not
possess a single property of those which now it has; seeing that it shall be

purged of every evil desire, and God shall reduce it to such a condition as was Adam's before he sinned. Two men serve one master in one and the same work. The one alone sees the work, and gives orders to the second, and the second performs all that the first commands. Seems it just to you, I say, that the master should reward only him who sees and commands, and should cast out of his house him who wearied himself in the work? Surely not.

How then shall the justice of God bear this? The soul and the body with sense of man serve God: the soul only sees and commands the service, because the soul, eating no bread, fasts not, [the soul] walks not, feels not cold and heat, falls not sick, and is not slain, because the soul is immortal: it suffers not any of those corporal pains which the body suffers at the instance of the elements. Is it, then, just, I say, that the soul alone should go into paradise, and not the body, which has wearied itself so much in serving God?" Peter answered: "O master, the body, having caused the soul to sin, ought not to be placed in paradise. Jesus answered: "Now how shall the body sin without the soul? Assuredly it is impossible. Therefore, in taking away God's mercy from the body, you condemns the soul to hell."

Chapter 174

As God lives, in whose presence my soul stands, our God promises his mercy to the sinner, saying: "In that hour that the sinner shall lament his sin, by myself, I will not remember his iniquities for ever." Now what should eat the meats of paradise, if the body go not thither? The soul? Surely not, seeing it is spirit." Peter ;answered: "So then, the blessed shall eat in paradise;; but how shall the meat be voided without uncleanness?"

Jesus answered: "Now what blessedness shall the body have if it eat not nor drink? Assuredly it is fitting to give glory in proportion to the thing glorified. But you err, Peter, in thinking that such meat should be voided in uncleanness, because this body at the present time eats corruptible meats, and thus it is that putrefaction comes forth: but in paradise the body shall be incorruptible, impassible, and immortal, and free from every misery; and the meats, which are without any defect, shall not generate any putrefaction.

Chapter 175

God says this in Isaiah the prophet, pouring contempt on the reprobate: My servants shall sit at my table in my house and shall feast joyfully, with gladness and with the sound of harps and organs, and I will not suffer them to have need of anything. But you that are my enemies shall be cast away from me, where you shall die in misery, while every servant of mine despises you..

Chapter 176

To what does it serve to say, "They shall feast"?' said Jesus to his disciples. 'Surely God speaks plain. But to what purpose are the four rivers of precious liquor in paradise, with so many fruits? Assuredly, God eats not;, the angels eat not, the soul eats not, the sense eats not, but rather the flesh, which is our body. Wherefore the glory of paradise is for the body the meats, and for the soul and the sense God and the conversation of angels and blessed spirits. That glory shall be better revealed by the Messenger; of God, who (seeing God has created all things for love of him) knows all things better than any other creature.'

Said Bartholomew;: 'O master, shall the glory of paradise be equal for every man? If it be equal, it shall not be just, and if it be not equal the lesser will envy the greater.' Jesus answered: 'It will not be equal, for that God is just; and everyone shall be content, because there is no envy there. Tell me, Bartholomew;: there is a master who has many servants, and he clothes all of those his servants in the same cloth. Do then the boys, who are clothed in the garments of boys, mourn because they have not the apparel of grown men? Surely, on the contrary, if the elders desired to put on them their larger garments they would be wroth, because, the garments not being of their size, they would think themselves mocked. Now, Bartholomew, lift your heart to God in paradise, and you shall see that all one glory, although it shall be more to one and less to another, shall not produce ought of envy.'

Chapter 177

Then said he who writes : 'O master, has paradise light from the sun as this world has?' Jesus answered: 'Thus has God said to me, O Barnabas: 'The world wherein you men that are sinners dwell has the sun and the moon and the stars that adorn it, for your benefit and your gladness; for this have I created. " Think you, then, that the house where my faithful dwell shall not be better? Assuredly, you err, so thinking: for I, your God, am the sun of paradise;, and my Messenger ;is the moon ;who from me receives all; and the stars are my prophets which have preached to you my will. Wherefore my faithful, even as they received my word from my prophets [here] , shall in like manner obtain delight and gladness through them in the paradise of my delights."

Chapter 178

And let this suffice you,' said Jesus, 'for the knowledge of paradise.' Whereupon Bartholomew ;said again: 'O master, have patience with me if I ask you one word.' Jesus answered: 'Say that which you desire.' Said Bartholomew: 'Paradise is surely great: for, seeing there be in it such great goods, it needs must be great.' Jesus answered: 'Paradise is so great that no man can measure it. Truly I say to you that the heavens are nine, among which are set the planets;, that are distant one from another five hundred years' journey for a man: and the earth in like manner is distant from the first heaven five hundred years' journey.

But stop you at the measuring of the first heaven, which is by so much greater than the whole earth as the whole earth is greater than a grain of sand. So also the second heaven is greater than the first, and the third than the second, and so on, up to the last heaven, each one is likewise greater than the next. And truly I say to you that paradise is greater than all the earth and all the heavens [together], even as all the earth is greater than a grain of sand.' Then said Peter: 'O master, paradise must needs be greater than God, because God is seen within it.' Jesus answered: 'Hold your peace, Peter, for you unwittingly blaspheme.'

Chapter 179

Then the angel Gabriel came to Jesus and showed him a mirror shining like the sun, in which he beheld these words written:

'As I live eternally, even as paradise is greater than all the heavens and the earth, and as the whole earth is greater than a grain of sand, even so am I greater than paradise; and as many times more as the sea has grains of sand, as there are drops of water upon the sea, as there are [blades of] grass upon the ground, as there are leaves upon the trees, as there are skins upon the beasts; and as many times more as the grains of sand that would go to fill the heavens and paradise and more.'

Then Jesus said: "Let us do reverence to our God, who is blessed for evermore." They bowed their heads a hundred times and prostrated themselves to earth upon their face in prayer. When the prayer was done, Jesus called Peter and told him and all the disciples what he had seen. And to Peter he said: "Your soul, which is greater than all the earth, sees through one eye the sun which is a thousand times greater than all the earth." "It is true," said Peter. Then Jesus said: "Even so, through [the eye of] paradise, shall you see God our Creator." And having said this, Jesus gave thanks to God our Lord, praying for the House of Israel and for the holy city. And everyone answered: "So be it, Lord."

Chapter 180

One day, Jesus being in Solomon's porch, a scribe, one of them that made discourse to the people, drew near to him and said to him: "O master, I have many times made discourse to this people; in my mind there is a passage of scripture which I am not. able to understand." Jesus answered: "And what is it?" The scribe said: "That which God said to Abraham your father, I will be your great reward. Now how could man merit [such reward]?"

Then Jesus rejoiced in spirit, and said: "Assuredly you are not far from the kingdom of God! Listen to me, for I will tell you the meaning of such teaching. God being infinite, and man finite, man cannot merit God and is this [the reason for] your doubt, brother?" The scribe answered, weeping: "Lord, you know my heart. Speak, therefore, for my soul desires to hear your voice." Then Jesus said: "As God lives, man cannot merit [even] a little breath which he receives every moment."

The scribe was beside himself, hearing this, and the disciples marvelled as well, because they remembered that which Jesus said, that whatever they gave for love of God, they should receive a hundredfold [in return]. Then he said: "If someone should lend you a hundred pieces of gold, and you should spend those pieces, could you say to that man: 'I give you a decayed vine-leaf; therefore give me your house, for I merit it'?" The scribe answered: "No, Lord, for he should first pay that which he owed, and then, if he wished for anything, he should give him good things, but what good is a corrupted leaf ?"

Chapter 181

Jesus answered: "You have spoken well, O brother; so tell me, Who created man out of nothing? Surely it was God, who also gave [man] the whole world for his benefit. But man by sinning has spent it all, for because of sin the world is turned against man, and man in his misery has nothing to give to God but works corrupted by sin. For, sinning every day, he makes his own work corrupt, as Isaiah the prophet says: Our righteousnesses are as a menstruous cloth.

How, then, shall man have merit, seeing he is unable to give satisfaction? Is it, perhaps, that man does not sin? It is certain that our God says by his prophet David: Seven times a day falls the righteous. How then falls the unrighteous? And if our righteousnesses are corrupt, how abominable are our unrighteousnesses! As God lives, there is nothing that a man should shun more than this saying: 'I merit.' Brother, let a man know the works of his hands, and he will straightway see his merit. Every good thing that comes out of a man, truly, man does not do it, but God works it in him; for his being is of God who

created him. That which man does is to contradict God his creator and to commit
sin, [and so] he merits not reward, but torment.

Chapter 182

'Not only has God created man, as I say, but he created him perfect. He has
given him the whole world; after the departure from paradise he has given him
two angels to guard him, he has sent him the prophets, he has granted him the
Law, he has granted him the faith, every moment he delivers him from Satan, he
is fain to give him paradise; no more, God wills to give himself to man.
Consider, then, the debt, if it is great! [a debt] to cancel which you would
need to have created man of yourselves out of nothing, to have created as many
prophets as God has sent, with a world and a paradise, no, more, with a God
great and good as is our God, and to give it ne all to God. So would the debt be
cancelled and there would remain to you only the obligation to give thanks to
God. But since you are not able to create a single fly, and seeing there is but
one God who is lord of all things, how shall you be able to cancel your debt?
Assuredly, if a man should lend you an hundred pieces of gold, you would be
obliged to restore an hundred pieces of gold.

Accordingly, the sense of this, O brother, is that God, being lord of paradise
and of everything, can say that which pleases him, and give whatsoever pleases
him. Wherefore, when he said to Abraham: "I will be your great reward," Abraham
;could not say: "God is my reward," but "God is my gift and my debt." So when
you discourse to the people, O brother, you ought thus to explain this passage:
that God will give to man such and such things if man works well. When God shall
speak to you, O man, and shall say: "O my servant, you have wrought well for
love of me; what reward seek you from me, your God?" answer you: "Lord, seeing I
am the work of your hands, it is not fitting that there should be in me sin,
which Satan ;loves. Therefore, Lord, for your own glory, have mercy upon' the
works of your hands.

And if God say: "I have pardoned you, and now I would fain reward you"; answer
you: "Lord, I merit punishment for what I have done, and for what you have done
you merit to be glorified. Punish, Lord, in me what I have done, and save that
which you have wrought." And if God say: "What punishment seems to you fitting
for your sin?" do you answer; "As much, O Lord, as all the reprobate shall
suffer." And if God say: "Wherefore seek you so great punish. men, O my faithful
servant?" answer you: "Because every one of them, if they had received from you
as much as I have received, would have served you more faithfully than I [have
done]." And if God say: "When will you receive this punishment, and for how long
a time?" answer you: "Now, and without end." As God lives, in whose presence my
soul stands, such a man would be more pleasing to God than all his holy angels.
For God loves true humility, and hates pride.'

Then the scribe gave thanks to Jesus, and said to him, 'Lord, let us go to the
house of your servant, for your servant will give meat to you and to your
disciples.' Jesus answered: 'I will come thither when you will promise to call
me "Brother" and not "Lord,"; and shall say you are my brother, and not my
servant.' The man promised, and Jesus went to his house.

Chapter 183

While they sat at meat the scribe said: 'O master, you said that God loves true
humility. Tell us therefore what is humility, and how it can be true and false.'
[Jesus replied:] "Truly I say to you that he who becomes not as a little child
shall not enter into the kingdom of heaven." Every one was amazed at hearing

this, and they said one to another: 'Now how shall he become a little child who is thirty or forty years old? Surely, this is a hard saying.'

Jesus answered: 'As God lives, in whose presence my soul stands, my words are true. I said to you that [a man] has need to become as a little child: for this is true humility. For if you ask a little child: "Who has made your garments?" he will answer: "My father." If you ask him whose is the house where he lives, he will say: "My father's." If you shall say: "Who gives you to eat?" he will reply: "My father." If you shall say: "Who has taught you to walk and to speak?" he will answer; "My father." But if you shall say: "Who has broken your forehead, for that you have your forehead so bound up?" he will answer: "I fell down, and so did I break my head."

If you shall say: "Now why did you fall down?" he will answer: "See you not that I am little, so that I have not the strength to walk and run like a grown man? so my father must needs take me by the hand if I would walk firmly. But in order that I might learn to walk well, my father left me for a little space, and I, wishing to run, fell down." If you shall say: "And what said your father?" he will answer: "Now why did you not walk quite slowly? See that in future you leave not my side."

Chapter 184

Tell me, is this true?' said Jesus. The disciples and the scribe answered: 'It is most true.' Then Jesus said: 'He who in truth of heart recognizes God as the author of all good, and himself as the author of sin, shall be truly humble. But whoever shall speak with the tongue as the child speaks, and shall contradict [the same] in act, assuredly he has false humility and true pride. For pride is then at its height when it makes use of humble things, that it be not reprehended and spurned of men.

True humility is a lowliness of the soul whereby man knows himself in truth; but false humility is a mist from hell which so darkens the understanding of the soul that what a man ought to ascribe to himself, he ascribes to God, and what he ought to ascribe to God, he ascribes to himself. Thus, the man of false humility will say that he is a grievous sinner, but when one tells him that he is a sinner he will wax wroth against him, and will persecute him. The man of false humility will say that God has given him all that he has, but that he on his part has not slumbered, but done good works. And these Pharisees of this present time, brethren, tell me how they walk.'

The scribe answered, weeping: "O master, the Pharisees of the present time have the garments and the name of Pharisees, but in their heart and their works they are Canaanites. And would to God they usurped not such a name, for then would they not deceive the simple! O ancient time, how cruelly have you dealt with us, that have taken away from us the true Pharisees and left us the false!'

Chapter 185

Jesus answered: 'Brother, it is not time that has done this, but rather the wicked world. For in every time it is possible to serve God in truth, but by companying with the world, that is with the evil manners in each time, men become bad. Now know you not that Gehazi, servant of Elisha the prophet, lying, and shaming his master, took the money and the raiment of Naaman the Syrian? And yet Elisha had a great number of Pharisees to whom God made him to prophesy.

Truly I say to you that men are so inclined to evil working, and so much does
the world excite them thereto, and work Satan entice them to evil, that the
Pharisees of the present day avoid every good work and every holy example: and
the example of Gehazi is sufficient for them to be reprobated of God. 'The
scribe answered: "It is most true"; whereupon Jesus said: "I would that you
would narrate to me the example of Haggai and Hosea, both prophets of God, in
order that we may behold the true Pharisee." The scribe answered: "O master,
what shall I say? Surely many believe it not, although it is written by Daniel
the prophet; but in obedience to you I will narrate the truth.

Haggai was fifteen years old when, having sold his patrimony and given it to the
poor, he went forth from Anathoth to serve Obadiah the prophet. Now the aged
Obadiah, who knew the humility of Haggai, used him as a book wherewith to teach
his disciples. Wherefore he oftentimes presented him raiment and delicate food,
but Haggai ever sent back the messenger, saying: "Go, return to the house, for
you have made a mistake. Shall Obadiah send me such things? Surely not: for he
knows that I am good for nothing, and only commit sins.

And Obadiah, when he had anything bad, used to give it to the one next to
Haggai, in order that he might see it. Thereupon Haggai. when he saw it, would
say to himself: "Now, behold, Obadiah has certainly forgotten you, for this
thing is suited to me alone, because I am worse than all. And there is nothing
so vile but that, receiving it from Obadiah, by whose hands God grants it to me,
it were a treasure."

Chapter 186

When Obadiah desired to teach any one how to pray, he would call Haggai and say:
"Recite here your prayer so that every one may hear your words." Then Haggai
would say: "Lord God of Israel, with mercy look upon your servant, who calls
upon you, for that you have created him. Righteous Lord God, remember your
righteousness and punish the sins of your servant, in order that I may not
pollute your work. Lord my God, I cannot ask you for the delights that you grant
to your faithful servants, because I do nought but sins. Wherefore, Lord, when
you would give an infirmity to one of your servants, remember me your servant,
for your own glory." And when Haggai did so,' said the scribe, 'God so loved him
that to every one who in his time stood by him God gave, [the gift of] prophecy.
And nothing did Haggai ask in prayer that God withheld.'

Chapter 187

The good scribe wept as he said this, as the sailor weeps when he sees his ship
broken up. And he said: "Hosea, when he went to serve God, was prince over the
tribe of Naphtali, and aged fourteen years. And so, having sold his patrimony
and given it to the poor, he went to be disciple of Haggai. Hosea was so
inflamed with charity that concerning all that was asked of him he would say:
'This has God given me for you, O brother; accept it, therefore!' For which
cause he was soon left with two garments only namely, a tunic of sackcloth and a
mantle of skins. He sold, I say, his patrimony and gave it to the poor, because
otherwise no one would be suffered to be called a Pharisee.

Hosea had the Book of Moses, which he read with greatest earnestness. Now one
day Haggai said to him: "Hosea, who has taken away from you all that you had?"
He answered: "The Book of Moses." It happened that a disciple of a neighbouring
prophet wanted to go to Jerusalem, but did not have a mantle. Wherefore, having
heard of the charity of Hosea, he went to find him, and said to him: 'Brother, I

would want to go to Jerusalem to perform a sacrifice to our God, but I have not a mantle, wherefore I know not what to do.'

When he heard this, Hosea said: 'Pardon me, brother, for I have committed a great sin against you: because God has given me a mantle in order that I might give it to you, and I had forgotten. Now therefore accept it, and pray to God for me.' The man, believing this, accepted Hosea's mantle and departed. And when Hosea went to the house of Haggai, Haggai said: 'Who has taken away your mantle?' Hosea replied: 'The Book of Moses.' Haggai was much pleased at hearing this, because he perceived the goodness of Hosea.

It happened that a poor man was stripped by robbers and left naked. Whereupon Hosea, seeing him, stripped off his own tunic and gave it to him that was naked; himself being left with a little piece of goat-skin over the privy parts. Wherefore, as he came not to see Haggai, the good Haggai thought that Hosea was sick. So he went with two disciples to find him: and they found him wrapped in palm-leaves. Then said Haggai: 'Tell me now, why have you not been to visit me?' Hosea answered: "The Book of Moses has taken away my tunic, and I feared to come thither without a tunic." Whereupon Haggai gave him another tunic.

It happened that a young man, seeing Hosea read the Book of Moses, wept, and said: 'I also would learn to read if I had a book.' Hearing which, Hosea gave him the book, saying: 'Brother, this book is yours; for God gave it me in order that I should give it to one who, weeping, should desire a book.' The man believed him, and accepted the book.

Chapter 188

There was a disciple of Haggai near to Hosea; and he, wishing to see if his own book was well written, went to visit Hosea, and said to him: "Brother, take your book and let us see if it is even as mine. " Hosea answered: "It has been taken away from me." " Who has taken it from you?" said the disciple. Hosea answered: "The Book of Moses," Hearing which, the other went to Haggai ;and said to him: "Hosea has gone mad, for he says that the Book of Moses has taken away from him the Book of Moses." Haggai answered: "Would to God, O brother, that I were mad in like manner, and that all mad folk were like to Hosea!"

Now the Syrian robbers, having raided the land of Judea, seized the son of a poor widow, who dwelt hard by Mount Carmel, where the prophets and Pharisees abode. It chanced, accordingly, that Hosea having gone to cut wood met the woman, who was weeping. Thereupon he straightway began to weep; for whenever he saw any one laugh he laughed, and whenever he saw any one weep he wept. Hosea then asked the woman touching the reason of her weeping, and she told him all.

Then said Hosea: 'Come, sister, for God wills to give you your son." And they went both of them to Hebron;, where Hosea ;sold himself, and gave the money to the widow;, who, not knowing how he had gotten that money, accepted it, and redeemed her son. He who had bought Hosea took him to Jerusalem, where he had an abode, not knowing Hosea. Haggai;, seeing that Hosea was not to be found, remained afflicted thereat. Whereupon the angel of God told him how he had been taken as a slave to Jerusalem. The good Haggai, when he heard this, wept for the absence of Hosea as a mother weeps for the absence of her son. And having called two disciples he went to Jerusalem. And by the will of God, in the entrance of the city he met Hosea, who was laden with bread to carry it to the labourers in his master's vineyard.

Having recognized him, Haggai said: "Son, how is it that you have forsaken your old father, who seeks you mourning?" Hosea answered: "Father, I have been sold." Then said Haggai in wrath: "Who is that bad fellow who has sold you?" Hosea answered: "God forgive you, O my father; for he who has sold me is so good that if he were not in the world no one would become holy." 'Who, then, is he?" said Haggai;. 'Hosea answered: "O my father, it was the Book of Moses;."Then the good Haggai remained as it were beside himself, and said: "Would to God, my son, that the Book of Moses; would sell me also with all my children, even as it has sold you!"

And Haggai went with Hosea to the house of his master, who when he saw Haggai said: "Blessed be our God, who has sent his prophet to my house"; and he ran to kiss his hand. Then said Haggai: "Brother, kiss the hand of your slave whom you have bought, for he is better than I." And he narrated to him all that had passed; whereupon the master gave Hosea his freedom. 'And that is all that you desired, O Master,' [said the scribe].

Chapter 189

Then Jesus said: "This is true, because I am assured of it by God. Therefore, that every one may know that this is the truth, in the name of God let the sun stand still, and not move for twelve hours!" And so it came to pass, to the great terror of all Jerusalem and Judea.

And Jesus said to the scribe: "O brother, what seek you to learn from me, seeing you have such knowledge? As God lives, this is sufficient for man's salvation, inasmuch as the humility of Haggai, with the charity of Hosea, fulfils all the Law and all the prophets. Tell me, brother, when you came to question me in the Temple, did you think, perhaps. that God had sent me to destroy the Law and the prophets? It is certain that God will not do this, seeing he is unchangeable, and therefore that which God ordained as man's way of salvation, this has he caused all the prophets to say.

As God lives, in whose presence my soul stands, if the Book of Moses with the book of our father David had not been corrupted by the human traditions of false Pharisees and doctors, God would not have given his word to me. And why speak I of the Book of Moses and the book of David? Every prophecy have they corrupted, in so much that today a thing is not sought because God has commanded it, but men look whether the doctors say it, and the Pharisees observe it, as though God were in error, and men could not err.

Woe, therefore, to his faithless generation, for upon them shall come the blood of every prophet and righteous man, with the blood of Zechariah son of Berachiah, whom they slew between the Temple and the altar! What prophet have they not persecuted? What righteous man have they suffered to die a natural death? Scarcely one! And they seek now to slay me. They boast themselves to be children of Abraham, and to possess the beautiful Temple. As God lives, they are children of Satan, and therefore they do his will: therefore the Temple, with the holy city, shall go to ruin, in so much that there shall not remain of the Temple one stone upon another.'

Chapter 190

'Tell me, brother, you that are a doctor learned in the Law in whom was the promise of the Messiah made to our father Abraham? In Isaac or in Ishmael." The scribe answered: 'O master, I fear to tell you this, because of the penalty of death.' Then Jesus said: 'Brother, I am grieved that I came to eat bread in your house, since you love this present life more than God your creator; and for this cause you fear to lose your life, but fear not to lose the faith and the life eternal,

which is lost when the tongue speaks contrary to that which the heart knows of the Law of God. Then the good scribe wept, and said: "O master, if I had known how to bear fruit, I should have preached many things which I have left unsaid lest sedition should be roused among the people."

Jesus answered: "You should respect neither the people, nor all the world, nor all the holy ones, nor all the angels, when it should cause offence to God. Wherefore let the whole [world] perish rather than offend God your creator, and preserve it not with sin. For sin destroys and preserves not, and God is mighty to create as many worlds as there are sands in the sea, and more."

Chapter 191

The scribe then said: "Pardon me, O master, for I have sinned." Jesus said: "God pardon you. for against him have you sinned."

Whereupon said the scribe: I have seen an old book; written by the hand of Moses and Joshua ;(he who made the sun stand still; as you have done), servants and prophets of God, which book is the true Book of Moses. Therein is written that Ishmael is the father of Messiah, and Isaac the father of the messenger of the Messiah. And thus says the book, that Moses said: "Lord God of Israel, mighty and merciful, manifest to your servant the splendour of your glory."

Whereupon God showed him his Messenger in the arms of Ishmael, and Ishmael in the arms of Abraham. Near to Ishmael stood Isaac, in whose arms was a child, who with his finger pointed to the Messenger of God, saying: "This is he for whom God has created all things." Whereupon Moses cried out with joy: "O Ishmael, you have in your arms all the world, and paradise! Be mindful of me, God's servant, that I may find grace in God's sight by means of your son, for whom God has made all."

Chapter 192

In that Book it is not found that God eats the flesh of cattle or sheep; in that Book it is not found that God has locked up his mercy in Israel alone, but rather that God has mercy on every man that seeks God his creator in truth. All of this book I was not able to read, because the high priest, in whose library I was, forbade me, saying that an Ishmaelite had written it.'

Then Jesus said: "See that you never again keep back the truth, because in the faith of the Messiah God shall give salvation to men, and without it shall none be saved." And there did Jesus end his discourse. Whereupon, as they sat at meat, lo! Mary, who wept at the feet of Jesus, entered into the house of Nicodemus (for that was the name of the scribe), and weeping placed herself at the feet of Jesus, saying: 'Lord, your servant, who through you has found mercy with God, has a sister, and a brother who now lies sick in peril of death.'

Jesus answered: 'Where is your house? Tell me, for I will come to pray God for his health.' Mary answered: 'Bethany is [the home] of my brother and my sister, for my own house is Magdala: my brother, therefore, is in Bethany;.' Jesus said to the woman: 'Go you straightway to your brother's house, and there await me, for I will come to heal him. And fear you not, for he shall not die.' The woman

departed, and having gone to Bethany found that her brother had died that day,
wherefore they laid him in the sepulchre of their fathers.

Chapter 193

Jesus abode two days in the house of Nicodemus, and the third day he departed
for Bethany; and when he was near to the town he sent two of his disciples
before him, to announce to Mary his coming. She ran out of the town, and when
she had found Jesus. said, weeping: 'Lord, you said that my brother would not
die; and now he has been buried four days. Would to God you had come before I
called you, for then he had not died!'

Jesus answered: 'Thy brother is not dead, but sleeps, therefore I come to awake
him.' Mary answered, weeping: 'Lord, from such a sleep he shall be awakened on
the day of judgment by the angel of God sounding his trumpet.' Jesus answered:
'Mary, believe me that he shall rise before [that day], because God has given me
power over his sleep; and truly I say to you he is not dead, for he alone is
dead who dies without finding mercy with God.' Mary returned quickly to announce
to her sister Martha the coming of Jesus.

Now there were assembled at the death of Lazarus ;a great number of Jews from
Jerusalem, and many scribes and Pharisees. Martha;, having heard from her sister
Mary of the coming of Jesus, arose in haste and ran outside, whereupon the
multitude of Jews, scribes, and Pharisees followed her to comfort her, because
they supposed she was going to the sepulchre to weep over her brother. When
therefore she arrived at the place where Jesus had spoken to Mary, Martha
weeping said: 'Lord, would to God you had been here, for then my brother had not
died!' Mary then came up weeping; whereupon Jesus shed tears, and sighing said:
'Where have you laid him?' They answered: 'Come and see.'

The Pharisees said among themselves: 'Now this man, who raised the son of the
widow ;at Nain;, why did he suffer this man to die, having said that he should
not die?' Jesus having come to the sepulchre, where every one was weeping, said:
'Weep not, for Lazarus sleeps, and I am come to awake him.' The Pharisees said
among themselves: 'Would to God that you did so sleep!' Then Jesus said: 'My
hour is not yet come; but when it shall come I shall sleep in like manner, and
shall be speedily awakened.' Then Jesus said again: 'Take away the stone from
the sepulchre.' Said Martha: 'Lord, he stinks, for he has been dead four
days.'Jesus said: 'Why then am I come hither, Martha? Believe you not in me that
I shall awaken him?' Martha answered: 'I know that you are the holy one of God,
who has sent you into this world.'

Then Jesus lifted up his hands to heaven, and said: ' God of our fathers, God of
Abraham;, God of Ishmael ;and Lord of Isaac;, have mercy upon the affliction of
these women, and give glory to your holy name.' And when every one had answered
'Amen,' Jesus said with a loud voice: 'Lazarus, come forth!' Whereupon he that
was dead arose; and Jesus said to his disciples: 'Loose him.' For he was bound
in the grave-clothes with the napkin over his face, even as our fathers were
accustomed to bury [their dead].

A great multitude of the Jews and some of the Pharisees believed in Jesus,
because the miracle was great. Those that remained in their unbelief departed
and went to Jerusalem and announced to the chief of the priests the resurrection
of Lazarus;, and how that many were become Nazarenes;; for so they called them
who were brought to penitence through the word of God which Jesus preached.

Chapter 194

The scribes and Pharisees took counsel with the high priest to slay Lazarus; for many renounced their traditions and believed in the word of Jesus, because the miracle of Lazarus was a great one, seeing that Lazarus had conversation with men, and ate and drank. But because he was powerful, having a following in Jerusalem, and possessing with his sister Magdala and Bethany, they knew not what to do.

Jesus entered into Bethany, into the house of Lazarus, and Martha, with Mary, ministered to him. *Mary, sitting one day at the feet of Jesus, was listening to his words, whereupon Martha said to Jesus: 'Lord, see you not that my sister takes no care for you, and provides not that which you must eat and your disciples?' Jesus answered: 'Martha, Martha, do you take thought for that which you should do; for Mary has chosen a part which shall not be taken away from her for ever.

Jesus, sitting at table with a great multitude that believed in him, spoke, saying: 'Brethren, I have but little time to remain with you, for the time is at hand that I must depart from the world. Wherefore I bring to your mind the words of God spoken to Ezekiel ;the prophet, saying: "As I, your God, live eternally, the soul that sins, it shall die, but if the sinner shall repent he shall not die but live." Wherefore the present death is not death, but rather the end of a long death: even as the body when separated from the sense in a swoon, though it have the soul within it, has no other advantage over the dead and buried save this, that the buried [body] awaits God to raise it again, but the unconscious waits for the sense to return. Behold, then, the present life that it is death, through having no perception of God.

Chapter 195

'They that shall believe in me shall not die eternally, for through my word they shall perceive God within them, and therefore shall work out their salvation. What is death but an act which nature does by commandment of God? As it would be if one held a bird tied, and held the cord in his hand; when the head wills the bird to fly away, what does it? Assuredly it commands naturally the hand to open; and so straightway the bird flies away. "Our soul," as says the prophet David,

"is as a sparrow freed from the snare of the fowler," when man abides under the protection of God. And our life is like a cord whereby nature holds the soul bound to the body and the sense of man. When therefore God wills, and commands nature to open, the life is broken and the soul escapes in the hands of the angels whom God has ordained to receive souls.

Let not, then, friends weep when their friend is dead; for our God has so willed. But let him weep without ceasing when he sins, for [so] the soul dies, seeing it separates itself from God, the true Life. If the body is horrible without its union with the soul, much more frightful is the soul without union with God, who with his grace and mercy beautifies and quickens it.' And having said this Jesus gave thanks to God; whereupon Lazarus said: 'Lord, this house belongs to God my creator, with all that he has given into my keeping, for the service of the poor. Wherefore, since you are poor, and have a great number of disciples, come you to dwell here when you please, and as much as you please, for the servant of God will minister to you as much as shall be needful, for love of God.'

Chapter 196

Jesus rejoiced when he heard this, and said: 'See now how good a thing it is to
die! Lazarus has died once only, and has learned such doctrine as is not known
to the wise men in the world that have grown old among books! Would to God that
every man might die once only and return to the world, like Lazarus;, in order
that men might learn to live.' John answered: 'O master, is it permitted to me
to speak a word?'

'Speak a thousand,' answered Jesus, 'for just as a man is bound to dispense his
goods in the service of God, so also is he bound to dispense doctrine: and so
much the more is he bound [so to do) inasmuch as the world has power to raise up
a soul to penitence, whereas goods cannot bring back life to the dead. Wherefore
he is a murderer who has power to help a poor man and when he helps him not the
poor man dies of hunger; but a more grievous murderer is he who could by the
word of God convert the sinner to penitence, and converts him not, but stands,
as says God, "like a dumb dog." Against such says God: "The soul of the sinner
that shall perish because you have hidden my word, I will require it at your
hands, O unfaithful servant."

In what condition, then, are now the scribes and Pharisees who have the key and
will not enter, no hinder them who would fain enter, into eternal life? 'You ask
me, O John;, permission to speak one word, having listened to an hundred
thousand words of mine. Truly I say to you, I am bound to listen to you ten
times for every one that you have listened to me. And he who will not listen to
another, every time that he shall speak he shall sin; seeing that we ought to do
to others that which we desire for ourselves, and not do to others that which we
do not desire to receive.' Then said John: 'O master, why has not God granted
this to men, that they should die once and return as Lazarus has done, in order
that they might learn to know themselves and their creator?'

Chapter 197

Jesus answered: 'Tell me, John; there was an householder who gave a perfect axe
;to one of his servants in order that he might cut down the wood which
obstructed the view of his house. But the labourer forgot the axe, and said: "If
the master would give me an old axe I should easily cut down the wood." Tell me,
John, what said the master? Assuredly he was wroth, and took the old axe and
struck him on the head, saying: Fool and knave! I gave you an axe wherewith you
might cut down the wood without toil, and seek you this axe, wherewith one must
work with great toil, and all that is cut is wasted and good for nought? I
desire you to cut down the wood in such wise that your work shall be good." Is
this true?'

John answered: 'It is most true.' [Then Jesus said:] 'As I live eternally,'
said God, 'I have given a good axe to every man, which is the sight of the
burial of one dead. Whoso wield well this axe remove the wood of sin from their
heart without pain; wherefore they receive my grace and mercy; giving them merit
of eternal life for their good works. But he who forgets that he is mortal,
though time after time he see others die, and says. "If I should see the other
life, I would do good works," my fury shall be upon him, and I will so smite him
with death that he shall never more receive any good.' 'O John;,' said Jesus,
'how great is the advantage of him who from the fall of others learns to stand
on his feet!'

Chapter 198

Then said Lazarus: 'Master, truly I say to you, I cannot conceive the penalty of which he is worthy who time after time sees the dead borne to the tomb and fears not God our creator. Such an one for the things of this world, which he ought entirely to forsake, offends his creator who has given him all.'

Then Jesus said to his disciples: 'You call me Master, and you do well, seeing that God teaches you by my mouth. But how will you call Lazarus? Truly he is here master of all the masters that teach doctrine in this world. I indeed have taught you how you ought to live well, but Lazarus will teach you how to die well. As God lives, he has received the gift of prophecy; listen therefore to his words, which are truth. And so much the more ought you to listen to him, as good living is vain if one die badly.'

Said Lazarus: 'O master, I thank you that you make the truth to be prized; therefore will God give the great merit.' Then said he who writes this: 'O master how speaks Lazarus the truth in saying to you "You shall have merit," whereas you said to Nicodemus that man merits nought but punishment? Shall you accordingly be punished of God?' Jesus answered: 'May it please God that I receive punish. men of God in this World, because I have not served him so faithfully as I was bound to do.

But God has so loved me, by his mercy, that every punishment is withdrawn from me, in so much that I shall only be tormented in another person. For punishment was fitting for me, for that men have called me God; but since I have confessed, not only that I am not God, as is the truth, but have confessed also that I am not the Messiah, therefore God has taken away the punishment from me, and will cause a wicked one to suffer it in my name, so that the shame alone shall be mine. wherefore I say to you, my Barnabas, that when a man speaks of what God shall give to his neighbour let him say that his neighbour merits it: but let him look to it that, when he speaks of

what God shall give to himself , he say: God will give me." And let him look to it that he say not, I have merit, because God is pleased to grant his mercy to his servants when they confess that they merit hell for their sins.

Chapter 199

God is so rich in mercy that the water of a thousand seas, if so many were to be found, could not quench a spark of the flames of hell, yet a single tear of one who mourns at having offended God quenches the whole of hell, by the great mercy wherewith God succours him. God, therefore, to confound Satan and to display his own bounty, wills to call merit in the presence of his mercy every good work of his faithful servant, and wills him so to speak of his neighbour. But of himself a man must beware of saying: "I have merit"; for he would be condemned.'

Chapter 200

Jesus then turned to Lazarus, and said: 'Brother, I must needs for a short time abide in the world, wherefore when I shall be near to your house I will not ever go elsewhere, because you will minister to me, not for love of me, but for love of God.' It was near to the Passover of the Jews, [so] Jesus said to his disciples: "Let us go to Jerusalem to eat the paschal lamb." And he sent Peter and John to the city, saying: "You shall find an ass near the gate of the city with a colt: loose her and bring her here; for I must ride [on her] into Jerusalem. And if any one ask you saying, "Why [do] you loose her?" say to them: "The Master has need [of her]," and they will permit you to bring her."

The disciples went, and found all that Jesus had told them, and accordingly they brought the ass and the colt. The disciples [then] placed their mantles upon the colt, and Jesus rode [on her]. And it came to pass that, when the men of Jerusalem heard that Jesus of Nazareth was coming, the men went forth with their children eager to see Jesus, bearing in their hands branches of palm and olive, singing: 'Blessed be he that comes to us in the name of God; hosanna son of David!'

Jesus having come into the city, the men spread out their garments under the feet of the ass, singing: "Blessed be he that comes to us in the name of the Lord God; hosanna, son of David!" The Pharisees rebuked Jesus, saying: 'See you not what these say? Cause them to hold their peace!' Then Jesus said: 'As God lives, in whose presence my soul stands, if men should hold their peace, the stones would cry out against the unbelief of malignant sinners.' And when Jesus had said this all the stones of Jerusalem cried out with a great noise: 'Blessed be he who comes to us in the name of the Lord God!' Nevertheless the Pharisees remained still in their unbelief, and, having assembled themselves together, took counsel to catch him in his talk.

Chapter 201

Jesus having entered into the Temple, the scribes and Pharisees brought to him a woman taken in adultery. They said among themselves: 'If he save her, it is contrary to the Law of Moses, and so we have him as guilty, and if he condemn her it is contrary to his own doctrine, for he preaches mercy.' Wherefore they came to Jesus and said: 'Master, we have found this woman in adultery. Moses commanded that [such] should be stoned: what then say you?'

Thereupon Jesus stooped down and with his finger made a mirror on the ground wherein every one saw his own iniquities. They still pressed for the answer, Jesus lifted up himself As and, pointing to the mirror with his finger, said: 'He that is without sin among you, let him be first to stone her.' And again he stooped down, shaping the mirror. The men, seeing this, went out one by one, beginning from the eldest, for they were ashamed to see their abominations.

Jesus having lifted up himself, and seeing no one but the woman, said: 'Woman, where are they that condemned you?' The woman answered, weeping: 'Lord, they are departed; and if you will pardon me as God lives, I will sin no more.' Then Jesus said: 'Blessed be God! Go your way in peace and sin no more, for God has not sent me to condemn you.'

Then, the scribes and Pharisees being assembled, Jesus said to them: 'Tell me: if one of you had an hundred sheep, and should lose one of them, would you not go to seek it, leaving the ninety and nine? And when you found it, would you not lay it upon your shoulders and, having called together your neighbours, say to them: "Rejoice with me, for I have found the sheep which I had lost"? Assuredly you would do so. Now tell me, shall our God love less man, for whom he has made the world? As God lives, even so there is joy in the presence of the angels of God over one sinner that repents; because sinners make known God's mercy.'

Chapter 202

'Tell me, by whom is the physician more loved: by them that have never had any sickness, or by them whom the physician has healed of grievous sickness?' Said the Pharisees to him: 'And how shall he that is whole love the physician?

assuredly he will love him only for that he is not sick; and not having knowledge of sickness he will love the physician but little.'

Then with vehemence of spirit Jesus spoke, saying: 'As God lives, your own tongues condemn your pride, inasmuch as our God is loved more by the sinner that repents, knowing the great mercy of God upon him, than by the righteous. For the righteous has not knowledge of the mercy of God. Wherefore there is more rejoicing in the presence of the angels of God over one sinner that repents than over ninety and nine righteous persons. Where are the righteous in our time? As God lives, in whose presence my soul stands, great is the number of the righteous unrighteous; their condition being like to that of Satan.'

The scribes and Pharisees answered: 'We are sinners, wherefore God will have mercy on us.' And this they said tempting him; for the scribes and Pharisees count it the greatest insult to be called sinners. Then Jesus said: 'I fear that you be righteous unrighteous. For if you have sinned and deny your sin, calling yourselves righteous, you are unrighteous; and if in your heart you hold yourselves righteous, and with your tongue you say that you are sinners, then are you doubly righteous unrighteous.'

Accordingly the scribes and Pharisees hearing this were confounded and departed, leaving Jesus with his disciples in peace, and they went into the house of Simon the leper, whose leprosy he [had] cleansed. The citizens had gathered together the sick to the house of Simon and prayed Jesus for the healing of the sick. Then Jesus, knowing that his hour was near, said: 'Call the sick, as many as there be, because God is mighty and merciful to heal them.' They answered: 'We know not that there be any other sick folk here in Jerusalem.'

Jesus weeping answered: 'O Jerusalem, O Israel, I weep over you, for you know not your visitation; because I would fain have gathered you to the love of God your creator, as a hen gathers her chickens under her wings, and you would not! Wherefore God says thus to you

Chapter 203

O city, hard-hearted and perverse of mind, I have sent to you my servant, to the end that he may convert you to your heart, and you may repent; but you, O city of confusion, have forgotten all that I did upon Egypt and upon Pharaoh for love of you, O Israel. Many times weep you that my servant may heal your body of sickness; and you seek to slay my servant because he seeks to heal your soul of sin.

Shall you, then, alone remain unpunished by me? Shall you, then, live eternally? And shall your pride deliver you from my hands? Assuredly not. For I will bring princes with they shall surround you with might, an army against you, and in such wise will I give you over into their hands that your pride shall fall down into hell.

I will not pardon the old men or the widows, I will not pardon the children, but I will give you all to famine, the sword, and derision and the Temple, whereon I have looked with mercy, I will make desolate with the city, insomuch that you shall be for a fable, a derision, and a proverb among the nations. So is my wrath abiding upon you, and my indignation sleeps not."

Chapter 204

Having said this, Jesus said again: 'Know you not that there be other sick folk? As God lives, they be fewer in Jerusalem that have their soul sound than they that be sick in body. And in order that you may know the truth, I say to you, O sick folk, in the name of God, let your sickness depart from you! And when he had said this, immediately they were healed.

The men wept when they heard of the wrath of God upon Jerusalem, and prayed for mercy; when Jesus said: "'If Jerusalem shall weep for her sins and do penance, walking in my ways, said God, "I will not remember her iniquities any more, and I will not do to her any of the evil which I have said. But Jerusalem weeps for her ruin and not for her dishonouring of me, wherewith she has blasphemed my name among the nations. Therefore is my fury kindled much more. As I live eternally, if Job, Abraham, Samuel, David, and Daniel my servants, with Moses, should pray for this people, my wrath upon Jerusalem will not be appeased."' And having said this, Jesus retired into the house, while every one remained in fear.

Chapter 205

While Jesus was supping with his disciples in the house of Simon the leper, behold Mary the sister of Lazarus entered into the house, and having broken a vessel, poured ointment over the head and garment of Jesus. Seeing this, Judas the traitor was fain to hinder Mary from doing such a work, saying: "Go and sell the ointment and bring the money that I may give it to the poor.' Jesus said: 'Why hinder you her? Let her be, for the poor you shall have always with you, but me you shall not have always.'

Judas answered: 'O master, this ointment might be sold for three hundred pieces of money now see how many poor folk would be helped.' Jesus answered: 'O Judas, I know your heart: have patience, therefore, and I will give you all.' Every one ate with fear, and the disciples were sorrowful, because they knew that Jesus must soon depart from them. But Judas was indignant, because he knew that he was losing thirty pieces of money for the ointment not sold, seeing he stole the tenth part of all that was given to Jesus.

He went to find the high priest, who assembled in a council of priests, scribes, and Pharisees; to whom Judas spoke, saying: 'What will you give me, and I will betray into your hands Jesus, who would fain make himself king of Israel?' *They answered: 'Now how will you give him into our hand?' Judas said: 'When I shall know that he goes outside the city to pray I will tell you, and will conduct you to the place where he shall be found; for to seize him in the city will be impossible without a sedition.' The high priest answered: 'If you will give him into our hand we will give the thirty pieces of gold and you shall see how well I will treat you.'

Chapter 206

When day was come, Jesus went up to the Temple with a great multitude of people. Whereupon the high priest drew near, saying: 'Tell me, O Jesus, have you forgotten all that you did confess, that you are not God, nor son of God, nor even the Messiah?' Jesus answered: 'No, surely, I have not forgotten; for this is my confession which I shall bear before the judgment seat of God on the day of judgment. For all that is written in the Book of Moses is most true, inasmuch as God our creator is [God] alone, and I am God's servant and desire to serve God's Messenger whom you call Messiah.'

Said the high priest: 'Then what boots it to come to the Temple with so great a multitude of people? Seek you, perhaps, to make yourself king of Israel? Beware lest some danger befall you!' Jesus answered: 'If I sought my own glory and desired my portion in this world, I had not fled when the people of Nain would fain have made me king. Believe me, truly, that I seek not anything in this world.' Then said the high priest: 'We want to know a thing concerning the Messiah.' And then the priests, scribes, and Pharisees made a circle round about Jesus.

Jesus answered: 'What is that thing which you seek to know about the Messiah? Perhaps it is the lie? Assuredly I will not tell you the lie. For if I had said the lie I had been adored by you, and by the scribes [and] Pharisees with all Israel: but because I tell you the truth you hate me and seek to kill me.' Said the high priest: 'Now we know that you have the devil at your back; for you are a Samaritan;, and have not respect to the priest of God.'

Chapter 207

Jesus answered: 'As God lives, I have not the devil at my back, but I seek to cast out the devil. Wherefore, for this cause the devil stirs up the world against me, because I am not of this world, but I seek that God may be glorified, who has sent me into the world. Hearken therefore to me, and I will tell you who has the devil at his back. As God lives, in whose presence my soul stands, he who works after the will of the devil, he has the devil at his back, who has put on him the bridle of his will and rules him at his pleasure, making him to run into every iniquity.

Even as a garment changes its name when it changes its owner, although it is all the same cloth: so also men, albeit they are all of one material, are different by reason of the works of him who works in the man. 'If I (as I know) have sinned, wherefore do you not rebuke me as a brother, instead of hating me as an enemy? Truly the members of a body succour one another when they are united with the head, and they that are cut off from the head give it no succour. For the hands of one body do not feel the pain of another body's feet, but that of the body in which they are united. As God lives, in whose presence my soul stands, he who fears and loves God his Creator has the feeling of mercy over them [over] whom God his head has mercy: and seeing that God wills not the death of the sinner, but waits for each one to repent, if you were of that body wherein I am incorporate, as God lives, you would help me to work according to my head.

Chapter 208

If I work iniquity, reprove me, and God will love you, because you shall be doing his will, but if none can reprove me of sin it is a sign that you are not sons of Abraham as you call yourselves, nor are you incorporate with that head wherein Abraham was incorporate. As God lives, so greatly did Abraham love God, that he not only brake in pieces the false idols and forsook his father and mother, but was willing to slay his own son in obedience to God.

The high priest answered: "This I ask of you, and I do not seek to slay you, wherefore tell us: Who was this son of Abraham?" Jesus answered: "The zeal of your honour, O God, inflames me, and I cannot hold my peace. Truly I say, the son of Abraham was Ishmael, from whom must be descended the Messiah promised to Abraham, that in him should all the tribes of the earth be blessed." Then was the high priest wroth, hearing this, and cried out: "Let us stone this impious fellow, for he is an Ishmaelite, and has spoken blasphemy against Moses and against the Law of God."

Whereupon every scribe and Pharisee, with the elders of the people, took up stones to stone Jesus, who vanished from their eyes and went out of the Temple. And then, through the great desire that they had to slay Jesus, blinded with fury and hatred, they struck one another in such wise that there died a thousand men; and they polluted the holy Temple. The disciples and believers, who saw Jesus go out of the Temple (for from them he was not hidden), followed him to the house of Simon.

Thereupon Nicodemus came thither and counselled Jesus to go out of Jerusalem beyond the brook Cedron, saying: 'Lord, I have a garden with a house beyond the brook Cedron, I pray you, therefore, go thither with some of your disciples, to tarry there until this hatred of our priests be past; for I will minister to you what is necessary. And the multitude of disciples leave you here in the house of Simon and in my house, for God will provide for all.' And this Jesus did, desiring only to have with him the twelve first called apostles.

Chapter 209

At this time, while the Virgin Mary, mother of Jesus, was standing in prayer, the angel Gabriel visited her and narrated to her the persecution of her son, saying: "Fear not, Mary, for God will protect him from the world." Mary, weeping, departed from Nazareth, and came to Jerusalem to the house of Mary Salome, her sister, seeking her son.

But since he had secretly retired beyond the brook Cedron she was not able to see him any more in this world; except after the deed of shame, for [then] the angel Gabriel, with the angels Michael, Rafael, and Uriel, by [the] command of God, brought him to her.

Chapter 210

When the confusion in the Temple ceased by the departure of Jesus, the high priest ascended on high, and having beckoned for silence with his hands he said:, 'Brethren, what do we? See you not that he has deceived the whole world with his diabolical art? Now, how did he vanish, if he be not a magician? Assuredly, if he were an holy one and a prophet, he would not blaspheme against God and against Moses [his] servant, and against the Messiah, who is the hope of Israel. And what shall I say? He has blasphemed all our priesthood, wherefore truly I say to you, if he be not removed from the world Israel will be polluted, and our God will give us to the nations. Behold now, how by reason of him this holy Temple has been polluted.'

And in such wise did the high priest speak at many forsook Jesus, wherefore the secret persecution was converted into an open one, insomuch that the high priest went in person to Herod, and to the Roman governor, accusing Jesus that he desired to make himself king of Israel, and of this they had false witnesses.

Thereupon was held a general council against Jesus, forasmuch as the decree of the Romans made them afraid. For so it was that twice the Roman Senate had sent a decree concerning Jesus: in one decree it was forbidden, on pain of death, that any one should call Jesus of Nazareth;, the prophet of the Jews, either God or Son of God; in the other it forbade, under capital sentence, that any one should contend concerning Jesus of Nazareth, prophet of the Jews. Wherefore, for this cause, there was a great division among them. Some desired that they should write again to Rome against Jesus; others said that they should leave Jesus alone, regardless of what he said, as of a fool; others adduced the great miracles that he wrought.

The high priest therefore spoke that under pain of anathema none should speak a word in defence of Jesus; and he spoke to Herod, and to the governor, saying 'In any case we have an ill venture in our hands, for if we slay this sinner we have acted contrary to the decree of Caesar, and, if we suffer him to live and he make himself king, how will the matter go?' Then Herod arose and threatened the governor, saying: 'Beware lest through your favouring of that man this country be rebellious: for I will accuse you before Caesar ;as a rebel.'

Then the governor feared the Senate and made friends with Herod (for before this they had hated one another to death), and they joined together for the death of Jesus, and said to the high priest: 'Whenever you shall know where the malefactor is, send to us, for we will give you soldiers.' This was done to fulfil the prophecy of David who had foretold of Jesus, prophet of Israel, saying: The princes and kings of the earth are united against the holy one of Israel, because he announces the salvation of the world. Thereupon, on that day, there was a general search for Jesus throughout Jerusalem.

Chapter 211

Jesus, being in the house of Nicodemus ;beyond the brook Cedron, comforted his disciples, saying: 'The hour is near that I must depart from the world; console yourselves and be not sad, seeing that where I go I shall not feel any tribulation. 'Now, shall you be my friends if you be sad at my welfare? No, assuredly, but rather enemies. When the world shall rejoice, be you sad, because the rejoicing of the world is turned into weeping; but your sadness shall be turned into joy and your joy shall no one take from you: for the rejoicing that the heart feels in God its creator not the whole world can take away. See that you forget not the words which God has spoken to you by my mouth. Be you my witnesses against every one that shall corrupt the witness that I have witnessed with my gospel; against the world, and against the lovers of the world.

Chapter 212

Then lifting up his hands to the Lord, he prayed, saying: 'Lord our God, God of Abraham;, God of Ishmael ;and Isaac;, God of our fathers, have mercy upon them that you have given me, and save them from the world. I say not, take them from the world, because it is necessary that they shall bear witness against them that shall corrupt my gospel;. But I pray you to keep them from evil, that on the day of your judgment they may come with me to bear witness against the world and against the House of Israel that has corrupted your testament.

Lord God, mighty and jealous, that take vengeance upon idolatry against the sons of idolatrous fathers even to the fourth generation, do you curse eternally every one that shall corrupt my gospel that you gave me, when they write that I am your son. For I, clay and dust, am servant of your servants, and never have I thought myself to be your good servant; for I cannot give you aught in return for that which you have given me, for all things are yours.

Lord God, the merciful, that shows mercy to a thousand generations upon them that fear you, have mercy upon them which believe my words that you have given me. For even as you are true God, so your word which I have spoken is true; for it is yours, seeing I have ever spoken as one that reads, who cannot read save that which is written in the book that he reads: even so have I spoken that which you have given me.

'Lord God the Saviour, save them whom you have given me, in order that Satan may not be able to do aught against them, and save not only them, but every one that shall believe in them. Lord, bountiful and rich in mercy, grant to your servant to be in the congregation of your Messenger; on the Day of Judgment: and not me only, but every one whom you have given me, with all them that shall believe on me through their preaching. And this do, Lord, for your own sake, that Satan boast not himself against you, Lord.

'Lord God, who by your providence provides all things necessary for your people Israel, be mindful of all the tribes of the earth, which you have promised to bless by your Messenger, for whom you did create the world. Have mercy on the world and send speedily your Messenger, that Satan your enemy may lose his empire.' And having said this, Jesus said three times: 'So be it, Lord, great and merciful!' And they answered, weeping: 'So be it," all save Judas, for he believed nothing.

Chapter 213

The day having come for eating the lamb, Nicodemus ;sent the lamb secretly to the garden for Jesus and his disciples, announcing all that had been decreed by Herod ;with the governor and the high priest. Whereupon Jesus rejoiced in spirit, saying: 'Blessed be your holy name, O Lord, because you have not separated me from the number of your servants that have been persecuted by the world and slain. I thank you, my God, because I have fulfilled your work.' And turning to Judas, he said to him: 'Friend, wherefore do you tarry? My time is near, wherefore go and do that which you must do."

The disciples thought that Jesus was sending Judas ;to buy something for the day of the Passover;: but Jesus knew that Judas was betraying him, wherefore, desiring to depart from the world, he so spoke. Judas answered: 'Lord, suffer me to eat, and I will go.' 'Let us eat,' said Jesus, 'for I have greatly desired to eat this lamb before I am parted from you.'

And having arisen, he took a towel and girded his loins, and having put water in a basin, he set himself to wash his disciples' feet. Beginning from Judas;, Jesus came to Peter. Said Peter;: 'Lord, would you wash my feet?' Jesus answered: 'That which I do you know not now, but you shall know hereafter.' Peter answered: 'You shall never wash my feet. Then Jesus rose up, and said: 'Neither shall you come in my company on the day of judgment.' Peter answered: 'Wash not only my feet, Lord, but my hands and my head.'

When the disciples were washed and were seated at table to eat, Jesus said: 'I have washed you, yet are you not all clean, for as much as all the water of the sea will not wash him that believes me not.' This said Jesus, because he knew who was betraying him. The disciples were sad at these words, when Jesus said again: 'Truly I say to you, that one of you shall betray me, insomuch that I shall be sold like a sheep; but woe to him, for he shall fulfil all that our father David said of such an one, that "he shall fall into the pit which he had prepared for others." '

Whereupon the disciples looked one upon another, saying with sorrow: 'Who shall be the traitor?' Judas then said: 'Shall it be I, O Master?' Jesus answered: 'You have told me who it shall be that shall betray me.' And the eleven apostles heard it not. When the lamb was eaten, the devil came upon the back of Judas;, and he went forth from the house, Jesus saying to him again: 'Do quickly that which you must do.'

Chapter 214

Having gone forth from the house, Jesus retired into the garden to pray,
according as his custom was to pray, bowing his knees an hundred times and
prostrating himself upon his face. Judas, accordingly, knowing the place where
Jesus was with his disciples, went to the high priest, and said: "If you will
give me what was promised, this night will I give into your hand Jesus whom you
seek; for he is alone with eleven companions." The high priest answered: "How
much do you seek?" Judas said, "Thirty pieces of gold."

Then straightway the high priest counted to him the money, and sent a Pharisee
to the governor to fetch soldiers, and to Herod, and they gave a legion of them,
because they feared the people; wherefore they took their arms, and with torches
and lanterns upon staves went out of Jerusalem.

Chapter 215

When the soldiers with Judas drew near to the place where Jesus was, Jesus heard
the approach of many people, wherefore in fear he withdrew into the house. And
the eleven were sleeping. Then God, seeing the danger of his servant, commanded
Gabriel;, Michael;, Rafael;, and Uriel;, his ministers, to take Jesus out of the
world. The holy angels came and took Jesus out by the window that looks toward
the South;. They bare him and placed him in the third heaven in the company of
angels blessing God for evermore.

Chapter 216

Judas entered impetuously before all into the chamber whence Jesus had been
taken up. And the disciples were sleeping. Whereupon the wonderful God acted
wonderfully, insomuch that Judas was so changed in speech and in face to be like
Jesus that we believed him to be Jesus. And he, having awakened us, was seeking
where the Master was. Whereupon we marvelled, and answered: 'You, Lord, are our
master; have you now forgotten us?'

And he, smiling, said: 'Now are you foolish, that know not me to be Judas
Iscariot!' And as he was saying this the soldiery entered, and laid their hands
upon Judas, because he was in every way like to Jesus. We having heard Judas'
saying, and seeing the multitude of soldiers, fled as beside ourselves. And
John, who was wrapped in a linen cloth, awoke and fled, and when a soldier
seized him by the linen cloth he left the linen cloth and fled naked. For God
heard the prayer of Jesus, and saved the eleven from evil.

Chapter 217

The soldiers took Judas ;and bound him, not without derision. For he truthfully
denied that he was Jesus; and the soldiers, mocking him, said: 'Sir, fear not,
for we are come to make you king of Israel, and we have bound you because we
know that you do refuse the kingdom.' Judas answered: 'Now have you lost your
senses! You are come to take Jesus of Nazareth;, with arms and lanterns as
[against] a robber; and you have bound me that have guided you, to make me
king!'

Then the soldiers lost their patience, and with blows and kicks they began to
flout Judas, and they led him with fury into Jerusalem. John ;and Peter
;followed the soldiers afar off; and they affirmed to him who writes that they
saw all the examination that was made of Judas by the high priest, and by the

council of the Pharisees, who were assembled to put Jesus to death. Whereupon Judas spoke many words of madness, insomuch that every one was filled with laughter, believing that he was really Jesus, and that for fear of death he was feigning madness. Whereupon the scribes bound his eyes with a bandage, and mocking him said: 'Jesus, prophet of the Nazarenes ;(for so they called them who believed in Jesus), 'tell us, who was it that smote you?' And they buffeted him and spat in his face.

When it was morning there assembled the great council of scribes and elders of the people; and the high priest with the Pharisees sought false witness against Judas, believing him to be Jesus: and they found not that which they sought. And why say I that the chief priests believed Judas to be Jesus? No all the disciples, with him who writes, believed it; and more, the poor Virgin mother of Jesus, with his kinsfolk and friends, believed it, insomuch that the sorrow of every one was incredible.

As God lives, he who writes forgot all that Jesus had said: how that he should be taken up from the world, and that he should suffer in a third person, and that he should not die until near the end of the world. Wherefore he went with the mother of Jesus and with John to the cross. The high priest caused Judas ;to be brought before him bound, and asked him of his disciples and his doctrine. Whereupon Judas, as though beside himself, answered nothing to the point. The high priest then adjured him by the living God of Israel that he would tell him the truth.

Judas answered: 'I have told you that I am Judas Iscariot, who promised to give into your hands Jesus the Nazarene; and you, by what are I know not, are beside yourselves, for you will have it by every means that I am Jesus.' The high priest answered: 'O perverse seducer, you have deceived all Israel, beginning from Galilee; even to Jerusalem here, with your doctrine and false miracles: and now think you to flee the merited punishment that befits you by feigning to be mad?

As God lives,' you shall not escape it!' And having said this he commanded his servants to smite him with buffetings and kicks, so that his understanding might come back into his head. The derision which he then suffered at the hands of the high priest's servants is past belief. For they zealously devised new inventions to give pleasure to the council. So they attired him as a juggler, and so treated him with hands and feet that it would have moved the very Canaanites to compassion if they had beheld that sight. But the chief priests and Pharisees and elders of the people had their hearts so exasperated against Jesus that, believing Judas to be really Jesus, they took delight in seeing him so treated.

Afterwards they led him bound to the governor, who secretly loved Jesus. Whereupon he, thinking that Judas was Jesus, made him enter into his chamber, and spoke to him, asking him for what cause the chief priests and the people had given him into his hands. Judas answered: 'If I tell you the truth, you will not believe me; for perhaps you are deceived as the (chief) priests and the Pharisees are deceived.'

The governor answered (thinking that he wished to speak concerning the Law): 'Now know you not that I am not a Jew? but the (chief) priests and the elders of your people have given you into my hand; wherefore tell us the truth, wherefore I may do what is just. For I have power to set you free and to put you to death.' Judas answered: 'Sir, believe me, if you put me to death, you shall do a great wrong, for you shall slay an innocent person; seeing that I am Judas

;Iscariot, and not Jesus, who is a magician, and by his are has so transformed
me.'

When he heard this the governor marvelled greatly, so that he sought to set him
at liberty. The governor therefore went out, and smiling said: 'In the one case,
at least, this man is not worthy of death, but rather of compassion.' 'This man
says,' said the governor, 'that he is not Jesus, but a certain Judas who guided
the soldiery to take Jesus, and he says that Jesus the Galilean has by his are
magic so transformed him. Wherefore, if this be true, it were a great wrong to
kill him, seeing that he were innocent. But if he is Jesus and denies that he
is, assuredly he has lost his understanding, and it were impious to slay a
madman.'

Then the chief priests and elders of the people, with the scribes and Pharisees,
cried out with shouts, saying: 'He is Jesus of Nazareth;, for we know him; for
if he were not the malefactor we would not have given him into your hands. Nor
is he mad; but rather malignant, for with this device he seeks to escape from
our hands, and the sedition that he would stir up if he should escape would be
worse than the former.' Pilate (of such was the governor's name), in order to
rid himself of such a case, said: 'He is a Galilean, and Herod is king of
Galilee: wherefore it pertains not to me to judge such a case, so take you him
to Herod.' Accordingly they led Judas to Herod, who of a long time had desired
that Jesus should go to his house. But Jesus had never been willing to go to his
house, because Herod was a Gentile, and adored the false and lying gods, living
after the manner of the unclean Gentiles. Now when Judas had been led thither,
Herod asked him of many things, to which Judas gave answers not to the purpose,
denying that he was Jesus. Then Herod mocked him, with all his court, and caused
him to be clad in white as the fools are clad;, and sent him back to Pilate,
saying to him, 'Do not fail in justice to the people of Israel!' * And this
Herod wrote, because the chief priests and scribes and the Pharisees had given
him a good quantity of money. The governor having heard that this was so from a
servant of Herod, in order that he also might gain some money, feigned that he
desired to set Judas at liberty.

Whereupon he caused him to be scourged by his slaves, who were paid by the
scribes to slay him under the scourges. But God, who had decreed the issue,
reserved Judas for the cross, in order that he might suffer that horrible death
to which he had sold another. He did not suffer Judas to die under the scourges,
notwithstanding that the soldiers scourged him so grievously that his body
rained blood. Thereupon, in mockery they clad him in an old purple garment;,
saying: 'It is fitting to our new king to clothe him and crown him': so they
gathered thorns and made a crown, like those of gold and precious stones which
kings wear on their heads. And this crown of thorns they placed upon Judas'
head, putting in his hand a reed for sceptre;, and they made him sit in a high
place.

And the soldiers came before him, bowing down in mockery, saluting him as King
of the Jews. And they held out their hands to receive gifts, such as new kings
are accustomed to give; and receiving nothing they smote Judas, saying: 'Now,
how are you crowned, foolish king, if you will not pay your soldiers and
servants?' *The chief priests with the scribes and Pharisees, seeing that Judas
died not by the scourges, and fearing lest Pilate should set him at liberty,
made a gift of money to the governor, who having received it gave Judas to the
scribes and Pharisees as guilty to death. Whereupon they condemned two robbers
with him to the death of the cross.

So they led him to Mount Calvary, where they used to hang malefactors, and there they crucified him naked;, for the greater ignominy. *Judas truly did nothing else but cry out: 'God, why have you forsaken me, seeing the malefactor has escaped and I die unjustly?' *Truly I say that the voice, the face, and the person of Judas were so like to Jesus, that his disciples and believers entirely believed that he was Jesus; wherefore some departed from the doctrine of Jesus, believing that Jesus had been a false prophet, and that by art magic he had done the miracles which he did: for Jesus had said that he should not die till near the end of the world; for that at that time he should be taken away from the world.

But they that stood firm in the doctrine of Jesus were so encompassed with sorrow, seeing him die who was entirely like to Jesus, that they remembered not what Jesus had said. And so in company with the mother of Jesus they went to Mount Calvary, and were not only present at the death of Judas, weeping continually, but by means of Nicodemus and Joseph of Abarimathia; they obtained from the governor the body of Judas to bury it. Whereupon, they took him down from the cross with such weeping as assuredly no one would believe, and buried him in the new sepulchre of Joseph; having wrapped him up in an hundred pounds of precious ointments.

Chapter 218

Then returned each man to his house. He who writes, with John and James his brother, went with the mother of Jesus; to Nazareth;.

Those disciples who did not fear God went by night [and] stole the body of Judas and hid it, spreading a report that Jesus was risen again; whence great confusion arose. The high priest then commanded, under pain of anathema;, that no one should talk of Jesus of Nazareth;. And so there arose a great persecution, and many were stoned and many beaten, and many banished from the land, because they could not hold their peace on such a matter.

The news reached Nazareth how that Jesus, their fellow citizen, having died on the cross was risen again. Whereupon, he that writes; prayed the mother of Jesus; that she would be pleased to leave off weeping, because her son was risen again. Hearing this, the Virgin Mary, weeping, said: 'Let us go to Jerusalem to find my son. I shall die content when I have seen him.'

Chapter 219

The Virgin returned to Jerusalem with him who writes, and James and John, on that day on which the decree of the high priest went forth. Whereupon, the Virgin, who feared God, albeit she knew the decree of the high priest to be unjust, commanded those who dwelt with her to forget her son. Then how each one was affected! God who discerns the heart of men knows that between grief at the death of Judas whom we believed to be Jesus our master, and the desire to see him risen again, we, with the mother of Jesus, were consumed.

So the angels that were guardians of Mary ascended to the third heaven;, where Jesus was in the company of angels, and recounted all to him. Wherefore Jesus prayed God that he would give him power to see his mother and his disciples. Then the merciful God commanded his four favourite angels, who are Michael, Gabriel, Rafael;, and Uriel, to bear Jesus into his mother's house, and there keep watch over him for three days continually, suffering him only to be seen by them that believed in his doctrine.

Jesus came, surrounded with splendour, to the room where abode Mary the Virgin with her two sisters, and Martha and Mary Magdalen, and Lazarus, and him who writes, and John and James and Peter. Whereupon, through fear they fell as dead. And Jesus lifted up his mother and the others from the ground, saying: 'Fear not, for I am Jesus; and weep not, for I am alive and not dead.' They remained every one for a long time beside himself at the presence of Jesus, for they altogether believed that Jesus was dead. Then the Virgin, weeping, said: 'Tell me, my son, wherefore God, having given you power to raise the dead. suffered you to die, to the shame of your kinsfolk and friends, and to the shame of your doctrine? For every one that loves you has been as dead.'

Chapter 220

Jesus replied, embracing his mother: 'Believe me, mother, for truly I say to you that I have not been dead at all; for God has reserved me till near the end of the world.' And having said this he prayed the four angels that they would manifest themselves, and give testimony how the matter had passed.

Thereupon the angels manifested themselves like four shining suns, insomuch that through fear every one again fell down as dead. Then Jesus gave four linen cloths to the angels that they might cover themselves, in order that they might be seen and heard to speak by his mother and her companions. And having lifted up each one, he comforted them, saying: 'These are the ministers of God: Gabriel, who announces God's secrets; Michael, who fights against God's enemies; Rafael, who receives the souls of them that die; and Uriel, who will call every one to the judgment of God at the last day. Then the four angels narrated to the Virgin how God had sent for Jesus, and had transformed Judas, that he might suffer the punishment to which he had sold another.

Then said he who writes: 'O Master, is it lawful for me to question you now, as it was lawful for me when you dwelt with us?' Jesus answered: 'Ask what you please, Barnabas, and I will answer you.' Then said he who writes: 'O Master, seeing that God is merciful, wherefore has he so tormented us, making us to believe that you were dead? and your mother has so wept for you that she has been near to death; and you, who are an holy one of God, on you has God suffered to fall the calumny that you were slain amongst robbers ;on the Mount Calvary?'

Jesus answered: 'Believe me, Barnabas, that every sin, however small it be, God punishes with great punishment, seeing that God is offended at sin. Wherefore, since my mother and my faithful disciples that were with me loved me a little with earthly love, the righteous God has willed to punish this love with the present grief, in order that it may not be punished in the flames of hell. And though I have been innocent in the world, since men have called me "God," and "Son of God," God, in order that I be not mocked of the demons on the day of judgment, has willed that I be mocked of men in this world by the death of Judas;, making all men to believe that I died upon the cross. And this mocking shall continue until the advent of Muhammad;, the Messenger ;of God, who, when he shall come, shall reveal this deception to those who believe in God's Law. Having thus spoken, Jesus said: 'You are just, O Lord our God, because to you only belongs honour and glory without end.'

Chapter 221

Jesus turned himself to him who writes, and said: "Barnabas, see that by all means you write my gospel concerning all that has happened through my dwelling in the world. And write in a similar manner that which has befallen Judas, in order that the faithful may be undeceived, and every one may believe the truth."

Then answered he who writes: "I will do so, if God wills, O Master; but I do not know what happened to Judas, for I did not see it."

Jesus answered: "Here are John and Peter who saw everything, and they will tell you all that has passed." And then Jesus commanded us to call his faithful disciples [so] that they might see him. So James and John called together the seven disciples with Nicodemus and Joseph, and many others of the seventy-two, and they ate with Jesus.

The third day Jesus said: "Go to the Mount of Olives with my mother, for there I will ascend again to heaven, and you will see who shall bear me up." So they all went there except twenty-five of the seventy-two disciples, who for fear had fled to Damascus. And as they all stood in prayer, at midday Jesus came with a great multitude of angels who were praising God: and the splendour of his face made them greatly afraid and they fell with their faces to the ground. But Jesus lifted them up, comforting them, and saying: "Do not be afraid, I am your master."

And he reproved many who believed that he had died and risen again, saying: "Do you hold me and God for liars? I said to you that God has granted to me to live almost to the end of the world. Truly I say to you, I did not die; it was Judas the traitor. Beware, for Satan will make every effort to deceive you. Be my witnesses in Israel, and throughout the world, of all things that you have heard and seen."

And having said this, he prayed God for the salvation of the faithful, and the conversion of sinners and [then], his prayer ended, he embraced his mother, saying: "Peace be to you, my mother. Rest in God who created you and me." And having said this, he turned to his disciples, saying: "May God's grace and mercy be with you." Then before their eyes the four angels carried him up into heaven.

Chapter 222

After Jesus had departed, the disciples scattered through the different parts of Israel and of the world, and the truth, hated of Satan, was persecuted, as it always is, by falsehood. For certain evil men, pretending to be disciples, preached that Jesus died and rose not again. Others preached that he really died, but rose again. Others preached, and yet preach, that Jesus is the Son of God, among whom is Paul deceived. But we - as much as I have written - we preach to those that fear God, that they may be saved in the last day of God's Judgment. Amen.

www.ingramcontent.com/pod-product-compliance
Lightning Source LLC
Chambersburg PA
CBHW060346100426
42812CB00003B/1141